Studies in the Torah
Vol. 2

שְׁמוֹת • Exodus

Studies in the Torah
שְׁמוֹת • Exodus

Tim Hegg

Copyright © 2014 by TorahResource • Tacoma WA
All rights reserved
Printed in the United States of America

ISBN 978-0-9889581-9-7

torahresource.com
torahresourceinstitute.com
trradio.com

PO Box 7701 • Tacoma WA • 98417
800-508-3566

A special word of gratitude is extended to
all who have faithfully supported the work at TorahResource,
making the publication of *Studies in the Torah* possible.

Table of Contents

Forward 9

Main Headings [in bold] indicate the Annual Cycle of readings.
Sub-headings indicate the Triennial Cycle readings.

Parashah Thirteen: שְׁמוֹת **– Shemot – 1:1–6:1**..13
Triennial Parashah 46 – 1:1–2:25 15
Triennial Parashah 47 – 3:1–4:13 21
Triennial Parashah 48 – 4:14–6:1 29

Parashah Fourteen: וָאֵרָה **– Va'eirah – 6:2–9:35** 37
Triennial Parashah 49 – 6:2–7:18 39
Triennial Parashah 50 – 7:19–8:19[15] 47
Trieenial Parashah 51 – 8:20[16] – 9:35 51

Parashah Fifteen: בֹּא **– Bo' – 10:1–13:16** 55
Triennial Parashah 52 – 10:1–12:12 57
Triennial Parashah 53 – 12:13–28 65
Triennial Parashah 54 – 12:29–51 71
Triennial Parashah 55 – 13:1–20 75

Parashah Sixteen: בְּשַׁלַּח **– B'shalach – 13:17–17:16** 79
Triennial Parashah 56 – 13:21–15:18 81
Triennial Parashah 57 – 15:19–16:24 89
Triennial Parashah 58 – 16:25–17:16 97

Parashah Seventeen: יִתְרוֹ **– Yitro – 18:1–20:26**...101
Triennial Parashah 59 – 18:1–20:26 103

Parashah Eighteen: מִשְׁפָּטִים **– Mishpatim – 21:1–24:18** 127
Triennial Parashah 60 – 21:1–22:24 129
Triennial Parashah 61 – 22:25–23:33 137
Triennial Parashah 62 – 24:1–18 145

Parashah Nineteen: תְּרוּמָה **– Terumah – 25:1–27:19** 153
Triennial Parashah 63 – 25:1–26:30 155
Triennial Parashah 64 – 26:31–27:19 163

Parashah Twenty: תְּצַוֶּה **– T'tzaveh – 27:20–30:10**....................................171
Triennial Parashah 65 – 27:20–28:43 173
Triennial Parashah 66 – 29:1–46 179
Triennial Parashah 67 – 30:1–10 187

Table of Contents

Parashah Twenty-One: כִּי תִשָּׂא – **Ki Tissa' – 30:11–34:35** 195
   Triennial Parashah 68 – 30:11–38 197
   Triennial Parashah 69 – 31:1–32:14 205
   Triennial Parashah 70 – 32:15–34:26 217

Parashah Twenty-Two: וַיַּקְהֵל – **Vayaqheil – 35:1–38:20** 225
   Triennial Parashah 71 – 34:27–36:38 227
   Triennial Parashah 72 – 37:1–38:20 235

Parashah Twenty-Three: פְקוּדֵי – **Pequdei – 38:21–40:38** 245
   Triennial Parashah 73 – 38:21–31 247
   Triennial Parashah 74 – 38:21–40:38 255

Indexes 259
   Index of Haftarot 259
   Index of Apostolic Readings 260

Foreword

This second volume of *Studies in the Torah* comprises the teaching notes on the book of Exodus (*Sh^emot*) I have used for our weekly Shabbat studies at Beit Hallel in Tacoma, WA. When we first gathered as a synagogue on Shabbat 25 years ago, we naturally adopted the Annual Cycle of Torah readings (*parashot*), along with the traditional *haftarah* portions (selections from the Prophets) assigned to each Torah *parashah*. But we soon came to realize that the portions of the Annual Cycle were often too large to allow serious study and discussion of the passage at our Shabbat gatherings. So after completing the Annual Cycle that first year, we decided to use the Triennial Cycle of readings which naturally had smaller sections, allowing a more in-depth study of each weekly *parashah*. Since the Triennial Cycle is, in the estimation of most scholars, the older lectionary of the synagogue, it also made sense to utilize it as we considered how the synagogues of The Way might have read through the Torah in the pre-destruction era.[1]

We realized, of course, that the Triennial Cycle of readings was not nearly as uniform as the later Annual Cycle. Indeed, the Annual Cycle was formulated at a time when the Rabbis were seeking to establish uniformity among the dispersed Jewish communities of the post-destruction era and thus was created to assure that the diverse synagogue communities would all be reading the same Torah selections on any given Shabbat. Given the fact that the earlier Triennial Cycle was not nearly so uniform, and that variations existed among the extant lists, we were forced to make a decision as to which list would form the basis for our weekly Shabbat readings. In the end, we chose to follow the Triennial Cycle as described by the following scholars: Charles Perrot, "The Reading of the Bible in the Ancient Synagogue" in Martin Mulder, ed., *Mikra* (Fortress, 1988), pp. 139ff; Cecil Roth, "Triennial Cycle" in *Encyclopedia Judaica* (Keter, 1971), 15.1386–1389; and Jacob Mann, *The Bible as Read and Preached in the Old Synagogue*, 2 vols. (KTAV, 1971), which contains a very helpful Prolegomenon by Ben Zion Wacholder.

We then chose passages from the Apostolic Scriptures (New Testament) to accompany the weekly sections of the Torah and Prophets

---

[1] For a study on the reading of the Torah in 1st Century synagogues, see my essay, "The Public Reading of the Scriptures in the 1st Century Synagogue," available from the Articles in English page at TorahResource.com.

as listed in the Triennial Cycle. In choosing these readings from the Apostolic Scriptures, we allowed general themes or topics to be the primary factor.

The studies that follow, therefore, do not comprise a commentary on the book of Exodus, at least not as we usually think of a commentary that deals with the text on a verse-by-verse or section-by-section basis, giving a detailed explanation of the biblical text. Rather, I have concentrated on various themes that are apparent in Exodus and sought to show how the narrative highlights and carries forward these themes. Primary in this regard is the theme of the dwelling of God with Israel, and ultimately with mankind in the person of our Messiah, Yeshua. Thus, in volume one (Genesis) of Studies in the Torah, we saw the opening chapters of God's plan to redeem His fallen creation. In Exodus, we see the manner in which this redemption would be realized, i.e., by the giving of an innocent life sacrificially offered to atone for sin. The Tabernacle, its furnishings, the Priesthood, and the ceremonies initiated in the Tabernacle all are the first revelations of how God redeems sinners.

Obviously, Exodus likewise contains the narrative of the giving of the Torah at Sinai, and thus begins the wonderful story of how the Torah itself holds a central place in God's plan of salvation. It is obvious that we would never be able to understand and appreciate what God has done for us in and by His Son, Yeshua, if we fail to learn the important lessons regarding atonement and propitiation which the book of Exodus teaches.

As you read through the following chapters, you will see that I have spent the majority of time dealing with each of the Torah *parashot* and, in most cases, only outlining how the *haftarah* and Apostolic portions reinforce or carry forward the theme of the Exodus text. Surely the *haftarah* and Apostolic readings are worthy of their own more detailed study and application. My hope is that these thoughts on the text of Exodus will only whet the spiritual appetite of the reader to do his or her own further study, not only on the Torah section, but also on the accompanying *haftarah* and Apostolic portions.

As I noted above, these studies are the weekly notes utilized in our Torah community as together we have read and studied the Torah. The reader should therefore understand that when a given study occurred near or during a Festival, the theme of that Festival may inevitably find its way into the discussion of the biblical portions read that week. The whole question of what constituted the starting point for the Triennial Cycle is shrouded in history. In ancient times, did they begin the reading cycle (Genesis 1) during the first month, i.e., the month of Passover or did the cycle begin anew in the seventh month, i.e., the month of Yom Teruah or Rosh HaShanah? We really cannot be certain. But the greater weight of the data falls on the side of the seventh month being the beginning point for the cycle of readings. This means that every three years the Triennial Cycle and the Annual Cycle both read Genesis 1 on the same Shabbat.

Because so many synagogues and communities adhere to the Annual Cycle, I have arranged the following study according to the eleven *parashot* in the Annual Cycle of Exodus, naming each of the eleven chapters after their conventional names. Then each of the eleven sections of the Annual Cycle is divided into the portions as prescribed in the Triennial Cycle. I have done this in the hope that those who utilize the Annual Cycle will also find these notes suitable for their weekly study of the Torah portion.

Generally, the divisions of the Triennial Cycle coincide with a division in the Annual Cycle. There are, of course, a few times when this is not the case, and the Triennial Cycle breaks in a different place than the Annual Cycle. I have noted these differences on the opening page of the chapters in which they occur.

The studies that I present here have been formed and re-formed within the context of our weekly synagogue discussions and studies. I therefore acknowledge with gratefulness the many insights that have been offered from the community of Beit Hallel and how these have helped shape and advance my own understanding of the biblical text. Being part of the community of Beit Hallel is a privilege indeed, and my wife, Paulette, and I often give thanks to the Almighty for the blessings He gives us through our community of which we are privileged to be a part.

Tim Hegg
Av, 5774
August, 2014

Parashah Thirteen
שְׁמוֹת – Shemot

"These are the Names"
Exodus 1:1–6:1

In the Triennial Cycle there are Three Parashot

1:1–2:25 | 3:1–4:14 | 4:14–6:1

Parashah 46
Triennial Cycle

Exodus 1:1–2:25

HAFTARAH: ISAIAH 27:6–13 | APOSTOLIC: ROM 6:1–2; HEB 11:23

Whom the Father Loves, He Chastens

Shemot begins the story of the slavery of Jacob and his family under the oppressive hands of their enemies. Interestingly, the midrash begins its discussion on Shemot by quoting Prov. 13:24,

> He who spares his rod hates his son, but he who loves him disciplines him diligently.

The question lingering in the minds of the Sages is prompted by how this book begins—with a *vav*, וְאֵלֶּה שְׁמוֹת, "and these are the names." That means that it is directly connected with *B'reishit* (Genesis) and in fact, in Gen 46:8 these exact words are written:

> and these are the names of the sons of Israel who came from Egypt....

But in Gen 46:8 the travelling to Egypt is seen as a blessing in that a welcomed reception awaited Jacob and his sons, the best of the land was given to them, and their lives were maintained under the gracious hand of Joseph. Here, however, the words open the narrative of how the sons of Israel, coming to Egypt, are oppressed, their lives taken, and they are forced to live under the tyranny of the Egyptians. Why the change? Why blessing on one hand and apparent cursing on the other? The Sages answered this question with the quote, "whom the Father loves He chastens." The slavery of Egypt was the chastening of the Lord to bring His beloved first born to the full realization of what redemption is, and what it costs.

Our *parashah* links more than the literary units of *B'reishit* and *Shemot* (Genesis and Exodus). It also begins the necessary connection between the covenant made with Abraham and the one made with the nation at Sinai—the Abrahamic and the Mosaic covenants. At the end of this section we read:

> So God heard their groaning; and God remembered His covenant with Abraham, Isaac, and Jacob. And God saw the sons of Israel, and God took notice of them (*literally*, and God knew). (2:25-26)

When used in the context of a covenant, the words "remember" and "know" are often technical terms, where "remember" means remaining faithful to the stipulations of the covenant, and "know" emphasizes the relationship between the covenant partners. The final phrase in the Hebrew of v. 26 is just two words: וַיֵּדַע אֱלֹהִים, "and God knew." The English translation "and God took notice of them" is an attempt to make sense of what God knew, since no object is present in the sentence. But the word "know" should be understood as a covenant term paired with "remember," and meaning "to be loyal to the covenant," emphasizing the relationship that the covenant produces. If we understand these final words of our section to be "and God knew them (i.e., Israel)," it paints the picture of a faithful husband expressing fidelity to the covenant of marriage, demonstrated through loving and intimate relationship.

In fact, the first act of the Egyptians noted in the book is that the Pharaoh who arose "did not know Joseph" (וַיָּקָם מֶלֶךְ־חָדָשׁ עַל־מִצְרָיִם אֲשֶׁר לֹא־יָדַע אֶת־יוֹסֵף). In context, this must mean that the Pharaoh was unwilling to maintain the covenant that the former Pharaohs had made with Joseph and his family. To "not know Joseph" does not mean he was unaware of Joseph—Egyptians were big on history! It means that the current Pharaoh did not intend to honor the covenants made with Joseph and his family.

This sets the stage, then, for the whole book: God as Israel's husband will demonstrate His faithfulness to the covenant and will redeem her at great cost in order to restore her to Himself, and to maintain the faithful relations of marriage that the covenant demands.

In fact, the very first issue raised in the Exodus narrative is that of children—offspring, the gift of marital relations. Moses, the baby, is the prime example of thousands of other babies who become the focus of the opening story. Like the creation narrative in which the earth teams with life, Israel is described this way:

> But the sons of Israel were fruitful and increased greatly, and multiplied, and became exceedingly mighty, so that the land was filled with them. (1:7)

What this English translation hides is that "increased greatly" is the Hebrew וַיִּשְׁרְצוּ, the same word used in Genesis 1:20, "and let the waters swarm...." Like the life that filled the earth at creation, so Israel has increased to fill Egypt. God has been faithful to bless Israel, and the proof is that He has given her many, many children.

In contrast, the desire of Egypt, (God's enemy in this story) is to find a way to destroy the children by whom Israel is blessed. Interestingly, Egypt follows the same strategy as modern America. First, go to the medical people and instruct them to kill the children. When this failed, they commanded the people themselves to kill the children (throwing them in the Nile). When both of these measures failed, there was nothing left but to attempt to kill them through slavery and finally militarily (though by the time Pharaoh gives this final command the Israelites are already on their way out of Egypt.) Unfortunately, in America the first two measures have "worked." According to recently gathered statistics, 1.3 million children are murdered each year in the United States at the hands of doctors with the consent of mothers or fathers. If ever there will be a return to God in America, this is a sin for which there will need to be genuine repentance. Of course, there has already been genuine repentance in the hearts of some individuals, and this has brought God's healing mercies into their lives. But as a nation, this horrific sin continues to hang over us as a plague ravaging our spiritual life because it undermines the very sanctity of life which is foundational for any Godly society.

It is most interesting to note once again in our *parashah* that the value of children is first maintained by the "health care professionals" of the story. The midwives are the first major heroes in the story. But they are so because of their focus. Indeed, the Hebrew text sets this up nicely in the narrative by a possible play on the words "see" and "fear." In 1:16 Pharaoh proclaims to the midwives,

> When you are helping the Hebrew women to give birth and see them (וּרְאִיתֶן) upon the birthstool, if it is a son, then you shall put him to death; but if it is a daughter, then she shall live.

The very next phrase has "וַתִּירֶאןָ הַמְיַלְּדֹת אֶת־הָאֱלֹהִים, "but the midwives feared God…." In Hebrew, "see" (ראה) and "fear" (ירא) often look alike in their various forms. Indeed, the MT writes the word "fear" here without the normal final ה so that it looks even more like the word "see."

The point is this: a great deal rests upon our focus—what we look at—Whom we fear. Pharaoh wanted the mid-wives to concentrate upon the birth itself. In contrast, the midwives focused upon God. It is interesting to me to note historically how often God has used women to effect significant revivals and spiritual awakenings as well as to maintain morality and stability within His people. Throughout the history of Israel women have played a significant (even if at times a somewhat unapplauded) role in both the physical as well as the spiritual maintenance of the nation. The same has been true in our own country. And one can point to pivotal events in the life of God's people in which women have played the key roles. It is not surprising, then, that in the Torah movement of our day the women are often ahead of the men in pursuing God with a willingness to obey the Torah and teach their children to do the same. But as is always the case, unless obedience to God is the priority of the men as well, the Torah movement in our times will languish and ultimately have less than a full impact.

Some have suggested that the midwives were less than honest in their report to Pharaoh. Of course, in the matter of saving life it is permitted to hide the truth, and even to speak a falsehood, for the saving of life takes precedence. But there is another way to understand 1:19: the midwives simply did not make an effort to attend the births at the early stages of labor. God was merciful to the Israelite women and caused their births to come quickly and easily (after all, the text does state that God was the One who caused the number of Israel to multiply). By the time the midwives arrived, the child had already been born. Pharaoh's plan was that the midwives would kill the child and make it appear that the death was the result of the birthing process.

The manner in which Pharaoh made life miserable for Israel is also interesting and has historical as well a modern parallels. Goshen had been given to Joseph and his family. Thus, the first thing Pharaoh does is remove ownership of property which brings poverty. Without ownership of property, the Israelites became servants to the Egyptians upon whom they were dependent for food and life's necessities. The second step in Pharaoh's plan was economic: he required more work for the same benefits. Finally, he made it impossible to obtain the necessary things for life because he required of the Israelites more work than they could perform (making bricks as well as gathering the raw materials to make them). As such, he diminished them to indentured slaves.

But all of this only sets up the story to bring us to the conclusion of our *parashah*: the purposes and activities of God. While we may glean many important lessons from the story of Israel's enslavement in Egypt, the overarching emphasis of the narrative is God's activity in redeeming His people. This in itself is a reminder to us that in the midst of all of life's events, the person and work of God Himself is to be our primary focus.

2:24-25 contain four verbs that highlight God's activity at the beginning of our story. But the Hebrew is very interesting in its emphasis upon these four verbs, because it adds אֱלֹהִים to each of the verbs, where we might normally expect it only at the beginning of the phrases. "God heard ... God remembered ... God saw ... God knew." What might we learn from these?

God heard – The word "to hear" has become a well known word in the Torah community because we so often recite the *Shema*, "Hear O Israel...." We have become well aware of the fact that the Hebrew idiom "to hear the voice" (שָׁמַע בְּקוֹל) means "to obey." When we therefore see the verb "hear" applied to God it arrests our attention. What does it mean that God "heard their groaning"? It means much more than merely "paying attention." It means first that God is attentive to the needs of His people. How often it is easy to presume that somehow our cares and troubles are so insignificant when compared to God's greatness that He cannot be bothered with them. But the fact is that He is always attentive to the needs of His people. He is fully aware of our groanings and our calling out to Him. In fact, one of the often repeated motifs throughout the Psalms is the "cry/answer" motif. When the weak cry out to God, He answers them. When the Psalmist cries to God for help, He answers him. Granted, the answers are not always what is expected, but they are always what is best. So do not be afraid to call out to God, to express to Him the deepest cares and woes of your soul. He hears.

God remembered – God remembered the promises—the covenant He made with Abraham, Isaac, and Jacob. God is a covenant keeping God, and He never goes back on any of His promises. This you can count on. More often than not, when we have become despondent and are becoming weaker and weaker in our faith it is because we have failed to focus on *and rehearse* the promises of God.

By focusing on the promises of God I mean to emphasize the need to know them. All too often the people of God languish in weak faith because they are not aware of God's promises—they have never studied and understood the rich promises of the Scriptures, given to God's people for their safety, security, and comfort.

But secondly, we often fail to rehearse His promises. Musicians know that rehearsals are important, and if one intends to perform to close perfection, then rehearsals are essential. It is not the purpose of rehearsals to learn the instrument: this must be done in advance. Rehearsals rather have as their goal *the owning of the music by the musician*. Rehearsals take the notes from the page and make them the possession of the musician. The music becomes one's own, so that one might express through the music the inner thoughts and emotions of the individual performer. Of course, in ensemble each individual collectively adds his or her musical expression to the whole, so that the group collectively expresses in the music even more than the composer could have ever written.

The same is true of rehearsing the promises: we need to make them our own. Take the promises of God and realize that they are for you—they belong to you. And then find in them the expression of your own love to God and to your neighbor.

God saw – Nothing is more evident in this verb than God's on-going, careful and kind providence for His children. "God saw the children of Israel"—this means that He was engaged in their lives, attentive to their needs and their future. He had a plan for them, a plan He intended to accomplish. The same is true regarding all of His children—the Father's eye is upon us. He has plans for good and for blessing. And we may trust Him for that.

God knew – This final activity of God in response to His chosen ones is, of course, the goal to which the others move: intimate relationship with those He redeems. In the course of our studies and lives; in the day to day out-working of our various tasks and efforts, it is easy to forget that the ultimate goal of the ages is that God should have close and enduring communion with His people. God wants that with each of us, but He draws us by the welcoming fragrance of His love, and the delights of His smile. May we find in Him the companion Who defines the essence of friendship at every level!

As we enter into this second book of Moses, we rehearse, once again, the great Torah lesson of God's faithfulness and His intention to redeem His people. All of subsequent Scripture will use the exodus story as the paradigm for God's method of redemption. As we study through this great story, may we revel in the accomplished redemption won for us in our own exodus from slavery.

> For He rescued us from the domain of darkness,
> and transferred us to the kingdom of His beloved Son,
> in whom we have redemption, the forgiveness of sins.
> Colossians 1:13–14

Parashah 47
Triennial Cycle

Exodus 3:1–4:13

Haftarah: Isaiah 40:11–19 | Apostolic: Acts 10:9-28

The Name (HaShem)

The Torah section before us today contains the story of Moses' face-to-face encounter with the *Shekinah* in the form of a burning bush. The profound revelation of God's person through the giving and explanation of The Name was to impact not only Moses, but the entire nation of Israel from this point on through her history. Indeed, the sanctification of the Name remains the central focus in all true worship and life from a Torah perspective.

We may dismiss the humanistic discussions which attempt to explain the burning bush event as some natural phenomenon (spontaneous combustion of dry leaves in the desert; brightly "painted" leaves of a certain species of bush, which, from a distance, appear to be ablaze [St. Elmo's fire]; volcanic gases; etc., *ad infinitum, ad nauseam*). This is the Torah, and the experience of Moshe Rabbinu—it happened as it is recorded.

But what did happen? Let us look closer. Moses is tending the sheep of his father-in-law, Yitro. He comes to Mt. Choreb (another name for Mt. Sinai, cf. 17:6; 33:6) which was quite a distance from Midian (he was doing his best to find grazing for the flock, having been entrusted with the family's primary economic source). When he encounters the burning bush, he "turns aside" to get a closer look at what was, to him, an obvious miracle—the bush burned but was not consumed.

The God Who Separates Holy and Profane

The first utterance of God is to instruct Moses about the proper manner in which mankind would approach the Holy God: "Remove your sandals from your feet, for the place on which you are standing is holy ground" (v. 5).

The lesson is obvious. Moses' sandals represent walking in a fallen world, a place where the rebellion of mankind abounds. Moses himself was exiled from his enslaved people with a bounty on his head. If the

Egyptians could not strike directly at God, they would do all in their power to subdue and humiliate His people. Our "walking" in this world is proof that we are in need of "foot washing." Even as Yeshua, in one of His final acts, washed the feet of the disciples, so Moses needed to understand that his feet were "dirty" by the evil world in which he lived.

Such unholy aspects have no place in the presence of God. If a person would have communion with the Creator, then he must first divest himself of that which is profane. We must never think that God will accept our filth in His presence. Here, once again, the need for atonement is obvious. The uncleanness we bear is the result of sin, a characteristic of our own fallen nature and of the world in which we dwell, an uncleanness that can only be taken away through the death of an innocent life. From the symbol let us recognize the reality. Yeshua is our only means for approaching God whose holiness is a consuming fire. And only in the changed heart of redemption are we enabled to purify our conscience and serve Him as we should. Or to say it another way: the sandals must be removed, they cannot simply be cleaned up. Redemption is not reformation; it is accomplished through death of the old and creation of the new.

God Keeps His Promises

God next introduces Himself to Moses—He is the God of Abraham, Isaac, and Jacob, i.e., the God Who has entered into covenant with His chosen people and intends to keep His word (vv. 6-9). As in the *Amidah*, the Name "God" is repeated with each name of the Patriarchs to whom the covenant was established: "The God of your father, the God of Abraham, the God of Isaac, the God of Jacob." The emphasis is upon the personal, one-to-one relationship that God has with His chosen ones. Isaac's relationship in covenant with God was not via Abraham as father—it was directly with God, and so with Jacob and now with Moses and the nation as a whole.

This is what distinguishes the true and living God from all of man's fabrications (idols). The God of our fathers takes the initiative to come and be with His chosen ones—God met Moses in the wilderness, where he was. And this is the glory of it all—God moves to love mankind *first*, not *vice versa*. Moses did not go in search of God. God, as in the garden, comes looking for Moses. "We love Him because He first loved us."

But why? Why does God go "looking" for sinful man in order to enter into fellowship and covenant with him? The only answer to this question is God's own sovereign desire. It was His purpose to seek out those whom He would save. God acts in accordance with His sovereign plan to accomplish His eternal will—this and this alone is the motivation for His interaction with mankind. And He never fails to keep His promises. To suggest otherwise is in every way to deny the very essence of The Name.

God, in His own sovereign and free love, chose Abraham and His seed. As such, He promised blessing to them, and protection. Now that the Egyptians were treating His chosen people with contempt, He moves to fulfill His word to them—to come to their aid and to rescue them. His promises are no less certain today, for He never changes. And His relationship in these promises is no less personal. Our names are inscribed upon the breastplate and worn over the heart of our great High Priest.

God Has Chosen to Accomplish His Will through People

God is not dependent upon people. He can get His work done without the help of anyone. But He, more often than not, chooses to use people to accomplish His purposes. This, of course, is a supreme blessing, to be used by God to accomplish His purposes. It is for this reason that the *mitzvot* are a blessing, for *mitzvot* are the instructions of the King to those He has chosen as His servants.

God first informs Moses of the situation and that He (obviously) is aware of it. Then He informs Moses that he would be the divinely sent messenger—the one through whom God would accomplish His grand plan of the exodus.

Moses wasn't so sure. At first this appears as a healthy expression of humility, but it ends in a show of apparent faithlessness. Note the three questions Moses asks:

1. Who am I? (v. 11)
2. What is His name? (v. 13)
3. What if they will not believe me? (4:1)

Then note God's answers:

1. Certainly I will be with you. (v. 12) [It really doesn't matter what strengths or weaknesses you have as long as I'm there].
2. I AM WHO I AM (v. 14) [My character is the basis of your trust].
3. I will give you power (4:1-5) so they will believe.
   [Their responses are My concern, not yours].

How often do we have the same questions as Moses as we face the events of life? We consider ourselves and recognize our insufficiencies.

God promises to be with us (which ought always to be enough!). We lack an accurate understanding of who God really is (we're not as diligent as we should be in the study of the Scriptures). God graciously reveals to us more and more as we seek to "know His Name." We list all of the ways that we're quite sure we cannot succeed, and God counters with all of the ways He intends to make us successful! But through this dialog He asks us to be faithful, to demonstrate our faith in Him, to trust that His presence and power will accomplish His designed plan in us.

The God Who Is

What is the meaning of the four-letter name that God reveals to Moses? This, of course, is the long-standing question, and one that has given rise to a great many debates. I doubt that we will settle the dispute here! But knowing some of the data might help.

a. The four-letter Name is called the "Tetragrammaton" which is Latin meaning "four letters."

b. It is this Name that Jews and those worshipping with them from ancient times refused to pronounce, substituting circumlocutions such as "heaven," "Adonai," "HaMakom" (הַמָּקוֹם, "the place"), "HaShem" (הַשֵׁם, "the Name"), etc.

c. The four letters are י - ה - ו - ה, *yod, hey, vav, hey*. Each of these letters, at certain times in the history of the Hebrew language, functioned both as consonants as well as marking vowel sounds. *Yod* = long i, *hey*=short or long a, *vav* = long u or long o. Thus, the four letters by themselves do form the Name, but without knowing the vowels that are included, the four consonants could be pronounced a number of different ways. The reality is that in our day, no one knows for certain the original pronunciation of the Tetragrammton, and anyone who claims that they do is misinformed.

d. In the MT of the Hebrew Bible, the Masoretes often indicated a *qereketiv* (what is read instead of what is written) when the Name appears. In the text itself, they would write the vowels of the word that should be substituted for the Name. Thus, when Adonai was to be read in place of the Tetragrammaton, they would write YeHoVaH (יְהֹוָה or יֱהֹוָה). Not realizing this, later translators manufactured "Jehovah" as God's Name, but of course, this combines the consonants of the Tetragrammaton with the vowels of Adonai—a genuine misnomer! In certain instances, where YHVH is coupled with Adonai (e.g., Gen 15:2), it became the tradition to substitute Elohim for the Tetragrammaton, and thus the Name is written יְהוִה or יֱהוִה in the MT, putting the vowels of Elohim on the consonants of the Tetragrammaton.

e. Many scholars have taken the position that the Name is somehow tied to, or based upon, the Hebrew verb הָיָה, the verb "to be." Of course, in the Hebrew verb system there is no form that corresponds to our present tense verb "am," thus to write "I am" using the verb "to be" in ancient Hebrew was impossible. Instead, the simple pronoun אֲנִי, *ani*, "I," is understood to represent "I am" when the context demands it. The verb to be (הָיָה) shows up in the Tanach either in the Perfect ("was") or imperfect ("will be"), and only twice as a participle (Ex 9:3, Qal fem. sing.; Prov 13:19, Nif fem. sing.). The Qal masc. sing. participle form, הֹוֶה is not found in the Tanach.

f. The significant line of 3:14, אֶהְיֶה אֲשֶׁר אֶהְיֶה, is usually translated "I am who I am" though a more precise translation of the Hebrew would yield "I will be what I will be" since the verb "to be" is, in both cases, in the imperfect aspect. Indeed, the Stone Chumash translates it "I shall be as I shall be." Interestingly, the Lxx translates the phrase ἐγώ εἰμι ὁ ὤν, "I am the one being" or "I am the one who is." The Rabbinic commentaries offer this perspective: (note b.*Berachot* 9b for example),

> I am that I am. The Holy One, blessed be He, said to Moses, Go and say to Israel: I was with you in this servitude, and I shall be with you in the servitude of the [other] kingdoms. He said to Him, Lord of the Universe, sufficient is the evil in the time thereof! Thereupon the Holy One, blessed by He, said to him, Go and tell them I AM has sent me unto you. (Rashi's comments are a repeat of this).

But the point that must be made here, and one that is quite significant in my estimation, is that the Christian commentators (following a Greek ontology) read the Lxx "I am the one being" or "I am who I am" as a statement of essential being, while the Hebrew text emphasizes essential character revealed through doing. What the text stresses, then, is that just as God has fulfilled His promises to Israel in the past (and particularly in His faithfulness to preserve Jacob, his family, and the nation while under the rule of the Egyptians) so He will act in the future to fulfill His word and to be with Israel. God's character is therefore not affirmed primarily on philosophical terms (eternality, omnipotence, etc.) but by His actions on behalf of His people. God's character is known through His actions.

With these data in mind, how should we understand the meaning of the Name, based as it is upon Ex 3:14? The Name signifies the One Who has made a covenant and Who designs human history in order to fulfill that covenant. The God of Israel, by His very name (the Tetragrammaton) is the God Who not merely breaks into history, but Who ordains history to bring about His appointed purposes. He is the One through Whom, and by Whom, and to Whom all things exist. This is the revelation of the Name.

But most significant for our study is that the Name as revealed to Moses, "I will be what I will be," is best seen in the repeated use of אֶהְיֶה, "I will be" in the phrase "I will be with you" or "I will be with your mouth" (Ex 3:12; 4:12, 15). The very essence of God's character is seen in His promise to "be with" His chosen people. Indeed, the whole theme of Exodus can be summed up in the dwelling of God among His people, represented most clearly in the Tabernacle and the service of the Tabernacle. In short, the Name of God reveals His purpose to dwell with His people, and in His dwelling, to secure their destiny within the realm of His covenant promises.

"I AM" and Yeshua

A very interesting event is narrated by John in his Gospel, involving an encounter of Yeshua with a group of Pharisees. In John 8:12–20, the Pharisees remark that Yeshua is testifying about Himself when He states, "I am the light of the world" (v. 12). They argue that when one is one's own witness, it is invalid since the Torah requires two or three witnesses to verify something as true. Yeshua responds that there is a "second witness," and that witness is His Father Who sent Him. They ask Him, "Where is Your Father?" (v. 19) and Yeshua answers "You know neither Me nor My Father; if you knew Me, you would know My Father also." Later in the narrative when Yeshua says, "You will know the truth, and the truth will make you free," (v. 32), the Pharisees retort, "We are Abraham's descendants and have never yet been enslaved to anyone!" (v. 37), to which Yeshua responds, "If you are Abraham's children, do the deeds of Abraham" (v. 39). The conversation continues with Yeshua stating: "Your father Abraham rejoiced to see My day, and he saw it and was glad" (v. 56). Now comes the real question from the Pharisees: "You are not yet fifty years old, and have You seen Abraham?" (v. 57) to which Yeshua answers: "Truly, truly, I say to you, before Abraham was born, I am." On hearing this, the group of Pharisees took up stones to stone Yeshua.

We do not know whether Yeshua was speaking Hebrew, Aramaic, or Greek. All of these are possibilities. But one thing we do know, the words of John are inspired by the Ruach, and thus the Greek we have fully represents the intended meaning of Yeshua's words. And the Greek that stands behind the English words "I am" is ἐγώ εἰμι, the same two Greek words used by the Lxx in Ex 3:14 (ἐγώ εἰμι ὁ ὤν). But for John to have written this phrase in v. 58 the way he did is remarkable, because it is not the normal way we would expect the Greek to be written: ἀμὴν ἀμὴν λέγω ὑμῖν, πρὶν Ἀβραὰμ γενέσθαι ἐγὼ εἰμί, "Truly truly I say to you, Before Abraham came to be I AM." Mixing the aorist infinitive with the present verb "to be," is simply poor grammar if John intend to convey Yeshua's words as "Before Abraham came to be I was." What is more, not only does Yeshua begin with ἀμὴν ἀμὴν, "amen amen" (which is a way to make His statement emphatic), but He uses the same emphatic form (with the added 1st person pronoun) that the Lxx used to translate Ex 3:14. Add to this the reaction of the Pharisees, who sought to kill Him for His words, and it is very clear what John intended us to know by the words he used to convey Yeshua's testimony of Himself: Yeshua identified Himself as יהוה in the flesh.

Of course, from the perspective of human reasoning, this seems impossible. But what is impossible from man's perspective is not impossible for God. We affirm, then, that the Father, the Son, and the Spirit are divinely revealed to us as distinct yet infinitely One.

The Practical Ramifications of Knowing God's Name

What are the practical applications of our study regarding the revealed Name of God? First, the Sacred Name of God emphasizes that He always does what He says He will do, and He never goes back on His promises. To suggest that God has not kept His word (e.g., in teaching that the covenant made with Israel has now been abandoned, or that the eternal nature of the Torah has now been changed) is in essence to besmirch the Name—to drag it down to a level comparable with man himself. Moreover, to live as though the eternal word of God has somehow fallen out of importance, or that the commands which He revealed as eternal have now been put aside, is likewise to disregard the very meaning of His Name. It is an egregious error that so many people who confess a true faith in God and His Messiah Yeshua can, at the same time, dismiss parts of His eternal word as though somehow they are temporal and currently inapplicable. Is God with us now? And does He remain the eternal, unchanging God Who was likewise with Moses and ancient Israel? Then how could it be suggested that the word of the Eternal One has somehow become irrelevant and no longer in need of being obeyed? Rather, encapsulated in the very Name of God, the revelation of His eternal nature and being, is the promise that He will always be with His people, and that therefore His unchanging word is likewise the possession and guiding light for all of those who are part of His family through the miracle of His grace. "For I, Y-H-V-H, do not change; therefore you, O sons of Jacob, are not consumed" (Mal 3:6).

Secondly, then, we sanctify the Name by living out the reality of its meaning—we live on the basis that what He has said is true. We keep the *mitzvot* and we live a life of faith based upon what He has said He will do. If we live as though what He has said is actually irrelevant, then we have lived in a way that defames the Name and fails to sanctify it.

Thirdly, our life of faith has as its focus His Name, and Yeshua is the revealer of His Name, for it is by Yeshua that the covenant is ultimately realized for Israel and for all attached to her. No one can truly sanctify the Name apart from a full acceptance of God's Messiah Who has come to reveal the Name. The oft repeated verse (Ps 118:25) in connection with Yeshua's role as Messiah is, "Blessed is He Who comes in the Name of Y-H-V-H." To "come in the Name of Y-H-V-H" means to come with divine authority and power, revealing the Almighty and accomplishing those things that only He can do. Therefore, to disregard Yeshua, or to discount His role as the bearer of the Name, is likewise to disregard the One Who sent Him. Note these statements of Yeshua in John's Gospel: "Everyone who has heard and learned from the Father, comes to Me" (John 6:45); "…if you knew Me, you would know My Father also" (John 8:19); "…If God were your Father, you would love Me" (John 8:42); "…He who hates Me hates My Father also" (John 15:23); "I am no longer in the world; and yet they themselves are in the world, and I come to You. Holy Father, keep them in Your Name, the Name which You have given Me, that they may be one even as We are" (John 17:11). Yeshua is the incarnation of the Name, and thus a sanctification of the Name is equally a reception of, and submission to, the Messiah Who is the revelation of the Name incarnate.

The mystery of the Divine nature is therefore found in the singular "Name" found in the commission of Yeshua to His disciples: "Go therefore and make disciples of all the nations, baptizing them in the Name of the Father and the Son and the Holy Spirit…" (Matt 28:19). The text does not say "in the names" but "in the Name" (singular). The mystery of the oneness of God is therefore expressed in the fact that Father, Son and Spirit equally bear "the Name" yet function as a plurality within the eternal oneness of God. This is not presented as an ontological or philosophical axiom, but rather as the reality of God with us, Immanuel. For Yeshua goes on to promise "…and look, I AM WITH YOU always, even to the end of the age" (Matt 29:20). In the phrase "I am with you," He reiterates the essence of אֶהְיֶה ("I will be what I will be") in our Torah *parashah*. In the same manner, Yeshua promised His disciples that the Spirit would abide with them: "…the Spirit of truth, whom the world cannot receive, because it does not see Him or know Him, but you know Him because He abides with you and will be in you" (John 14:17).

The proof that God never changes is found in the reality that He remains eternally with His people. It is the abiding and unchanging presence of God with His people that secures their salvation. And it is God's desire to dwell with His people that reveals the very essence of His nature as revealed in His Name.

PARASHAH 48
TRIENNIAL CYCLE

EXODUS 4:14–6:1

HAFTARAH: ISAIAH 55:12-56:7 | APOSTOLIC: ACTS 7:35–37

Preparing Moses

Our *parashah* continues from the dialog between Moses and Adonai with which the previous *parashah* ended. Though God had chosen Moses to be His spokesman, Moses had complained that he was "slow of speech and slow of tongue" (4:12). Even after God had assured Moses "I will be with your mouth," Moses replies, "send the message by whomever You will." This was a polite way of saying "no" to God, but actually, there's no polite way to rebuff the Almighty! Such *chutzpah* aroused the anger of the Almighty, as the opening verse of our *parashah* states: "Then the anger of Adonai burned against Moses…." Moses' refusal to believe that God could overcome whatever language deficiencies he had resulted in the loss of privilege. If Moses were unwilling, God would find someone else to speak for Him. That someone else was Moses' brother, Aaron. The Sages suggest that had Moses willingly complied with Adonai's request, he, rather than Aaron, would have also occupied the privileged position as High Priest (כֹּהֵן הַגָּדוֹל, *cohen hagadol*).

The fact that Aaron is called "the Levite" (4:14) is curious because it seems superfluous. Surely Moses knew that he and his older brother were from the tribe of Levi! Perhaps the designation is added in order to emphasize the future office of the High Priest which would be from Aaron's line, or the priesthood in general which would be from the tribe of Levi. It is possible to translate the Hebrew אַהֲרֹן אָחִיךָ הַלֵּוִי as "Aaron your Levite brother," which would emphasize that Aaron, like Moses, qualified for the task of addressing Pharaoh in some specific way (though what these specific qualifications might have been is not mentioned).

God then outlines how Aaron will function as the mouthpiece of Moses (4:15–16): God will communicate to Moses, Moses to Aaron, and Aaron to Pharaoh. Moreover, though Aaron would receive the messages from Moses, he was to accept them as though they were directly from God. He could thus address Pharaoh by saying "Thus says Adonai" (cf. 5:1; 7:17, etc). The fact that in the subsequent narrative both Moses and

Aaron address Pharaoh (e.g., 5:1, "And afterward Moses and Aaron came and said (plural) to Pharaoh...") could just as well be understood as Aaron speaking for both of them. This arrangement, of Moses being "as God" to Aaron, giving Aaron the words and having him address Pharaoh, was understood by the Sages as the paradigm for the office of the prophet. Indeed, this is explicitly stated in 7:1, "Then Adonai said to Moses, 'See, I make you as God to Pharaoh, and your brother Aaron shall be your prophet." The basic duty of the prophet, then, was to take the words of God, given directly to him, and faithfully proclaim them to the people.

Besides having the assurance that Aaron would be his spokesman to Pharaoh, Moses was also instructed to take the staff by which God had promised to perform confirming miracles in the sight of the Egyptians. The fact that the text repeats the notice that Moses took the staff (4:17, 20) is a portend of the fact that Pharaoh would rebuff Moses and Aaron, and thus two witnesses (Aaron's words and the miracles performed via the staff of Moses) would confirm the reality of the message.

Moses thus makes plans to return to Egypt. He receives confirmation from Yitro, his father-in-law, as well as divine revelation that those who were seeking his life in Egypt had died. So, together with his wife and sons, he begins the journey back to the land of Egypt where his people are enslaved.

But God not only assures Moses that it is safe for him to return, He also informs him in advance that Pharaoh will not listen to his request to let the people go. The reason for Pharaoh's recalcitrance, however, is at first confusing—Pharaoh will reject Moses' request because God Himself will harden his heart (4:21): "... but I will harden his heart so that he will not let the people go." Here we come face to face with the age-old question of God's sovereignty and man's will. If God hardened Pharaoh's heart even before Moses ever approached him, how could Pharaoh be held responsible for his actions? This is the very question asked by the Apostle Paul (Rom 9:19): "You will say to me then, 'Why does He still find fault? For who resists His will?'" In other words, if God controls the heart, then is the individual responsible for his or her responses? Paul's answer is clear (9:20): "On the contrary, who are you, O man, who answers back to God? The thing molded will not say to the molder, 'Why did you make me like this,' will it?" In other words, the sovereignty of God is beyond our ability to understand and give full explanation. Even as a pot has no ability to question the will of the potter, so mankind lacks the ability to understand the mystery and greatness of God. In the end, we must affirm both sides of the equation: God is the One Who controls all things, and each individual person is held responsible for his or her choices. The fact that we cannot reconcile these two realities in no way diminishes either of them. All who are truly redeemed by God's grace, however, have no difficulty confessing that their salvation is in every way the result of God's grace, not something they deserved or earned.

In general, the debates that have ensued over the issue of God's hardening Pharoah's heart have taken two different perspectives. On the one hand, some have found the whole idea that God would harden a person's heart against Himself so repugnant that they cannot accept this as true. As such, they either reject the Bible's revelation of God ("I can't accept a God Who would diminish a person's free will"), or they seek to find ways to reinterpret those passages that affirm God's sovereign control in the affairs of men. One such approach for our specific text is to say that Pharaoh hardened his own heart, and those verses that say God hardened it should be understood to mean not that God was *active* in hardening Pharoah's heart, but that He simply *allowed* Pharaoh to harden his own heart.

Both of these perspectives, however, begin with a view of God that is clearly not biblical. The Bible does not present God as someone who must answer to anyone other than Himself. God is not required to submit Himself to any law or standard which resides above Him. He is, by nature, fully consistent with His own character, but does not "play second fiddle" to any other sovereign or law. As such, all that is righteous is determined by God Himself. It is therefore both unbiblical and illogical to subject God and His actions to the scrutiny of some supposed standard of "fairness." God, and all He does, is the standard of righteousness and fairness.

The idea that God only confirmed what Pharaoh had already decided is not satisfying either, for the simple reason that salvation is only possible where God breaks in and overrides man's decisions. That is to say, for God to allow man to go his own way is in every case to condemn that person to damnation, for only when God breaks into one's life and overpowers the will does that person turn from wickedness to serve God with a pure heart. But even from the perspective of a humanist, a God who has the power to save from damnation but does not, is as guilty as if He had condemned the person outright.

The Exodus texts make the following amply clear:
1. God hardened Pharaoh's heart so that he would reject the pleas of Moses and Aaron, so that God's power in bringing Israel out of Egypt would be manifested (7:3-5, cf. Rom 9:17–18).
2. God promised Moses that He would harden Pharaoh's heart before Moses ever stood before Pharaoh (4:21).
3. Pharaoh participated in the hardening of his own heart (8:15, 32; 9:34)

4. The story makes it clear that a "hardened heart" manifests itself in rejecting God's commands.

There are three different words used in the texts relating to the hardening of Pharaoh's heart: חזק (*chazaq*), קשה (*qashah*) and כבד (*kabad*). The three words have various shades of meaning. חזק (*chazaq*), the most often used word, simply means "to be or make strong." It can be in a good or evil sense; in this case Pharaoh's heart was strengthened against God. קשה (*qashah*) means "to be difficult or heavy" and is used of "oppression, hard labor" and even of "labor in birth." This term might be best used to describe Pharaoh's heart as "obstinate." כבד (*kabad*) generally means "to encourage or honor" or "to be heavy." From a Hebrew perspective, to make someone or something "heavy" is to laden that thing or person with praise.

It should be noted that the only word used in connection with Pharaoh "hardening" his own heart is כבד (*kabad*), "to honor or encourage." Pharaoh's actions proceed from his pride and desire to establish his own greatness. The word most often used of HaShem's part is חזק (*chazaq*), "to strengthen or make strong." In other words, God strengthened Pharaoh's heart to remain rebellious against His command. The one time HaShem "encourages" Pharaoh in his pride (10:1) makes it clear that God acts sovereignly to accomplish His purposes and plans. While it may seem that God "dirties" His hands by encouraging Pharaoh's pride, the reality is simply that God encourages Pharaoh to be what he in fact is: selfish and prideful. In this regard we may have an illustration of what the Apostle Paul speaks of in Romans 1:28, "And just as they did not see fit to acknowledge God any longer, God gave them over to a depraved mind …." In other words, apart from God's gracious intervention in the life of an individual, drawing that person to Himself, no one would ever come to Him (cf. Jn 6:44; Rom 3:9–18).

The following chart lists each occurrence in Exodus of the hardening of Pharaoh's heart. Where the subject of the verb is clearly known, it is indicated. Blanks indicate the subject of the verb is ambiguous.

חזק (chazaq)	קשה (qashah)	כבד (kabad)
4:21 HaShem	7:3 HaShem	8:15 Pharaoh
7:13	13:15	8:32 Pharaoh
7:14		9:7
7:22		9:34
8:19		10:1 HaShem
9:12 HaShem		
9:35		
10:20 HaShem		
10:27 HaShem		
11:10 HaShem		
14:4 HaShem		
14:8 HaShem		
14:17 HaShem		

In 4:22 we find the first clear use of the name "Israel" to designate the nation formed from the sons of Jacob. Moreover, Israel is designated as the firstborn son of Adonai: "Israel is My son, My firstborn." This statement is foundational for the subsequent exodus story, for Adonai saves His "firstborn" but takes the life of each firstborn of the Egyptians. This important use of "firstborn" may also help us understand another difficult passage in our *parashah,* namely, the encounter between God and Moses as he and his family made their way to Egypt.

As Moses and his family stopped for the night, the text states that "Adonai met him and sought to put him to death." The pronouns are ambiguous. Was God angry with Moses or with his son? Whom was He about to put to death? It would seem that the divine anger was directed toward Moses, not his son, but was HaShem about to take the life of the son because of Moses? But why would God be angry with Moses when He had clearly sent him to Egypt and Moses had complied with Adonai's directions? This reminds us of the Balaam Oracles where Balaam is instructed by God to travel with the men who are about to arrive, and then the text says that God was angry with Balaam because he was going and the Angel of Adonai stood in his way to stop him (Num 22:20–22).

Even more puzzling is the manner in which the anger of God against Moses is assuaged. The issue revolves around the fact that one of the sons of Moses was not yet circumcised. The Sages are divided as to which son this was. Some (cf. b.*Ned* 32a; Mid. Rab. *Exodus* 5.8) taught that Eliezar, the second-born, was born on the way to Egypt, and since (like the Israelites who did not perform circumcision in the wilderness) circumcising an infant while traveling presented possible life-threatening dangers, Moses had put off the circumcision until later. But this would not explain God's wrath over the whole matter. Others of the Sages (Saadia, Ramban) believe it was Gershom, the firstborn, who remained uncircumcised, and a number of factors could have contributed to this neglect on Moses' part. In some of the Ancient Near Eastern cultures, circumcision was ridiculed, and this may have contributed to Moses' hesitation to circumcise Gershom on the eighth day as God had commanded. Or it is possible that Gershom was very weak as a newborn, and the circumcision was put off for health reasons but then neglected. Whatever the case, it may be the bold statement regarding Israel as God's firstborn son (v. 22) that informs this perplexing story. Here is Moses, on his way to lead God's firstborn son out of Egypt, His covenant people who would soon stand at Sinai and receive the Torah. Yet Moses himself had neglected to circumcise his own firstborn son. He had, in this sense, diminished the importance of the covenant made with Abraham, Isaac, and Jacob, the very covenant that would form the basis for God's decisive action on behalf of Israel. If Moses were to lead the people in strength, then he would have to show himself to be faithful to God's commandments. Neglecting to circumcise his own firstborn son would severely draw into question his own allegiance to the God he confessed to serve. Indeed, the exodus itself is centered in the covenant faithfulness of God toward His people, and thus it was incumbent upon His chosen leader, Moses, that the covenant also be held in highest regard.

Zipporah apparently understood this. Taking a flint knife, she circumcises her son. It should not go unnoticed that the normal word for "circumcising" (מול) is not used here but rather the common word "to cut" (כרת). Perhaps this is to parallel the common Hebrew expression for making a covenant, i.e., כרת ברית, *karat b'rit*, "to cut a covenant." Then, in some kind of ceremonial act, Zipporah touches the severed foreskin of her son to "his feet (or legs)" (4:25), but once again we are not sure to whom the pronoun refers. The NASB inserts "feet of Moses" and the NIV puts "Moses" in brackets, while the ESV includes "Moses" but adds a marginal note. But the Hebrew has only "his feet," and it may well be that this refers to the feet of the son, not of Moses. If so, this may have been done in order to show that the circumcision had been completed. Does this putting of the blood upon the feet parallel the putting of the blood upon the doorposts in the exodus from Egypt? In both cases, the blood acts as a sign which preserves life.

Then Zipporah proclaims (apparently to Moses): "Surely you are a bridegroom of blood for me" (כִּי חֲתַן־דָּמִים אַתָּה לִי). All of this seems very strange, and no clear explanation can be given for the meaning of Zipporah's words. It may be that by "bridegroom of blood" she implies that Moses' life was spared through her having accomplished the circumcision of her son. Though some commentators have tried to link this with the custom in other semitic peoples who circumcised a male just prior to his marriage, there is nothing in the context to warrant such a connection. Though perplexing, this story most likely is included here to emphasize the fact that obedience to maintain the covenant was all-important as the exodus event drew near, and particularly important for Moses who would be acting as God's direct agent in leading the exodus of Israel from Egypt. He could not rightly be God's covenant agent to His firstborn if he had neglected to administer the sign of the covenant to his own firstborn son.

The story continues by alerting us to the fact that God also instructed Aaron to go to the desert to meet Moses. Their meeting takes place at "the mountain of God" which is Sinai, the very region where Moses encountered the burning bush and received his instructions to return to Egypt. After meeting Aaron, they inform the "elders" as well as the people about God's plan. Performing the miracles in their sight confirmed that God was active on their behalf, and thus "the people believed" and bowed and worshipped God Who had shown His faithfulness to help them in accordance with the promises He had made (4:31).

Chapter 5 gives us the account of Moses and Aaron's first approach to Pharaoh. We already know that he will refuse their request to send the people forth to worship Adonai. Pharaoh makes it clear that he has no allegiance to Adonai ("I do not know Adonai," 5:2) and thus is not required to obey His commands. Instead, he accuses Moses and Aaron of subversion and makes the servitude of the people more harsh. Instead of supplying them with the necessary materials for making sun-hardened brick, he requires them to gather their own materials, but keeps the daily quota the same. The people were therefore required to do far more work than before. Moreover, those foremen who had been appointed to oversee the work were beaten when the quota was not met. Clearly, rather than bringing hope to the people, the meeting which Moses and Aaron had with Pharaoh had resulted in a much, much worse situation.

From the posture of worship, the people turned upon Moses and Aaron: "They said to them, "May Adonai look upon you and judge you, for you have made us odious in Pharaoh's sight and in the sight of his servants, to put a sword in their hand to kill us" (5:21). Such dire straits brought Moses to address the Almighty: "Why have You brought harm to this people? Why did you ever send me? ...You have not delivered Your people at all!" (5:23). It is easy for us to shake our heads at the apparent unbelief, both of the people as well as of Moses. Had not God promised to deliver them? Had not God promised to be with Moses and Aaron and to make their mission successful? Yet if we can, for a moment, put ourselves in their situation, we might wonder how we would have fared in our own belief and the stamina of our faith. How often do we, in far less difficult situations, fail to exercise a persevering faith in God and succumb rather to complaint and discouragement?

But note well God's response to Moses. He does not rebuke Moses, nor chastise him for his apparent lack of understanding and faith. Rather, He reaffirms His own plan to deal sovereignly with Pharaoh and with Egypt as a whole. "Now you will see what I will do to Pharaoh..." (5:23). Often God must bring us to the end of ourselves before we will acknowledge and trust His greatness. The exodus would not be effected by Moses or Aaron, even if they were valiant leaders. The redemption from Egypt would be by the sovereign, omnipotent hand of God Himself. And this could have only been the case, for the exodus was forever to stand as an historical drama revealing God's way of redemption. God, and God alone, is the One Who saves, and the exodus, in every detail, will emphasize this over and over again.

Parashah Fourteen
וָאֵרָא – VA'EIRAH
"and I appeared"
Exodus 6:2–9:35

In the Triennial Cycle there are
Three Parashot

6:2–7:18 | 7:19–8:19[15] | 8:20[16]–9:35

Parashah 49
Triennial Cycle

Exodus 6:2–7:18

Haftarah: Ezekiel 28:25-29:21 | Apostolic: Acts 7:17-22

The Character of the Redeemed Soul

If one looks at the Scriptures as a whole, nothing is more clear than this: the exodus from Egypt forms the paradigm or the pattern for the whole concept of "redemption." After this momentous event, the exodus would remain in the traditions and beliefs of Israel as the undisputed action of God in redeeming His people. A simple definition of redemption is "regaining ownership through payment of a price." This basic meaning of גָּאַל, *ga'al*, the Hebrew verb most often translated by our English word "redeem," by extension can also mean "to right something that is wrong." In either case, a consistent part of redemption is the paying of a price. A modern day illustration of the basic meaning of "redemption" may be found in a pawn shop. An item which has been left in the hands of the owner is redeemed when (1) proof of ownership is provided, and (2) the required price of redemption is remitted.

Now here is a very important aspect of redemption: the one doing the redeeming has prior ownership of that which is being redeemed. Israel belonged to God before she ever descended to Egypt. As the text states (Ex 4:22): "Israel is My son, My first born." This being the case, we must ask a fundamental question: "Why did God allow Israel to be under the bondage of slavery in the first place?" If He already had ownership of Israel, if indeed Israel was His son, His first-born, why would He allow Israel to be subjected to such an ordeal? This is the basic question in the minds of the Sages who wrote the midrashim. They answer by quoting from the Wisdom literature of the Tanach: "Whom the father loves, he chastens" (Prov. 13:24; note also Prov 3:12, cf. Heb 12:8, cp. Mid. Rab. *Exodus* 1.1).

> 'But he that loves him chastens him diligently' (Prov. 13:24). This refers to the Holy One, blessed be He; because of His love for Israel, as it is written: *I have loved you, says the Lord* (Mal. 1:2), does He heap upon them chastisements. You will find that the three precious gifts which

God gave unto Israel were all given after much suffering: The Torah, Eretz Israel, and the Life to Come.

The chastening hand of the Lord upon Israel was needed, for she had a natural tendency to believe in "self-redemption" (as indeed all mankind has such a tendency)—that she was self-sufficient and could pull herself up by the boot-straps. Indeed, it is when we are faced with trouble and calamity that we once again admit that we are unable and weak, and we cry out to God for help.

But the fact that God brings us under the rod of chastening by putting us into a difficult or troublesome situation does not negate the fact that we belong to Him, nor does it call into question His love for us. Indeed, the very place of trouble is where He intends to demonstrate His outstretched arm of redemption, not only to assure us of His unfailing faithfulness to His promises, but also to prove to us once again that apart from Him we can do nothing.

This is one clear characteristic of the redeemed soul, of the one who has true, saving faith: a willingness to (1) admit one's inabilities, and (2) to entrust oneself into God's care. Self-reliance is diametrically opposed to biblical faith.

Now God often has to bring us into situations of dire straits before we are willing to admit that we cannot make it on our own! Our hearts (minds, wills) are still affected by the natural thinking—by the depraved self or "flesh" who, in the strength of the remaining tendency to rebellion, tends to believe that one can get along fine without God. Yet it is the indwelling Ruach, the Spirit, who enlivens the redeemed soul to face the truth and willingly admit it—without God I can do nothing. If the difficulties of life are that which bring us to this place of truth and confession, then certainly we have come to understand why we would give thanks to God for such trials and tribulations—they bring us to appreciate the redemption God has made for us. Thus James writes:

> Consider it all joy, my brethren, when you encounter various trials, knowing that the testing of your faith produces endurance. And let endurance have its perfect result, so that you may be perfect and complete, lacking in nothing. (James 1:2–4)

But once the soul that belongs to God has reckoned with its innate inability, faith working within causes that soul to rest in the all-sovereign One and His promised care. The two parts go hand in hand: admitting my inability and relying upon God.

Not so with the unbeliever. The unbelieving heart may be forced to admit its inability, but there will still be an unwillingness to lay oneself upon God and trust Him for His care. Rather, the unbelieving heart hardens in rebellion against God for it reasons that God has arbitrarily brought the calamity, and this for selfish reasons. Like the sin entered into by Adam and Chavah (Eve), the heart of unbelief questions the very goodness and love of God. The lie of the evil one, "has God said?" was received by Adam and Chavah as a valid questioning of God's goodness. Had God given the prohibition regarding the tree of knowledge of good and evil for selfish reasons? Was God trying to hide the truth from Adam and Chavah, that they could be equal with Him if they but ate of that tree? The first sin, therefore, was that of unbelief. They questioned the goodness of God. The core element of the unbelieving heart, then, is a self-centered reliance based upon the suspicion that God is not always good. This being the case, how one interprets the struggles and troubles of life will depend ultimately upon whether one has faith or not. The heart of faith eventually confesses that even the tribulations in life are a mark of God's love. The unbelieving heart thinks just the opposite.

This does not mean that one who has genuine faith fails to experience the woes and despair of tribulations. The Psalmist demonstrates often that at first, when trouble came upon him, he cried out in pain and confusion about why God would allow such a thing. But inevitably, after contemplating what he knew to be true, his heart of faith was able to accept the tribulations of life, and even to be strengthened and encouraged through them.

This picture of redemption of the soul is graphically laid out before us in the exodus story. Israel, the possession of God, is brought by His hand into slavery and bondage. This trial brought Israel to realize that she was powerless to overcome the hardship in which she found herself, and thus she cried out to God. Would she have called out to Him had the trouble not arisen? Or would she have willingly remained in the pagan culture of her rulers, foregoing the full, outward worship of HaShem? All indications are that she would have remained content to abide in pagan Egypt. But the love of HaShem for His people could not allow such spiritual apathy. His love for her is demonstrated in His willingness to bring Israel under the rod of His chastening, that she might cry out to Him and experience the power of His redemption.

The picture given to us in the exodus is not only of God's redemptive hand, but also of the depraved heart of unbelief. Pharaoh, in contrast to Moses, Aaron, and the people of Israel, displays the characteristics of the natural heart, given to unbelief.

In our *parashah* the first three signs and wonders (cf. 7:3) that God sent are listed: (1) the Nile and the water in Egypt turns to blood, (2) an infestation of frogs followed, (3) and then an infestation of insects.

Previously, the transformation of Moses' rod into a snake and its return to the form of a stick (cf. 4:5) had apparently been received by the people of Israel as a mark of authenticity of Moses' authority and power from God. The same sign, however, in the presence of Pharaoh and His court, only produced further hardness of heart in them.

The same may be true of the signs and wonders that Moses and Aaron displayed. The Nile turning to blood was a devastating plague, for it hit at the very center of the Egyptian social and religious foundation. Like a woman with a flow of blood is unclean for seven days (cf. Lev 15:19), so the Nile became "unclean"—unfit to drink and thus the "life" flow of Egypt was defiled. Rather than a life-giving source, it was turned into the stench of death. But even though every Egyptian had nothing but blood in watering buckets and bowls, the Israelites apparently were unaffected by the plague and had fresh water to drink. Only newly dug wells or even troughs beside the Nile afforded drinkable water to the Egyptians. But there was no humility in Pharaoh and his court—they considered the whole thing to be some sort of magic that Moses and Aaron had performed. They duplicated the phenomenon through their magical arts. But like the last plague, the first one had the portends of death.

The second wonder was frogs—frogs, frogs, and more frogs! And the third was like it: flying insects. The frog, living in the Nile, was viewed by the Egyptians as connected to the divine power of the River. They were, as it were, the god's offspring. As such, they too were sacred. But instead of affording the Egyptians life and health, they brought disease and trouble. The text says that they would come "into you and your people and in all your servants" וּבְכָה וּבְעַמֶּךָ וּבְכָל־עֲבָדֶיךָ, (Heb 7:29; Eng. 8:4). Now while this may be understood as "upon" rather than "into," the preposition could surely be taken either way. It stands to reason that such an infestation of frogs must surely have led to disease, for the people must have ingested parts of the frogs! Yet in their rebellion, the magicians of Egypt add to the calamity by adding to the frogs! The best they could do was make the situation worse.

Even Moses (who carefully constructs the divine removal of the frogs so as to leave no question by Whose power it was done), when he removes the frogs through prayer to HaShem, the piles of dead frogs cause a great stench throughout the land. Such insanitary conditions are just what insects enjoy. The dead frogs were the perfect carrion to support maggots, producing the flying insects that overtook the land as Pharaoh refused to believe, and broke his pledge to send the people of Israel forth from his land.

Now in this third wonder, the magicians and Pharaoh are confronted with the obvious: this wonder could not be duplicated by the workers of magic—it was indeed, the work of HaShem. If we could excuse Pharaoh for his unbelief of the first two wonders, there is no excuse for denying this third one. He and his court knew beyond doubt that what was taking place was the direct action of the God of Abraham, Isaac, and Jacob. Yet he willfully turns his back and walks in blatant unbelief.

Here then we have, in stark contrast, the distinct characteristics of faith versus unbelief. And as such we are given a litmus test of our own faith. True faith in God admits one's utter inability and thus turns to rely entirely upon God for one's eternal salvation, a salvation that not only has the *olam haba* (the world to come) in view, but also the life of salvation in the *olam haze* (this world). Unbelief tries to find one's own way, and to secure one's own redemption. The life of faith is just the opposite: it is one of humility, while unbelief is marked by self-reliance. Faith says "there dwells in me, that is in my flesh, not one good thing" (Rom 7:18), while unbelief proudly affirms "Who is Adonai, that I should obey His voice?" (Ex. 5:2). Only faith saves; everything else will perish.

A Note on Exodus 6:3

The opening of our *parashah* contains a statement of Adonai to Moses which has been used by liberal scholarship to support the notion that the Torah as we now have it is actually a compilation of divergent documents, put together in the 6th Century BCE or even later.

> God spoke further to Moses and said to him, "I am Adonai; and I appeared to Abraham, Isaac, and Jacob, as El Shaddai, but by My name, Y-H-V-H, I did not make Myself known to them. (Ex 6:2–3)

From this text, some scholars reasoned that the revealed Name of God, יהוה, the Tetragrammaton, was not used until the time of the exodus, and that its appearance in Genesis was the result of combining documents which utilized different names of God, thus anachronistically putting יהוה into the patriarchal narratives when, in fact, that Name was not used until later. This liberal theory of the compilation of the Torah came to be known as the "Documentary Hypothesis" and developed into a discipline within the study of the Tanach known as "source criticism."

But if we take the Bible to be the inspired word of God and therefore that the Torah came by the hand of Moses (cf. Matt 8:4; 19:7; Mk 12:26; John 1:17; 7:19), then we must seek an interpretation of this Exodus text which is in harmony with that understanding. The issue is quite obvious: Ex 6:3 seems to say that the Name, יהוה, was unknown until the time of the exodus, but in fact we find the Name יהוה 165 times in the book of Genesis! What then can be meant by Adonai's words that He was not known to Abraham, Isaac, and Jacob by the Name יהוה?

The key is to understand what is meant when HaShem speaks of being "known" by someone: "... but by My name, יהוה, I did not make Myself known to them." To "be known" means far more than simply having knowledge about something or someone. From a Semitic or Hebraic perspective, to "know" someone or to make oneself "known" means to enter into a close, even intimate, relationship.

So when we take this into consideration, the verse before us can be understood as Moses intended. Surely the Tetragrammaton was known by the Patriarchs long before the exodus event. But God had not yet made known the broader meaning revealed in the Name, for it was through the exodus event itself that the covenant faithfulness of God to Abraham's descendants *as His chosen nation* would be made known. Surely He revealed the meaning of the Name El Shaddai to the Patriarchs, for in each case where women were barren and sought the Lord to give them children, the Name El Shaddai is used (cf. Gen 28:3; 35:11; 43:14; 48:3). And the Name El Shaddai most likely relates to the "God Who gives children," i.e.,"the God who brings a baby to a mother's breast."[1]

In like manner, the exodus event in which God brings plagues against Egypt in order to free His nation from the servitude of Egypt, each plague was specifically performed against one of the so-called gods of the Egyptian pantheon in order to show that they were no gods at all, being utterly incapable of overcoming the hand of Israel's God. In this way, God demonstrated ("made known") His Name יהוה by establishing the promises of the covenant He made with Abraham, and doing so in dramatic ways. Moreover, this was the first time that God demonstrated His covenant faithfulness to the nation formed from Abraham's descendants. Previously He had shown His covenant faithfulness to individuals (Abraham, Isaac, Jacob), but now the descendants of Jacob had been formed into a nation called Israel which constituted Adonai's "first born son" (Ex 4:22). This was therefore the first time that God would reveal Himself as the covenant faithful God on a national scale.

Thus, the exodus event would stand forever as the fuller revelation of God's Name, יהוה, the covenant-keeping God Whose covenant embraced a nation called Israel. And this is why the exodus becomes the foundational paradigm revealing God's redemptive plan, for in the same way that the nation of Israel was taken out of Egypt by God's outstretched arm, so all of those chosen from the nations would likewise be "rescued from the domain of darkness, and transferred to the kingdom of His beloved Son, in whom we have redemption, the forgiveness of sins" (Col 1:13–14).

---

1   See my *Studies in the Torah: Genesis*, pp. 117–18.

The *haftarah* for this *parashah* (Ezek 28:25-29:21) was chosen for obvious reasons. Using the language of the exodus, Ezekiel prophesies of the future days when Israel will once again be gathered from the nations and live in their own land which God gave to Jacob His servant (28:25). For even though Israel was historically taken out of Egypt and settled in their own land, it was often tempting to seek an alliance with Egypt in order to be strengthened against other nations which continued to expand their territories by conquest. Such alliances were strictly against the expressed command of God announced to Israel through His prophets, but these warnings went unheeded by Israel's kings.

So, relying upon the strength of foreign powers rather than upon God, Judah was defeated and exiled by Babylon. Ezekiel 28 begins with a woe oracle against the King of Tyre, describing his defeat at the hands of the Babylonian forces. Next (vv. 20ff) is a woe oracle against Sidon which was dependant upon Tyre and would thus likewise be overthrown. Thus, even as the Almighty defeated Pharaoh and his Egyptian forces, so He would demolish Tyre and Sidon.

In contrast, God's covenant faithfulness to Israel is once again announced, even in light of Israel's own disobedience and waywardness. The prophet Ezekiel speaks of a regathering of Israel to their own land, and the manner in which He will fight against the nations that have humbled Israel. Thus, the exodus motif continues to be used by the later prophets as a fitting description of God's covenant loyalty to His chosen nation, emphasizing once again that He acts in this way for His own Name sake:

> Therefore say to the house of Israel, 'Thus says the Lord ADONAI, "It is not for your sake, O house of Israel, that I am about to act, but for My holy name, which you have profaned among the nations where you went. I will vindicate the holiness of My great name which has been profaned among the nations, which you have profaned in their midst. Then the nations will know that I am ADONAI," declares the Lord ADONAI, "when I prove Myself holy among you in their sight. (Ezek 36:22–23)

The Apostolic portion chosen for this *parashah* is Acts 7:17–22, a section from the speech of Stephen in which he recounts highlights of Israel's history and God's faithfulness to Israel throughout their generations. These few verses from Stephen's speech focus on the severe enslavement put upon the Israelites by the Egyptians, for the former promise or covenant made with Joseph had been disregarded by a new Egyptian king who did not *know* Joseph. The language would suggest, not that the new Egyptian king had never heard of Joseph or the compact an earlier Pharaoh had made with him and his family, but that the new Pharaoh refused to honor the covenant previously made with Joseph and instead enslaved the descendants of Jacob.

This Apostolic reading, then, not only recounts the harsh slavery under which Israel labored as a nation in Egypt, but also contrasts the covenant faithfulness of God to Israel with the actions of the Pharaoh who refused to honor the covenant made by one of his predecessors.

In all of this, the unflinching faithfulness of the God of Israel to keep His covenant promises is highlighted. Surely we may rest confidently in the unfailing love of our God, Who has brought us close to Him through the work of His Son, our Messiah, Yeshua!

Parashah 50
Triennial Cycle

Exodus 7:19–8:19 [Hebrew 8:15]

Haftarah: Joel 3:9–21 [Heb. 4:9–21] | Apostolic: Romans 9:17–18

The Unseen Battle

Our *parashah* this week focuses on the first three of the ten plagues: the Nile turned to blood, an infestation of frogs, and an infestation of flying insects. We also see the first stages of Pharaoh's heart becoming hardened against Moses and Aaron, and against the people of Israel, but most importantly against God.

The first plague was against the River, known historically as the Nile. For the Egyptians, the Nile was the god Hapi. Another god, Osiris, was credited with the annual flooding of the Nile, which caused the surrounding land to be fertile for the next year's crops. This annual inundation occurs in September/October and was celebrated by the Egyptians as the gracious manifestation of their gods in supplying food for the nation. It is significant that the first plague was against the Nile, for it announced divine judgment against the Egyptians for the merciless killing of Israelite infant males at the command of the Pharaoh. Furthermore, it could not have been lost upon the Egyptians that when the God of Israel struck the Nile, it announced divine judgment against the gods of Egypt as well.

Modern scholars, who deny the presence of miracles in our world, find a number of natural explanations for what the biblical text describes as turning the Nile into blood. Some postulate the growth of red algae that turned the water red. Others suggest that the waters which flowed into the Nile from the mountains in Ethiopia gathered the red soil, thus making the River appear red as blood. But such explanations overlook the fact that not only was the water of the Nile red in color, but also water in all the wooden and stone vessels (7:19, cf. 7:21 which indicates the blood was throughout the whole land of Egypt). The only explanation for such a phenomenon is that God miraculously turned all the water in Egypt into blood, just as the text says. Moreover, the fact that the water containers of the Israelites remained clear could only be accounted for through a miracle. The God of Israel is the God of the miraculous. If He created the heavens and the earth, turning the water of the Nile to blood was nothing too difficult for Him!

The text indicates that the magicians of Egypt were able to perform a similar fete. It is not clear if they also turned water to blood, or if they were able to turn the bloody water back to its normal state. The latter is more likely, since by their demonic craft Pharaoh's heart was strengthened (חָזַק, *chazak*). This must mean that Pharaoh was encouraged to believe that his gods were able to overturn the work of the God of Israel. But God had already told Moses and Aaron that Pharaoh would not listen (7:4). Indeed, 7:23 literally says that Pharaoh did not "set his heart even to this." In other words, he gave the whole matter not a moment's thought.

The text indicates that the first plague lasted for seven days (7:25). The Hebrew literally says "seven days were filled up after Adonai struck the Nile." The divinely ordained period of a week, set forth initially in the creation account, is the signature of the God of Israel.

God therefore again gives the command to Moses and Aaron to approach Pharaoh with the divine edict: "send forth My people that they may serve Me" (8:1 [Eng]; 7:26 [Heb]). This command was immediately followed by imposing the second plague, that of frogs. The Egyptians worshipped a goddess named Heqt, the consort of the god Khnum. This frog-headed goddess was believed to be the goddess of fertility, and thus the massive death of the frogs was a divine retribution against the edict commanding the mid-wives to kill the male babies of the Israelites.

Since the frogs' natural habitat for reproduction was the Nile itself, now clogged with dead fish, the amphibians were forced to the land carrying the disease of the Nile, and died *en masse*.

Once again, the magicians of Egypt were able to reproduce the phenomenon, but not in causing the infestation of frogs to cease. Rather, they were only able to bring more frogs up to the land (8:7, Eng; 8:3, Heb). As a result, Pharaoh recognized that reliance upon his gods was futile, and he thus requested of Moses and Aaron that they entreat their God to remove the frogs. Moses gives Pharaoh the privilege of determining the time when the frogs should be removed, adding proof that when such occurred, it was truly the God of Israel Who made it happen. Incredibly, Pharaoh opts for "tomorrow" (8:10, Eng; 8:6, Heb)! Was he holding out hope that his magicians could work some relief in the meantime?

The intercessory work of Moses is portrayed with the words "Then Moses cried to Adonai concerning the frogs" (8:12). Moses as the mediator between God and man will become a significant theme in the book of Exodus, revealing the work of the priesthood who would represent Israel "before Adonai." God acts in accordance with Moses' request, and the frogs "died from the houses, the courts, and the fields." Once again, the death of the frogs *en masse* just at the time of Moses' prayer makes it clear that the God of Israel was in control and performing miracles to bring about these events.

But the hardness of Pharaoh's heart is seen in that once the major problem of the infestation is alleviated, he "honored" (כָּבֵד, *kabeid*) his heart and refused to listen to the demand given to him by God through His servants, Moses and Aaron. Once again, the text emphasizes that this was exactly what God had indicated would happen ("just as Adonai had said," 8:15 Eng; 8:11 Heb).

This sets up the third plague of flying insects. But this time, Moses and Aaron are not instructed to approach Pharaoh with the demand to "send forth My people" before evoking this devastation. The third plague therefore comes upon Pharaoh and Egypt as the immediate judgment for Pharaoh's unwillingness to heed the command of Adonai given before the second plague.

Aaron alone strikes the "dust of the earth" to evoke the third plague, whereas in the first two, both Aaron and Moses are viewed as acting. The Sages note that it was inappropriate for Moses to strike the dust of the land, since he had previously used it to cover the body of the Egyptian he had killed. It is not certain exactly what the flying insects were (כִּנִּם, *kinim* from the root כֵּן, *kein*), but some scholars suggest mosquitos. Others translated the word with "lice." The Lxx appears to have understood the words as "gnats." Regardless, the infestation of flying insects continued to inundate Egypt with disease. The magicians of Egypt once again attempt to duplicate the phenomenon, but are unable, and concede to Pharaoh that "this is the finger of Elohim" (8:19, Eng; 8:15, Heb). No one could deny the reality that the God of Israel was personally in control of the situation. Yet, for a third time, Pharaoh's heart was hardened. In spite of the obvious, that Israel's God was in control, Pharaoh refused to bow. In the hardness of his heart, he still believed he could overcome the hand of the Almighty.

It is clear that in these opening three plagues, the battle is only secondarily between Egypt and Israel. The primary battle is being waged between God and demonic forces. The sorcerers (מְכַשְּׁבִים, *mᵉkashbim*) and magicians (חַרְטֹם, *chartom*) utilize their "secret arts" (לְהָטִים, *lᵉhatim*) in attempting to duplicate the work of God. The word "secret arts" is formed on the root להט (*lahat*, an alternate form of לָט, *lat*) having the meaning "to burn." This most likely connects their work with sacrifices to the pagan gods, which we know are actually demons (cf. 1Cor 10:20). Did the magicians use slight of hand or trickery, or were the demonic powers able to actually duplicate the substance of the first plagues? Most likely both were involved, for the evil one is the father of lies (John 8:44).

The work of the demons is primarily a deception. Yet such deception is powerful, for the mind given over to it believes that the deception is real. Moreover, it is clear that demonic forces have power, and that they can manipulate things in this fallen world to appear as though they actually have divine power. This, of course, is their motivation, to "be like God" in the sense of having equal or even greater power than the Almighty. Yet they win their battle only when one believes their lies.

It would be one thing if the battle of the "heavenlies" (Eph 6:12) were contained in the heavens. But it is also fought in the realm of this world. God has designed that His people should also engage the battle with the evil one, and by His power, win over his deceptions. But the ability to discover and expose the deception of the evil one and his cohorts is vested in God's gracious revelation of the truth. As long as the heart of man remains in the darkness of falsehood, he stands no chance to see the enemy's deceptions for what they truly are. Therefore, it is God's revelation of Himself that shines forth and exposes the weapons of the enemy to be puny and futile. It is no wonder, then, that the evil one always attempts first to discredit the revelation of God in the Scriptures and in His Son, Yeshua. The sad state of affairs evident in mainline Christianity of our world may be traced first to the prevailing position among scholars and religious leaders of our day, that the Bible cannot be trusted. When the brilliant light of God's divine revelation is diminished, the shadows in which the enemy lurks grow all the more dominant. It should come as no surprise that the enemy's first attacks against the current Torah movement is to undermine the divine inspiration of the Scriptures.

But the fullest revelation of God to man came in the incarnation of our Savior. Yeshua is the full outshining of the glory of God, and provides an exact representation of the Almighty (Heb 1:3). Once again, it should be no surprise that in the Torah movement of our times, the eternal nature and divinity of our Messiah would come under attack. If we are to remain valiant soldiers in the spiritual battle in which we are engaged, we must always affirm as our foundation the divine truth of the Scriptures, and the mysterious, eternal and divine nature of the Messiah, Yeshua. For it is "in Messiah" that we find our primary identification. As Paul wrote:

> *Therefore if anyone is in Messiah, he is a new creature;*
> *the old things passed away;*
> *behold, new things have come.*
> (2Cor 5:17)

PARASHAH 51
TRIENNIAL CYCLE

EXODUS 8:20[Hebrew 8:16]–9:35

HAFTARAH: ISAIAH 34:11–35:4 | APOSTOLIC: HEBREW 12:14–17

Serving the Almighty: His View vs. Man's View

Nothing stands out more in our Torah text this week than the repeated emphasis upon God as the One Who makes distinctions. We read of the 4th, 5th, 6th, and 7th plagues (מַגֵּפָה, *magephah*, 9:14; נֶגַע, *nega'*, 11:1; נֶגֶף, *negeph*, 12:13 – all terms used to describe the plagues) waged against Egypt, and each time the text makes it clear that while the plague fell upon every level of Egyptian society (from Pharoah on down), not one Israelite was touched by the destructive "finger" of God.

But the first example of how God makes a distinction comes at the very beginning of the *parashah*. He had given explicit instructions to Moses and through him to Pharaoh: send forth My people that they may worship Me (שַׁלַּח עַמִּי וְיַעַבְדֻנִי). The "sending forth" (which is much more forceful than the common English "let My people go") is necessary before there can be the kind of worship or service God demands and desires.

Pharaoh had a different idea. Note 8:21[English 8:25]: "Pharaoh called for Moses and Aaron and said, "Go, sacrifice to your God within the land." (וַיִּקְרָא פַרְעֹה אֶל־מֹשֶׁה וּלְאַהֲרֹן וַיֹּאמֶר לְכוּ זִבְחוּ לֵאלֹהֵיכֶם בָּאָרֶץ)). Actually, this text can be read two ways, since בָּאָרֶץ can just as well mean "in the Land (of Israel)" as "in the land (of Egypt)." That Pharoah meant that Israel should worship HaShem without leaving Egypt is obvious, but the veiled reference to the Promised Land is intriguing.

Moses' answer is very interesting and the standard English translations (NASB, NIV, NRSV) miss the point. It is not that the lamb was considered by the Egyptians an abomination, but this word is used in the Hebrew text (since it was written to Hebrews) to describe all pagan sacrifices and idolatry (cf. Deut 7:25-26). The Egyptians considered the lamb sacred and would never have used it as a sacrifice. Thus when Moses says "Behold if (translating הֵן as a questioning particle, cf. Ibn Ezra) we sacrifice the abomination of the Egyptians…," he is referring to the lamb as a sacred object in the Egyptians' eyes–one of their many gods. Moses most likely used a different term when actually speaking to Pharaoh, but when relating the story (which would be read by Hebrews) used the term "abomination" to refer to the lamb as "sacred" in an idolatrous way. The Stone Chumash thus gives the proper sense: "behold, if we were to slaughter the deity of Egypt in their sight, will they not stone us?"

Here we gain insight into God's definition of worship. It involves, at its core, a clear distinction between the Creator and the creation. Paul recognizes that all idolators have this in common: they worship the creation rather than the Creator:

> They exchanged the truth of God for a lie, and worshiped and served created things rather than the Creator — who is forever praised. Amen. (Romans 1:25)

All paganism begins with the creation rather than the Creator. That is, paganism considers what can be seen as all important, while God's worship begins with what cannot be seen as absolutely necessary to understand properly what can be seen. In other words, from God's perspective, faith is a prerequisite for genuine worship.

> And without faith it is impossible to please God, because anyone who comes to him must believe that he exists and that he rewards those who earnestly seek him. (Hebrews 11:6)

But there is another important insight we receive by looking closely at how Pharaoh defines worship. His suggestion that Moses and the Israelites could just as well offer sacrifices in the land of Egypt rather than going into the wilderness reveals the fact that for Pharaoh worship was a means to an end rather than the end itself. For Pharaoh (and all false religion) worship is a way of pleasing the gods, of getting them on your side, of gaining for yourself from the gods what otherwise you could never have. In many cases, worship of the pagan gods is "tricking" them into acting on behalf of the worshiper.

In contrast to this, worship as God describes it is purely an act of love for Him and not an attempt to gain something from Him or cause Him to do something He otherwise might not. Thus for Pharaoh, to follow God's prescriptions for worship was not that necessary. If it was sacrifice He wanted, then give it to Him, but do it in the most expedient way—no need to travel three days journey—just do it here and now.

And here is the crux of the matter: Pharaoh, like all who follow falsehood, do not take seriously the word of God. The Almighty had communicated to Moses that Israel was to travel out of the land of Egypt and worship Him via sacrifice in the wilderness. Moses told Pharaoh this, but Pharoah considered it unimportant. "Do the ceremony, but there is no need to do it exactly as God says. Modifications don't matter—do it my way."

So why did it matter? Could the Israelites have genuinely worshiped God in the land of Egypt? Could they have offered acceptable sacrifice to HaShem without going into the wilderness as He had instructed them to?

The answer is, of course, "no." They could not have offered acceptable sacrifice in Egypt. And the reason is because God had told them to do something different than that. Acceptable worship to the One true God can only be accomplished in the context of obedience. The worship God desires cannot be given in the realm of disobedience.

Moses knew this. When he says "it is not proper to do so" (לֹא נָכוֹן לַעֲשׂוֹת כֵּן) he shows us that he had taken God's word seriously. It was not merely that to do this would have raised the hackles of the Egyptians, but more that God had prescribed a different way. Of course Israel would not always take this position. Accepting the ways of the pagan nations and incorporating these into their worship would become the on-going bane of the nation's existence.

But why was it necessary for Israel to leave Egypt before she could offer acceptable sacrifice? Because an eternal picture was wrapped up in her leaving: redemption and deliverance must proceed acceptable worship. Only the redeemed can worship Him as He desires, because only the redeemed have come to the full realization that God, and God alone, can save. Worship in the context of redemption is worship that considers the Creator to be blessed forever, separate and above the creation. And only people who have been genuinely redeemed are in a position to worship God out of their love for Him and not to gain something for themselves.

There's another way to say this: only the redeemed are able to worship God in the context of covenant. God had already told Moses that the sign He would give to prove Himself was that the people would worship at the mountain where He had revealed Himself in the burning bush (Ex 3:12). The covenant that would function as Israel's *ketubbah* (marriage contract) could only be given after they were redeemed from Egypt, not before. God would take Israel as His wife, and in so doing He would separate her unto Himself. Symbolically she could not remain in Egypt and still be His wife. She would have to be sanctified, made holy, set apart, in order to be His chosen beloved. Worship would be the result of her redemption, not the cause of it.

Thus the remaining plagues, as enumerated in our *parashah*, have as one of the primary functions the separating of Israel as a distinct people from the Egyptians: "I shall make a distinction between My people and your people..." (8:19 [English 8:23]).

Note carefully as well that sacrifice is the key activity associated with worship. The command to Pharaoh is: "Send forth my people that they may worship (עָבַד, *'avad*) Me." And this worship is defined as offering sacrifice. Why sacrifice? Because redemption is accomplished via sacrifice. This is the key of the Pesach event: blood on the doorposts (which symbolize one's entire life) is the redemptive symbol distinguishing the Israelites from the Egyptians.

Pharaoh saw sacrifice as a means of placating the gods. It could thus be done whenever and wherever. God reveals that sacrifice is the means of redemption and must therefore be done according to His schedule and done His way.

> But when the time had fully come, God sent his Son, born of a woman, born under the Torah, to redeem those under the Torah, that we might receive the full rights of sons. (Gal 4:4-5)

Indeed, in the progressive revelation explaining God's way of redemption, sacrifice would be prescribed as acceptable only when done in connection with the *Mishkan* (Tabernacle), and finally only at the *Heichal* (Temple). These institutions would be the revelation of how God would dwell among His people—how He would effect full and complete redemption. It is the natural tendency to believe that redemption and worship can be had apart from sacrifice. Our sinful nature arrogantly thinks that we have something God counts as worthy—of attracting His forgiveness. But faith recognizes that redemption must be won by Someone other than ourselves. The symbolism of the pure and spotless lamb proclaimed this time and time again, and the sacrificial system made it clear to all who had faith to accept it, that God forgives on the basis of sacrifice, that is, the sacrifice of Messiah. It is in Him that God's people find their ultimate distinction—their true holiness.

Parashah Fifteen
בֹּא – Bo'

"GO"
Exodus 10:1–13:16

In the Triennial Cycle there are Four Parashot

10:1–12:12 | 12:13–28 | 12:29–51
13:1–20

(Note: the final *parashah* of the Triennial Cycle exceeds the end of the Annual Cycle by four verses.)

PARASHAH 52
TRIENNIAL CYCLE

EXODUS 10:1–12:12

HAFTARAH: ISAIAH 19:1–17 | APOSTOLIC: JOHN 1:29–34

The Awesome God of Israel

We come, now, in our journey through *Shemot* (Exodus), to the final judgments against Egypt, culminating with the death of the first born. All of the plagues caused discomfort and trouble to the Egyptians, but none of them had been directed at the people themselves. Now, however, the power of God is shown against the Egyptians themselves as the first born is taken. As our *haftarah* expresses, the awesome power of God is unleashed against His enemy.

The opening paragraph of our *parashah* describes the sovereignty of God in no uncertain terms. Here the question of Pharaoh's hardened heart is explicitly shown to be the work of the Almighty: "I have hardened his heart and the heart of his servants, that I may perform these signs of Mine among them...." That, in itself, should cause us to tremble before the Lord. How foolish for us to think that somehow we control the destiny of life! Far above us is the will of the Sovereign One, Who accomplishes His purposes in heaven and among men, and no one stays His hand or asks Him what He is doing (Daniel 4:35). *El Gibor* (Mighty Warrior) is His Name, and He regards the nations as nothing more than dust in the scales (Is 40:15). Egypt, in all of her grandeur and sophistication, will wilt before the pounding boots of this conquering Warrior.

But notice the purpose of God's conquest against Egypt (10:2-3): "that you may tell in the hearing of your son, and of your grandson, how I made a mockery of the Egyptians and how I performed My signs among them, that you may know that I am Adonai." The destruction of the Egyptians in the final plagues will forever stand as an indisputable testimony of how God deals with His enemies. This story, thus, must be passed down to son and grandson, from generation to generation, so that there would never be any doubt Who is the One true God, and that He is the God of Israel.

Moreover, the story of the Exodus cuts two directions. To the Israelites, the Warrior God had come to their rescue because He was keeping His promises to them. But to the Egyptians, the God of Israel would show their folly for trusting in make-believe gods who were nothing more than powerless demons when faced with the power of the Almighty. So as we read this story once again, we must decide where we stand. Are we attached to Israel through faith in her God, or do we stand outside of that circle of protection, and find ourselves amongst the enemies of this awesome Warrior?

There is a place of refuge from the wrath of God! It is not, however, to be found in a religion, nor in oneself, nor even in one's own attempts at being righteous, but in the Lamb. The most obvious and spectacular message of this *parashah* is that it was the Lamb that made the difference between salvation and destruction. It was not the blood that ran in the veins of Israelites that mattered, but the blood of the spotless Lamb that was applied to the doorposts and lintel of their dwellings. The unblemished Lamb sacrificed for the sake of Israel was the deciding factor.

Our text moves on to describe the eighth plague. Moses and Aaron go, as before, to Pharaoh and rebuke him for his failure to humble himself before the God of Israel. They once again command Pharaoh to send forth the people of Israel that they may worship God as He has commanded, and promise him that if he refuses, a plague of locust would ravish the land. The description of the locust plague is no fanciful exaggeration. The Ancient Near East was not unfamiliar with the devastation of locust plagues. When the pests descended upon a region, they ate everything in their path. Descriptions from historical documents describe the devastation as something like fire that consumes all the plants, leaving the ground blackened. Indeed, Pharaoh's servants understand the message, and realize that every other plague prophesied by Moses and Aaron had taken place just as they had said. Any logical person would realize that this plague likewise would bring sure disaster. Their counsel to Pharaoh is straightforward: "How long will this man be a snare to us? Let the men (אֲנָשִׁים, *'anashim*) go, that they may serve the Lord their God. Do you not realize that Egypt is destroyed?" Whether their counsel was that the adult males should be released or not, is uncertain. The Hebrew word *'anashim,* could just as well be "people" as "males." But it is certain that their advice to Pharaoh was that he should take seriously the threat that Moses and Aaron had given.

Thus, Pharaoh summons Moses and Aaron back to his court, and asks them who exactly would be leaving (10:8). The answer is clear: everyone of the Israelites must go, as well as all their flocks—no one would remain. This enrages Pharaoh. He responds with an outburst that can be taken two ways: "Thus may YHVH be with you, if ever I let you and your little ones go! Take heed, for evil is in your mind." Pharaoh's meaning was apparently: "You certainly will need the help of YHVH if ever I let you and your little ones go!" But the Hebrew could just as well mean "YHVH will be with you when I let you and your little ones go." Thus, though Pharaoh responded arrogantly in jest, he spoke what would be the reality: Adonai would go with the Israelites, and He would bring them up out of the land of slavery.

Though it seems that Pharaoh's counsellors advised him to let the "people" go, he turned the word "people" to its more restricted meaning of "men," and exclaims with a negative, "Not so," it won't happen as you request. Instead, Pharaoh restricts his permission to just the males. (The Egyptian word for "men" may also mean "people.")

This, of course, is not acceptable to Moses and Aaron, and so the plague of locust ensues. The strong east wind moved the locust cloud toward Egypt, and brought more locust in the land than ever before, or after (10:14). And the devastation was just as Moses and Aaron had said: nothing green remained before the marauding infestation.

Faced with utter defeat, Pharaoh once again summons Moses and Aaron, and as before, he feigns repentance (cf. 9:27). His words betray his hardened heart: (10:17) "Now therefore, please forgive my sin only this once, and make supplication to the Lord your God, that He would only remove this death from me." Pharaoh's sorrow is only in regard to the trouble. He hopes that his "humility" would solve the problem of the locust, but the real problem was with Pharaoh himself. Repentance that only seeks to alleviate the problem, but seeks no real change of heart, is not really repentance at all.

Once again, Moses intercedes on behalf of Pharaoh, and God removes the locust, this time with a strong westerly wind that drives the horde into the Red Sea. But at the same time, He hardens Pharaoh's heart. The awesome power of God was not yet fully demonstrated, for more plagues were still to come.

The ninth plague (which finishes this final set of three) comes without warning to Pharaoh and his court. The high god of Ra, the sun god in the pagan religion of the Egyptians, was next to be mocked. The Egyptians believed that there was a daily struggle between the supreme sun god, Ra, who brought daylight, and the demonic god Apophis, the embodiment of darkness. The rising of the sun each day signalled Ra's victory over Apophis. The ninth plague, therefore, must have struck a very real psychological impact upon the Egyptian populace.

Moses is instructed to lift the staff toward the sky, and a "thick darkness (חֹשֶׁךְ־אֲפֵלָה, *choshek 'apheilah*) fell upon the land. It was a darkness that could be felt (10:21), a metaphoric description or perhaps indicating that dust in the air contributed to the darkness. The darkness remained for three days, securing the fact that the supreme god in the Egyptian pantheon had been defeated. The text indicates that the Egyptians did not see one another for three days. Rambam suggests that the deep fog that occurred also snuffed out all flames as well, and that the Egyptians even lost track of the days.

Once again, Pharaoh summons Moses and offers a compromise. The people can go, but the flocks must remain. This, of course, was not acceptable. Moses reminds Pharaoh that the purpose of leaving was to worship the God of Israel, and this required sacrifice, which necessitated the flocks as well. Moses also tells Pharaoh that God had not yet given instructions on exactly what and how many sacrifices would be offered, and thus the flocks, not just a few animals, would need to be taken.

This outrages Pharaoh once again, and he gives a final ultimatum to Moses: "Get away from me! Beware, do not see my face again, for in the day you see my face you shall die!" (10:28). Pharaoh's hardened heart has reached its limit. In spite of the obvious power of Israel's God, Pharaoh draws a line in the sand: he has raised his fist against the Almighty and His representative, Moses. But once again, Pharaoh's words will come true—this will be last time he will see Moses' face: Moses said, "You are right; I shall never see your face again!" (10:29). There will be no turning back—the redemption of Israel is about to take place.

The order of the events as listed in chapters 11 and 12 pose an apparent problem. In 11:8, it appears that Moses returns once again to Pharaoh with yet another message: "All these your servants will come down to me and bow themselves before me, saying, 'Go out, you and all the people who follow you,' and after that I will go out." And he went out from Pharaoh in hot anger." And in 12:31 Pharaoh summons Moses and Aaron again to deliver the message that Israel was to leave Egypt. The Sages give various explanations. Regarding the statement of 11:8, they suggest that this actually occurred, not after Moses instructs the people (11:1–7), but before, and that God had given Moses a direct revelation while he still stood before Pharaoh. And regarding the summons in 12:31, they suggest that Pharaoh was not actually in attendance, but that the message of Pharaoh was delivered by his servants (court officials). Thus Moses' promise never to be seen by Pharaoh again was upheld.

The instructions given to the Israelites by Moses, that they were to ask for silver and gold from their Egyptian neighbors (11:2), is sometimes read as underhanded. In 3:22, it is foretold that the Israelites would ask for items of silver and gold, as well as clothing, and the Lxx and Samaritan Pentateuch add the word "clothing" to our text as well. This sounds like borrowing without the intention of returning the items. The Sages suggest several explanations. Since the text has noted that Moses was esteemed in the eyes of the people, but does not specify whether this refers to the Israelite or the Egyptians, some suggest that the Egyptian populace had come to revere Moses in his position as stronger than Pharaoh, and that they therefore willingly gave gifts to the Israelites in honor of Moses. Others suggest that the Egyptians gave items of value to the Israelites in order to encourage them to leave, because they knew that if they remained, the God of Israel would utterly demolish the Egyptian society and land. It might also be noted that Israel had been wrongfully enslaved, and that the acquiring of silver and gold (as well as clothing) was a repayment of wages that they should have been given for their work. Regardless, the prophecy of 3:22 was in the process of being fulfilled: Israel would, indeed, plunder the Egyptians. We should note that it was the silver and gold from the Egyptians that eventually was used to make the sacred articles of the Tabernacle.

Like the ninth plague of darkness, in which a clear distinction was made between Israel and Egypt, so the final plague would highlight this difference. Death would occur in every household of Egypt. The phrase "from the first born of the Pharaoh who sits on his throne, even to the first born of the slave girl who is behind the millstones" is a merism, a literary form that describes a totality, much like "heaven and earth," which in some cases means "everywhere." This would contradict the teachings of some of the Sages that the servants of Pharaoh, who approached Moses (11:8) were spared the death of their first born. In contrast, "against any of the sons of Israel a dog will not even bark, whether against man or beast" (11:7). The contrast would be fully evident: in the homes of the Egyptians, there would be great calamity and sorrow, but for the Israelites, there would be full protection. The God Who divides between holy and profane would show His sovereign hand in making a clear distinction between Israel and Egypt.

The event of the final judgment against Egypt in the killing of her first born (בְּכוֹר, *bichor,* can refer to either a son or a daughter, though in matters of inheritance, it most often refers to the first born son) and the subsequent deliverance of Israel from the slavery of Egypt, would stand forever as the paradigm for God's work of redemption. As such, God commands Moses and Aaron that this event would mark a change in the ordering of the months. It stands to reason that there would be no need to reckon the month of the exodus as the first month if it were, in fact, already the first month of the Israelite calendar. God's instructions here are specific (12:2): "This month shall be the beginning of months for you (הַחֹדֶשׁ הַזֶּה לָכֶם רֹאשׁ חֳדָשִׁים); it is to be the first month of the year to you (רִאשׁוֹן הוּא לָכֶם לְחָדְשֵׁי הַשָּׁנָה). This is the only time in the Tanach that רֹאשׁ, *rosh* ("head, beginning") is used in the singular with the word "months"

(חֳדָשִׁים, *chodashim*). The obvious meaning is that when it comes to reckoning the beginning and order of the months, the month in which the exodus occurred was to rank as first. From this time on in the Tanach, the designation "first month" (חֹדֶשׁ הָרִאשׁוֹן, *chodesh hari'shon*) refers to the month of the exodus. Yet the counting of the years as pertains to the sabbatical year (every seven years) and the Jubilee (יוֹבֵל, *yovel*) does not begin with the month of the exodus, but with the month in which Yom Kippur occurs (Lev 25:8–11). Thus, as pertains to months in the Hebrew calendar, the month of the exodus (Pesach) is first, while as regards the counting of years, the month in which Yom Kippur occurs is the beginning. The obvious importance of this is that redemption (pictured by the exodus) begins that story of God's covenant faithfulness to Israel which is then paralleled to the final fruit of redemption, the freedom portrayed in the Yovel (Jubilee) marked by Yom Kippur (the Day of Atonement). The picture we are to see in this is that Israel is redeemed from slavery in order to be free to worship God, and such freedom from slavery is to characterize the nation (as lived out in the Yovel), for the ultimate destiny of God's chosen people is that they should forever be free to worship Him.

The matter of the Pesach (Passover) lamb is detailed in 12:3-12. First, the lamb was to be selected on the 10th of the month, four days before it was slaughtered as a sacrifice. The lamb was thus "set apart" (note the command "you shall keep it," 12:6) in advance, even as Yeshua was chosen from before the foundations of the world to be our sacrifice (1Pet 1:20). Second, the lamb was to be a one year old male without blemish, selected from either the sheep or the goats. This speaks to the fitness of the lamb for sacrifice. Third, one lamb was sufficient for a complete household, and even beyond that limit, if the household was small. This emphasized the fact that the sacrifice of the lamb had corporate dimensions. One sacrifice for many people. But it also emphasizes that the efficacy of the sacrifice was limited. Only those within an Israelite household were protected by the blood of the lamb. This shows that God's redemption is not merely forensic but also historical. The locus of God's redemptive work is confined to His chosen ones. Only Israel is redeemed, and Israel is comprised of those God chooses, regardless of their ethnicity. Thus, a "mixed-multitude" leaves Egypt through God's saving power.

Fourth, this corporate aspect of the Pesach sacrifice is also highlighted by the fact that individual families did not perform the sacrifice, each by themselves. The text indicates (12:6) that "the whole assembly of the congregation of Israel is to kill it at twilight." Exactly how this was carried out is not specified, but it is on this basis that later, the Pesach lamb was sacrificed at the Tabernacle or Temple before it was roasted for eating.

Fifth, the sacrifice of the lamb was not sufficient in and of itself. Its blood needed to be applied the doorposts and lintel of the family's dwelling (12:7). Even as the blood of the Yom Kippur sacrifice did not avail to the atoning of sin until it was applied to the mercy seat of the Ark in the Most Holy Place, so the blood of the Pesach lamb did not protect the Israelites until it was applied to the doorposts and lintel. In like manner, the blood of our Messiah must be applied (as it were) to each individual who would be saved from the wrath of God. Whereas in Egypt, the blood was applied to the doorpost and lintel with a hyssop branch, in the eternal aspects of which this was a foreshadow, the blood of our Savior's death is applied to each believer by the work of the Spirit through the gift of faith and by the intercessory work of Yeshua as our heavenly Cohen HaGadol (High Priest).

Sixth, the meat of the Pesach lamb was to be roasted whole, not boiled or eaten raw (which was often done in pagan sacrifices). The roasting of the lamb paralleled the sacrifice by fire, which signified the full giving of the offering to God. Yet the fact that the meat is also eaten by those bringing the sacrifice connects it to the fellowship offering. This aspect of the Pesach sacrifice emphasizes the covenant relationship between God and Israel. That it was roasted with fire symbolized the upward dimension: the sacrifice was presented to God. The eating of the meat symbolized the covenant fellowship that existed between God and the individual worshipper as a result of the sacrifice.

Seventh, nothing of the lamb was to be left over until the morning. Whatever was not eaten was to be burned with fire. This eventually was understood by the Sages to mean that nothing was to be eaten after midnight. This symbolizes that there was a window of time in which the requirements for Israel's redemption could be accomplished. And so it is true for us. There is a "day" of salvation, but when it is over, night comes (cf. Is 49:8; 2Cor 6:2).

Finally, the Pesach meal was to be eaten in a manner that anticipated leaving Egypt (12:11): "Now you shall eat it in this manner: with your loins girded, your sandals on your feet, and your staff in your hand; and you shall eat it in haste—it is the Lord's Passover." The point is clear: the Pesach meal, initiated at the exodus, was forward-looking. It was to emphasize God's covenant faithfulness with His chosen covenant partner Israel, but it was not the end in itself. It spoke of the redemption that was about to become a reality and the ultimate freedom that would result as seen in Yom Kippur and the Yovel. The slavery of Egypt was imposed upon Israel by her enemies, while the slavery of debt (rectified in the Yovel, the Year of Jubilee) was self-imposed. This speaks to the fact that, spiritually speaking, freedom has two dimensions: freedom from the debt of sin inherited from Adam, and freedom from the condemnation incurred by our own willful sin.

In the same way, as we celebrate Pesach each year, we do so with the realization of our having been redeemed from the slavery of sin by the death and resurrection of Yeshua. Yet we still await our full redemption (Rom 8:21–22) when we will forever be free from the burden of our own sin, when mortal puts on immortality and we reign eternally with Yeshua in full conformity to His holiness.

Paul teaches us that as we celebrate Pesach, we proclaim Yeshua's death "until He comes" (1Cor 11:26). We too, in one sense, like Israel of old, await our final redemption. Yet we know that it is secure. The Lamb has been slain, His blood has been applied, the victory has already been won! We wait, then, prepared and ready for the coming of our Savior when death will be completely swallowed upon in victory (1Cor 15:50–58).

Parashah 53
Triennial Cycle

Exodus 12:13–28

Haftarah: Jeremiah 46:13-28 | Apostolic: Colossians 1:13-14

Lessons from Pesach

What Does the Verb פָּסַח (*pasach*) mean?

1. Two words for "pass over" in Exodus 12:
   a. עָבַר - *'avar*, "to cross over, pass over" This term is found in vv. 12 and 23. In both instances, יהוה is the subject of the verb: יהוה is the one who "passes through" or "passes over" the land.
   b. פָּסַח - *pasach*. The definition of this verb, however, is not universally agreed upon. The verb and corresponding noun are found 73 times in the Tanach, but only 20 times outside of the Torah.

The early Christian interpretation of the Exodus text has influenced the definition of the verb to a great extent. This interpretation considered יהוה to be the One who either destroyed (Egyptians) or *spared* (Israelites). In other words, He either destroyed or *skipped*, i.e., "passed over."

One other text seems to support this definition of "skip over": 1 Ki 18:21, "How long will you waver between two opinions?" These words, in the mouth of Eliyahu, encourage the people to put their complete faith in God and Him alone, and not to give any allegiance to Baal. The Lexicons consider the possibility that the verb *pasach* may have a base meaning of "limp," or "be lame." From this comes the idea of "waver" or "wobble," and thus the current translation of 1 Ki 18:21. But the word translated "opinions" is from a cluster of Hebrew nouns all based on the root סעף (*sa'aph*), which most likely means "branches" or even the "Y" of a branch. Note the following: Is 17:6; 27:10, "branch" (סְעִיף), Is 10:33, "trim branches" (מְסָעֵף); Ezek 31:6, 8, "slender branch" (סְעַפָּה). Add to this the fact that the preposition translated "between" is עַל (*'al*, "upon; over") when we would expect בֵּין (*bein*, "between"), and we have good cause to seek a better translation.

The use of the verb *pasach* in Is. 31:5 gives every indication that the base meaning is "to hover over," "to protect." Note the poetic lines:

> Like flying birds so Adonai of hosts will protect Jerusalem
> He will protect and deliver;
> He will *pasach* and rescue.

Here, the term obviously means to "hover over," "to protect." This is what a mother-bird does for her young, cp. Deut. 32:11.

Now we may retranslate 1 Ki 18:21 like this: "why do you hover over two branches,' that is, "How long will you go on hovering like a bird fluttering over two branches? Land already!"

In fact, the verb *pasach* fits every context in which it is used if the meaning given is "to hover over, to protect."

2. Who is the destroyer?

In vv. 12 and 23 Adonai is clearly the One who does the destroying of the Egyptian's first born. But in v. 23 there appears to be two individuals. Adonai both destroys and does not allow the destroyer to come into the houses marked by blood. Here, as often in the Tanach, Adonai is seen in a plurality. Who is the destroyer? Most certainly the Angel of the Lord, (cp. 2 Sam 24:16-17; 2 Kgs 19:35; Is 37:36; 1 Chr 21:12ff; 2 Chr 32:21; Ps 35:5-6) and possibly the pre-incarnate Messiah. (Note that in Rev. 1:18 Yeshua owns the keys to death and Hades.)

The clear indication of Ex 12:23 is that Adonai "hovers over" the house marked by blood, and protects its occupants from the death sentence of the destroyer. In this the picture of redemption is made known. God is both the destroyer and the protector of those He has chosen not to be destroyed.

3. In What Way is the Blood a Sign (v. 13)?

Verse 13 is specific: the blood on the doorpost is a sign to the Israelite family.

וְהָיָה הַדָּם לָכֶם לְאֹת עַל הַבָּתִּים אֲשֶׁר אַתֶּם שָׁם וְרָאִיתִי אֶת־הַדָּם וּפָסַחְתִּי עֲלֵכֶם וְלֹא־יִהְיֶה בָכֶם נֶגֶף לְמַשְׁחִית בְּהַכֹּתִי בְּאֶרֶץ מִצְרָיִם

"The blood shall be a sign for you upon the houses where you are; I shall see the blood and I shall pass over you; there shall not be a plague of destruction upon you when I strike in the land of Egypt."

But how is it a sign for the Israelite? It appears to function more as a sign for the Almighty. The Hebrew could just as well be understood to mean that the blood as a sign *belonged* to the Israelites—it was a sign that belonged to them and not to the Egyptians. It was not so much that the blood was for them to see as it was that the blood "belonged to them" or was a sign that they were to be spared.

Some of the Sages disagree. Rashi notes that the blood on the doorpost was considered as sign "for you" (the Israelites) which meant that the blood should be placed on the inside of the doorpost so it could be seen by those in the house, and not on the outside for the Egyptians to see. His point is that the Jewish firstborn were saved from the plague because the blood signified that those inside the house had involved themselves in doing God's will. The blood was proof of obedience, and it was this obedience that saved the Israelites. In the same vein, Rashi points out that an Egyptian firstborn staying in the house of an Israelite would not have been spared. For Rashi, it was devotion to the commandment, not the mere presence of a "safe house" that protected the Jews. (*Mechilta* takes a similar view by suggesting the blood was that of the Pesach sacrifice co-mingled with the blood of circumcision.)

This all sounds very pious. The problem with this interpretation, however, is what we are to do when Israel is entirely disobedient—like at Sinai and the building of the golden calf. If obedience is the bases of one's redemption, should not idolatry be the cause of one's destruction? Yet Israel is not destroyed over the well-known incident. The reality of the matter is clear: redemption is not based upon Israel's obedience, but upon God's willingness to accept the blood of the sacrificial lamb in the place of their firstborn sons. And since Israel is God's firstborn (Exodus 4:22) she is spared as a whole because of the blood on the *mezuzot*. "It will be a sign belonging to you ... and when I see the blood ...." The blood is a sign that belongs to Israel because it is the sign of her redemption. Redemption belongs to those HaShem chooses—it is not the possession of all peoples.

The exodus from Egypt would thus become the paradigm of redemption for all time. Forever, throughout the history of Israel, the redemption from Egypt would stand as the ultimate illustration of the eternal redemption God would accomplish in Messiah. So central and key is the exodus picture that it would form the first Mo'ed of the year, celebrated for seven days throughout the generations of Israel. What does Pesach teach us about redemption as God sees it?

In Exodus 6:6 the whole exodus experience is summed up in four verbs (which become the basis for the four cups in the Pesach seder). גָּאַל, *ga'al*, "to redeem" is one of the those key terms. *Ga'al* and פָּדָה (*padah*) are somewhat synonymous, conveying the concept of "redemption," but *ga'al* always has a family orientation—used for redeeming a family member. This idea is never lost in its use and informs us of an essential aspect of Israel's redemption by God's outstretched arm. God is seen as the Father Who redeems His children.

But a second aspect that cannot be lost sight of is that *ga'al* always has "payment of the necessary price" connected with it. Consider how the term is used for the redemption of property:

If a fellow countryman of yours becomes so poor he has to sell part of his property, then his nearest kinsman is to come and buy back what his relative has sold. Or in case a man has no kinsman, but so recovers his means as to find sufficient for its redemption, then he shall calculate the years since its sale and refund the balance to the man to whom he sold it, and so return to his property. But if he has not found sufficient means to get it back for himself, then what he has sold shall remain in the hands of its purchaser until the year of jubilee; but at the jubilee it shall revert, that he may return to his property. (Lev 25:25–28)

This and many other examples show that redemption is affected by payment of the necessary price. This has wide ramifications for the term as it is used with regard to eternal redemption—the payment for sins in order that God may dwell among His people. No matter how much we may want to think that somehow, someway we have contributed to our own redemption price, the fact of the matter is that the price required for our redemption was entirely out of our reach—beyond our means. For the payment necessary for our redemption (as clearly demonstrated in the Pesach lamb) was the death of an innocent substitute. Try as we might, we could never effect our redemption (the salvation of our life) because it could only be gained through death. "The soul that sins shall die." (Ezek 18:4)

The picture of leaven illustrates this same thing. Interestingly, two words are found in our text translated leaven: the common term, חָמֵץ, *chametz* and שְׂאֹר , *s'or*, found only 5 times and only in the Torah (Ex 12:15, 19; 13:7; Lev 2:11; Dt 16:4). שְׂאֹר (*s'or*) most likely denotes yeast itself, while חָמֵץ (*chametz*) means any food in which yeast is found. Our text becomes the basis for the ruling that leaven must be cleaned out of the house by the 14th of Nisan, for Ex 34:25 states clearly that the leaven must be removed before the Pesach offering may be offered, which was done the afternoon of the 14th (Ex 12:6, where בֵּין הָעַרְבַּיִם, *bein ha-arbaim*, means "between the evenings," i.e., at the closing of the day before the sunset and the beginning of the next day. This is the end of the 14th not the beginning of the 14th). Thus the Stone Chumash (following Rashi) renders בַּיּוֹם הָרִאשׁוֹן (*b'yom harishon*) of Ex 12:15 not as "on the first day" but "on the previous day" (cf. Job 15:7 where Rashi contends that הָרִאשׁוֹן should be understood as "previous.")

But what is the picture here? Why is the redemption illustrated by the exodus coupled with the removal of leaven? It is difficult (if not impossible) to show that leaven pictured "sin" in the early Tanach. The parallel between leaven and sin began to be used in the later post-exilic and even rabbinic eras (cf. *Yalkut,* Ex. 201 as noted in Jastrow's *Lexicon*). Paul's use of the concept in 1Cor 5:6f of leaven as a symbol of sin fits this later metaphoric usage, but it does not appear that leaven is viewed symbolically as sin in the passover narrative.

So if leaven is not a picture *per se* of "sin" in the Torah, what is the meaning in its connection with Pesach? The obvious emphasis is one of *haste*. Israel could not wait for bread to rise because she was being taken out of Egypt in haste.

> Now you shall eat it in this manner: with your loins girded, your sandals on your feet, and your staff in your hand; and you shall eat it in haste—it is ADONAI's Passover. (Ex 12:11, cf. 12:34)

This is why leaven is specifically added to the *minchah* of Shavuot:

> 'You shall bring in from your dwelling places two loaves of bread for a wave offering, made of two-tenths of an ephah; they shall be of a fine flour, baked with leaven as first fruits to the LORD. (Lev. 23:17)

Here, at Shavuot, there is no more need for haste—as the redeemed of the Lord, Israel is no longer a nation of slaves but of freemen. They may therefore eat at their leisure without the restraints of taskmasters setting their schedules.

This sets the agenda, then, for Pesach. Leaving in haste emphasizes that *the redemption was happening to Israel, not something she was doing herself*. If Israel were to be redeemed, it was because she was taken out of Israel by the mighty hand of God, not because she was effecting her own salvation. In the subsequent Festival, the house free of leaven was a picture of leaving Egypt in haste—of being snatched out of Egypt by God's omnipotence, not by the efforts (planning, time schedule, etc.) of Israel. If Israel were to be redeemed, she would have to do it on God's schedule, not her own. And it is easy to see how leaven could thus become a picture of sin—of self-reliance, of "doing it my way" as opposed to "doing it God's way." Since this picture is so central to God's unfolding picture of redemption, retained leaven during the week of Pesach would result in כָּרֵת, *karat*, being cut off. The two (God's way and man's way) cannot coexist.

Thus the *haftarah* (of the triennial cycle) chosen by the Sages to accompany this *parashah* emphasizes God's sovereign hand in the redemption of Israel. God is the One who redeems Israel—she cannot affect her own redemption. And it is this very core and central truth that the Apostle Paul emphasizes in the selected Apostolic Scripture:

> For He rescued us from the domain of darkness, and transferred us to the kingdom of His beloved Son, in whom we have redemption, the forgiveness of sins. (Col. 1:13-14)

The redemption of the soul, to which the ancient exodus offered the divine paradigm, is accomplished not by one's own efforts, but by the final and eternal sacrifice of the Lamb. This is our hope and our salvation.

לְדוֹר וָדוֹר - *L'dor v'dor: From Generation to Generation*

> "And when your children say to you, 'What does this rite mean to you?' (Ex 12:26).

The purpose of the Pesach seder, and the observing of the Feast of Unleavened Bread (חַג הַמַּצּוֹת, *chag hamatzot*) is that of memorial—of remembering the pivotal event in the life of Israel, and thus in all of our lives who are part of the covenant people. It is therefore of foundational importance that the story and message of the exodus, and its revelation of God's way of redemption, be passed on to our children.

We do this, in an initial sense, by following the commandment to make the festival of Pesach and Unleavened Bread a part of our lives as family and community. But simply observing the Festival is not sufficient, in and of itself. For if the redemption from Egypt is a central revelation of how God has redeemed us, then our lives must be changed in light of that redemption. Ultimately, the exodus points to a greater and eternal reality—our redemption in Yeshua. If we observe the Festival, but our lives remain laden with the leaven of slavery to the world, our observance rings hallow. What will be a lasting testimony to our children is when they observe us walking in righteousness, and humbly seeking forgiveness from God and others when we sin. Thus, passing this grand message of freedom in Yeshua to the next generation is a daily process, one in which they observe the life of Yeshua in us, not only in the major decisions of life, but even more importantly, in our everyday actions and manner of life.

Parashah 54
Triennial Cycle

Exodus 12:29-51

Haftarah: Isaiah 21:11-22:4 | Apostolic: 1Thessalonians 4:13-18

The *parashah* before us details the events of the first Pesach, and particularly the application of the blood upon the doorposts (מְזוּזוֹת, *mezuzot*) of the Israelite homes. A number of questions confront us from this text, and we should discuss them in the order in which they appear.

The first question is why the striking of the firstborn needed to be so comprehensive. The text before us is clear: "From the firstborn of Pharaoh who sits on the throne to the firstborn of the prisoner in the dungeon" (literally בּוֹר, *bor*, "pit"). But the killing extends even to the animals. Why? Why must the killing be so extensive? Would it not have sufficed to deal with the firstborn of Pharaoh alone?

We may presume that the primary reason was to show that God and God alone was the One who brought about this plague. Each of the other plagues may have been considered (at least by the Egyptians) as a mere consequence of nature (though this would have taken a vivid imagination). However, to have the firstborn of every household slain, as well as the firstborn of all the animals, all in the same night, could be construed as nothing less than the consequence of Divine action. This is doubly true by the fact that Moses had already indicated it would happen at night (12:12), and thus both the extent of the killing as well as the timing left no explanation except that HaShem had done it.

But we should not lose sight of the fact that the extensive killing of the firstborn is also an indication both of God's power and anger. "It is a terrifying thing to fall into the hands of the living God" (cf. Hebrews 10:31). Often in life God seems distant, or even nonexistent. The unbeliever says "Adonai does not see, nor does the God of Jacob pay heed" (Ps. 94:7). The Egyptians (represented by Pharaoh) up to this point had acted as though the God of Israel was not to be taken seriously. If He existed, He was simply a nuisance, but not a terrible threat. But God's hand is not weak—His power is not limited. Only those without true faith disregard His voice. "God is always in concert. But the audience is not always listening." Like the first Pesach, the wicked will be destroyed in a moment they least expect. Deep in the sleep of self-reliance, they will come face to face with the Almighty. All of their mockings will turn to woe, and their assurance that God is only the "make-believe" crutch of the weak will be turned to utter despair.

If ever there is a picture of the wrath of God upon His enemies, the Pesach night is it. Death in every house—mourning and wailing over the devastation—but all for naught. The hour is past, the opportunities gone. The mercy of God has been used up and only His wrath remains. The Egyptians have no hope and stand no chance of recovery. They have spit in the eye of the Sovereign Lord, and there is no taking back their insults. The judgement of God against His enemies is awesome and terrible.

The second question that confronts us is an ethical one. Were the Israelites justified in asking for silver and gold from the Egyptians, knowing full well they would never return it (v. 36)? But we should understand the word שָׁאַל, *sha'al* to mean "ask," not in the sense of a "loan" (though the word can have this meaning in some contexts), but in the sense of "ask for compensation or wages." The request of the Israelites to their Egyptian neighbors would have been absurd apart from the intervention of God. But the verse tells us explicitly that God did intervene: "And the Lord gave the people favor in the eyes of the Egyptians ...." Thus, against all odds, the Israelites (under direction from Moses) sought compensation from the Egyptian for their unjust enslavement, and received it.

We may therefore consider an alternative translation to the conclusion of v. 36. It is commonly translated "so they plundered the Egyptians." The word translated "plundered" is the piel of נָצַל, *natzal*, which usually has the meaning "save" or "deliver." Granted, in a situation where spoils of war are for the taking, it can be used in the sense of "pick up the articles left behind"— "to save them," and thus "to plunder" the enemy. But is it possible that we should understand it here to mean that by the Egyptians showing favor to Israel and giving her items of silver and gold, they actually were "delivered" from total annihilation? Is it possible that God would have entirely wiped Egypt off the face of the earth had they not compensated Israel in at least some small measure for their years of servitude? We may say that at least this is a possible understanding of the text.

A third question that this text raises is the thorny one of chronology. So emphatic is our text! "Now the time that the sons of Israel lived in Egypt was four hundred and thirty years. And at the end of four hundred and thirty years, to the very day, all the hosts of Adonai went out from the land of Egypt" (12:40-41). We all know that it is difficult to reckon 430 years for Israel's stay in Egypt. According to Gen 47:9 Jacob arrived in Egypt when he was 130 years old; he not only brought his son Levi with him, but also his grandson Kohath (Gen 46:11), and Moses was his grandson, the son of Amram. Thus, between Jacob, Levi and Moses we had only two generations. The life spans of Kohath and Amram were 133 and 137 respectively, and if we add 80 years of Moses till the Exodus (Ex 6:18, 20; 7:7), even the sum of these reaches only 350 years.

That this was a problem to ancient commentators is seen by the fact that both the Lxx and the Samaritan Pentateuch add a phrase to our verse to make sense of it: (Lxx) "which they spent in the Land of Egypt <u>and in the Land of Canaan</u>..."; the Sam. Pent. reads "And the sojourn of the sons of Israel <u>and their fathers in the Land of Canaan</u> and the Land of Egypt ...." Josephus (*Antiq.* II, 15.2) taught: "They left Egypt 430 years after our patriarch, Abraham, had come to Canaan, while Jacob's settlement there took place 215 years later." He thus divided the number 430 into two equal parts. Most modern commentators have either considered the notice in our text to be erroneous, or have opted to understand it in line with the Lxx, taking the 430 years to include all of the sojourning of Abraham and his descendents, both in the Land of Canaan and in the Land of Egypt. The explanation is given that the Masoretic text only included "Egypt" at this point because it is the end and final location of Israel's sojourning. Here is a problem of chronology that, like many similar problems, has no simple solution. We must continue to seek to understand the text more clearly, for surely the answer lies therein.

A fourth question that comes to us regards the stipulations for who can and cannot eat of the Pesach sacrifice (vv. 43-49). The following are stated categorically: **1)** a נֵכָר, *neichar,* cannot eat of the Pesach sacrifice. This word means "foreign" or "foreigner" and is often connected with foreign gods (cf. Gen 35:2; Deut 32:12) and foreign altars (2Chron 14:2). We may presume that its use here denotes a foreigner who is still an idolator and has not come to confess the God of Israel as the only and true God. **2)** a purchased slave, עֶבֶד, *'eved,* once he has been circumcised (indicating he had attached himself to the God of Israel and was thus a member of Israel's covenant) is permitted to eat the Pesach sacrifice. **3)** the תּוֹשָׁב, *toshav* and the שָׂכִיר, *sachir* may not eat of the Pesach sacrifice. While תּוֹשָׁב ("one who dwells") can be equated with the גֵר, *ger* ("sojourner"), the two words are sometimes also distinct (cf. Num 35:15). It seems that in contexts where תּוֹשָׁב is distinct from גֵר, then תּוֹשָׁב is someone just passing through the region, and may have stopped for lodging or for a short stay. That this word is paralleled by שָׂכִיר, "laborer, hired worker" also shows that these words can designate non-permanent residents—those passing through who had not joined themselves to Israel via a belief in Israel's God.

Here we have proof that from the Torah's perspective circumcision does not change a person's ethnic status. The circumcised servant is singled out necessarily as qualified to eat the Pesach. If his circumcision had granted him the ethnic status of a Jew, there would have been no need for this statement. Yet it should equally be emphasized that the circumcised slave has the same rights and privileges as the native born Jew in all matters relating to life and worship. "The same law shall apply to the native as to the stranger who sojourns among you" (v. 49). Thus from the very formation of the nation (via the Exodus through which HaShem redeemed Israel for Himself) the non-Jewish resident is viewed as the first fruits of the promise given to Abraham, "in your seed all the nations of the earth shall be blessed." The issue was not one of a change of ethnicity but a common bond in the life of faith—faith in the God of Israel and in His promises, all of which ultimately center upon the Messiah.

Parashah 55
Triennial Cycle

Exodus 13:1–20

Haftarah: Isaiah 46:3-13 | Apostolic: Colossians 1:15-23

Remembering our Redemption

In the final Pesach our Messiah celebrated upon the earth, He added to the Haggadah a section which had, for thousands of years previously, not been uttered. By stating that the *matzah* represented His flesh, and the third cup (cup of redemption) His blood, He forever interpreted the story of redemption set in the historical exodus of Israel from Egypt as ultimately speaking of His work of redemption, i.e., His own death and resurrection by which He would redeem all who would come to the Father by Him. In a ceremony entirely slated to be a זִכָּרוֹן, *zikaron*, a memory or memorial, Yeshua commanded His *talmidim* to remember His work of redemption each time they celebrated the Lord's festival of Pesach.

Why are we so prone to forgetfulness? Is it really possible that Israel could have forgotten this most momentous event in her history? Is it possible that, apart from the commandment to celebrate this remembrance, we would have forgotten all together our coming out of Egypt? In one sense, I would suggest the answer is "no," while in another, a resounding "yes!" I don't think we would have forgotten the event, in fact, we would have (and in some senses we actually may have) made the ceremony of Pesach with all of the trimmings of the seder and Haggadah an end in itself. We would have remembered the event and forgotten its true importance. We would have considered ourselves righteous for remembering our sacred history while at the same time heaping pride upon ourselves in that very act of remembering. Indeed, we would have, in the end, forgotten why we remember.

As an aside, we may consider the Christian Church's institution of "communion" derived from the Pesach seder, and the admonition to "remember." Here again, in our own sacred history as part of the Christian church, we find a "remembering" that has all but become a "forgetting." In making the Table a separate institution apart from the yearly celebration of Pesach, it became exactly opposite of what Pesach was to be. It became an end itself, and for a majority of the Church, a means of saving oneself, when it should have been a remembrance that redemption is something entirely of God's grace afforded entirely by the substitutionary death of the innocent Lamb.

So significant and central is the remembering of the Pesach that it becomes connected with the donning of *tefillin*. "It shall be a sign (אוֹת, *'ot*) for you upon your arm, and a reminder between your eyes…." (vv. 9, 16). In the בָּתִּים (*batim*, "boxes") of the *tefillin* are contained not only the two passages from the Shema (Deut 6:4ff; 11:13ff) that speak of "binding them upon the hand …" but also these two passages from our *parashah*. In the passages of the Shema, it is the *mitzvot* which are to be bound upon the arm and the forehead: "Bind them (i.e., the commandments) as a sign upon your arm and let them be ornaments (טוֹטָפֹת, *totaphot*) between your eyes." Thus, in the *tefillin* are contained two sets of texts: those which require the binding of the commandments upon arm and head, and those which require binding the remembrance of Pesach upon both. Is not the significance clear? Keeping the commandments and redemption go hand in hand. And this leads me to the main point: the keeping of the commandments, yea, the celebration of the festivals, is to be a means of knowing and loving God, not an end in itself. The "remembering" is not merely a recollection of the event itself, or a comprehension of the detailed *mitzvot* connected with the ceremony, as important as these are. No—the remembering is an understanding and appreciation of our God Who accomplished our redemption in the first place.

John Piper, a well known author and speaker in our times, has championed a most profound statement in many of his teachings: "God is most pleased with us when we are most satisfied with Him!" While listening to a sermon of his recently, I was reminded that our single duty in life is to know God better than we know anything, and to enjoy God more than we enjoy anything. Here is the essence of "remembering"—that we should be taken above (not away from) all of the secondary though vitally important things to the supremely important aspect of knowing and loving God. Here is the destination of our journey, the reward of our efforts, the goal of our being His creation.

Now this does not mean that the multitude of things and relationships in this life are unimportant or somehow to be avoided, like the monastic philosophies of the middle ages which attempted to rid oneself of all things and to live "outside" of this world. No, this is clearly wrongheaded. But it is to understand that all of these things which are good and which God created for our use and pleasure are nonetheless given to us as a means to know God and to embrace Him with the full energy of our heart.

How this changes the perspective of life! Everything in it becomes a divinely ordained means for knowing the Creator and having my every longing and expectation filled by His presence. With such a perspective my "ministry," my "service," becomes a means, not an end. It allows me to hold my ministry with a loose grip knowing that it is but a means to a much more noble end. "How," I might ask, "How can Paul, at the end of his life and facing execution, be able to say in calmness of spirit "according to my earnest expectation and hope, that I shall not be put to shame in anything, but that with all boldness, Messiah shall even now, as always, be exalted in my body, whether by life or by death. For to me, to live is Messiah, and to die is gain." How does he gain this most lofty perspective? Because he had come to know God in a full and accurate way through the revelation of the Tanach, and he had come to such a maturity so as to rejoice in HaShem more than he rejoiced in anything else.

So clear is the message of Pesach. For every generation following the one which first came out of Egypt, the first born of every womb, whether of animal or man, was to be consecrated to the Lord. Why? Because it was to be a constant reminder that redemption cost HaShem His firstborn. Let us never forget this: despite the many suggestions of the Sages as to why the firstborn was to be consecrated to HaShem, there remains one over arching reality—the slaughter of the firstborn, and the obvious substitution of the Pesach lamb for the firstborn of the Israelites, is a clear and precise foreshadowing of the Messiah who would die to obtain the redemption of His people. While the firstborn son of an Israelite family was spared by the substitution of the lamb, the Son of God was not spared, but bore our sins in His own body upon the execution stake. But even here we must see the whole picture: Yeshua's death is not the end in itself. It is the means by which we may know God and rejoice in Him. Even the supreme work of Yeshua in His death and resurrection is a means to an end, not an end in itself. He died so that we might know God better than we know anything else. He died so that we might rejoice in God more than we rejoice in anything else. And therefore, when we make even the celebration of Yeshua's death and resurrection an end in itself, we deny the very purpose for which He underwent such cruel and hideous punishment! What is more, when we make our doing—our ministry—our keeping of the *mitzvot*, an end in itself; when we rejoice in these things more than we rejoice in God Himself, then we have made all of these things primary and God Himself secondary, and we have entered into the most subtle form of idolatry.

The first verse of Alfred B. Smith's hymn, "My Goal is God Himself," says it well:

> My goal is God Himself
> Not joy, reward, or even blessing
> But Himself, my God
> 'Tis His to bring me there,
> Not mine, but His.
> By any path dear Lord,
> By any road.

This is remembering—when all of the events of life, all of the keeping of the *mitzvot*, every Shabbat and Festival, every donning of the *tallit*, or laying of the *tefillin*, every *b'rachah* (blessing)—when all of these things bring me to the ultimate goal of knowing God and rejoicing in Him more than I know or rejoice in anything else—here then is true shalom, where nothing can separate me from His love, demonstrated in Yeshua; where therefore I remain with Him and He with me and nothing can take me away from this realm of joy, for He is all my joy; where nothing can take me from the realm of truth, for He is all truth, and I know Him as He truly is. Here is stability and strength; here is preparation for an eternity where the Lamb is all the glory of Immanuel's Land.

We must ever have this in mind as we live out the days God has given each one of us. Our goal must constantly be to know Him, not primarily through the words and experience of others, but through the inspired words of Scripture as the Ruach enlivens them to our own soul, and through our own, personal walk with God through the experiences of our daily routines. As Paul confessed:

> But whatever things were gain to me, those things I have counted as loss for the sake of Messiah. More than that, I count all things to be loss in view of the surpassing value of knowing Messiah Yeshua my Lord… that I may know Him and the power of His resurrection and the fellowship of His sufferings, being conformed to His death in order that I may attain to the resurrection from the dead. (Phil 3:7–11)

Parashah Sixteen
בְּשַׁלַח – B'shalach

"When He Sent"
Exodus 13:17-17:16

In the Triennial Cycle there are
Three Parashot

13:21-15:18 | 15:19-16:24 | 16:25-17:16

(Note: the beginning verses of the Annual Cycle
[13:17–20] are contained in the
previous Triennial *parashah*)

Parashah 56
Triennial Cycle

Exodus 13:21–15:18

Haftarah: Jeremiah 49:1–22 | Apostolic: Romans 8:1–14

God's Mysterious Leading

In our *parashah* this week we encounter the well-known story of the crossing of the Red Sea. Its familiarity offers both an advantage and a disadvantage: an advantage because we already know the general flow of this wonderful narrative, and a disadvantage, because in its familiarity we may fail to receive the impact it is intended to have. Here, in our text, the miraculous salvation of Israel is displayed in all of its grandeur—a salvation that would forever mark the sovereign hand of God in the affairs of His people.

The opening verse of our portion immediately highlights the core issue: God dwells with His people. This is the primary theme of *Shemot* (Exodus), and is the over arching lesson we must not miss. The God of Israel has determined to dwell among His people, not in some far-off, remote place where they cannot know or commune with Him. Thus our text begins with ויהוה הֹלֵךְ לִפְנֵיהֶם, "And Adonai was walking before them...." His visible presence was seen in a pillar (עַמּוּד, *'amud*) of cloud by day, and of fire by night. Verse 22 emphasizes the constant presence of God with Israel: "He did not take away the pillar of cloud by day, nor the pillar of fire by night, from before the people." The Sages note that this indicates an overlapping of the appearance of the cloud and the fire: the pillar of fire appeared while the cloud yet remained, and the cloud reappeared in the morning while the fire was still visible (*Mekhilta* "Beshallach" ii [2.187 in Lauterbach]). Thus God was with His people at all times, and He manifested His presence continually.

The same is true for us, though admittedly we lack the visible manifestation of God's presence in the form of a pillar of cloud and fire. Yet His dwelling among us is nonetheless just as real, and just as constant. When our Master promised "Look, I am with you always, even to the end of the age" (Matt 28:20), He asks us both to believe He is present, and to live in the knowledge of that reality. Moreover, the indwelling Spirit as comforter and companion, continues to manifest the very presence of

God among His people.

The route of the exodus is much disputed, primarily because the sites listed in our text have yet to be positively identified. Exodus 14:1 notes that Moses was to command the Israelites to "turn back" (שׁוּב, *shuv*) and camp "before Pi-hahiroth, between Migdol and the sea; you shall camp in front of Baal-zephon, opposite it, by the sea." Pi-hahiroth (פִּי הַחִירֹת) has not been found. In Hebrew this means "the mouth of the canals," but it may also be an Egyptian name meaning "House or temple of Hat-Hor" or "temple of Hrt." Migdol ("fortress") may be a square tower on a height known as Jebel Abu Hasan overlooking the southern part of the small Bitter Lakes. It seems apparent that at one time, the water of the Red Sea (Suez) extended further north to include what was later the Bitter Lakes. Thus, the biblical account that has Israel crossing the Red Sea (יָם סוּף, *yam suf*) has historical foundations as well. Some claim that the Red Sea never had reeds (Egyptian *twf*), but elsewhere in the Tanach, *yam suf* refers to the Red Sea and the Gulf of Aqabah (Ex 10:19; Num 33:10–11; 14:25; Deut 1:40; 1Ki 9:26).

Even though the exact route is allusive, the obvious point in the text is that Israel was heading away from Egypt, and God instructed them through Moses to "turn back" and to camp in a place that made them vulnerable. God's ways are not our ways, and He does not always reveal to us the purpose for His leading. In this case, He intended to bring a final destruction upon Pharaoh and his army by luring them into pursuing after Israel. The military observers for Pharaoh doubtlessly reported to him that Israel was wandering about, and had apparently lost her way. Camped with the water before them, they had no place to go, and from a military standpoint were "sitting ducks."

Thus God hardened Pharaoh's heart again (14:4, 8) and so he mustered his best fighting forces in chariots and went to defeat Israel in order to enslave her as before. Having a few days of respite from the months of plagues, the Egyptian people also had a change of heart. After all, their economy, resting as it was upon the shoulders of slave labor, had just hit an all-time low. The best solution in their minds was once again to enslave Israel who now presented herself as a weak and lost people, wandering in the wilderness.

We may pause to consider this mysterious aspect of God's leading. Would the people themselves have chosen to take this route? One hardly thinks so! The best route out of Egypt was the shortest and straightest. To have turned back and camped against the wall of the sea could never have been thought a wise thing to do. We should never forget that as God leads us in paths of righteousness (note that Ps 23:3 uses the same word, נחה, *nachah* "to lead" as is found in Ex 13:21) the path may traverse "the valley of deepest darkness (shadow of death)." But He brings us there to demonstrate His power and greatness, as a matter of His grace. It is in the hour of our greatest need that His "outstretched" arm is most obvious. Indeed, the Sages note that Pi-Hahiroth is related to חֵירוּת, *cheyrut,* "freedom." The very place where it appeared Israel was entrapped was the place of their ultimate freedom.

The text (14:9) indicates that the Egyptians "overtook" (נשׂג, *nasag*) the Israelites as they camped by the sea. This should most likely be understood to mean "they arrived on the horizon." One can only imagine the terror that struck the hearts of the people as they immediately realized their indefensible position. Their first response was to cry out to the Lord in fear, and next to blame Moses for his ineptitude. He had led them in a way that appeared ill-conceived and that would lead to their ultimate demise. The irony in their words is evident, as they ask, "were there not sufficient graves in Egypt?" (14:11). Indeed, Egypt was known for her graves! And they conclude that slavery in Egypt, as terrible as that was, was still better than dying in the wilderness. If we put ourselves in their place, we can sympathize with their sentiments.

Yet it was this very issue that was crucial: is slavery in Egypt actually better than dying in the wilderness? Or to put it another way: is it worth one's life to worship God as He desires to be worshipped? This was the point of their leaving Egypt, that they might "serve God." It is easy to state the principle when one is not faced with the ultimate choice, but the principle still remains true: better to die in the wilderness where true worship can be expressed, than to be enslaved in paganism.

The faith of Moses shines forth in his reply to the people (14:13–14):

> But Moses said to the people, "Do not fear! Stand by and see the salvation of Adonai which He will accomplish for you today; for the Egyptians whom you have seen today, you will never see them again forever. Adonai will fight for you while you keep silent."

This was a battle that God Himself would fight for the Israelites while they "kept silent" (חרשׁ, *charash*). The picture here is one of complete trust. The most difficult thing for us to do is to rely entirely upon the Lord when we find ourselves in situations well beyond our control and abilities. Yet it is in these times when we find the Lord working His will and accomplishing His purposes.

Moses gives a prophetic word: "you will never see these Egyptians again forever." Their fight against the Almighty secures their final demise. We must never lose sight of the fact that God's enemies will never succeed. Finally, in the end, all who rise up against the Lord will be crushed.

It is therefore a firm and resolute faith in God that is able to accept the comforting command, "do not fear," in such a situation.

The text (14:15) indicates that Moses likewise was crying out to the Lord. Yet He responds with a rebuke: "Why are you crying out to Me?" The Sages offer two suggestions for this rebuke: "Now, when Israel is in distress, is no time for a lengthy prayer!" Alternatively, some suggest a different punctuation: "Why do you cry out (as though the situation is your responsibility)? *It is* "to Me," that is, "It is for Me to save the nation, therefore instruct them to move ahead and I will attend to their safety" (Rashi). Regardless of how we may understand this rebuke, the Lord's point to Moses is that now was the time to move forward, not to seek alternative solutions. God's way of saving Israel was unfolding just as He had planned. He would be honored (כבד, *kabad*) through the destruction of Pharaoh and his army. While all along Pharaoh "honored" his own heart, in the end, the honor would be the Lord's.

As the Israelites set out toward the sea, the pillar of cloud moved from before them to act as their rear guard. Here, the pillar is identified as the "angel of God" (מַלְאַךְ הָאֱלֹהִים, *mal'ach haElohim*), which corresponds to the "angel of His presence" in Isaiah 63:9 — "In all their affliction He was afflicted, and the angel of His presence saved them; in His love and in His mercy He redeemed them, and He lifted them and carried them all the days of old." The pillar of cloud apparently gave light on the Israelite side, but maintained darkness for the Egyptians. Thus Israel marched through the sea all night long without the Egyptians knowing (14:20).

Once again, the staff of Moses is used (14:16). He stretches his hand and staff over the sea, and the waters parted via a strong east wind that not only held the waters back as walls on both sides, but also dried the sea bottom for easy passage across. At the morning watch (Rashi considers this to be just before dawn) the Egyptians were able to see that Israel had escaped through the sea, and they took up pursuit. God confused them by making their chariot wheels swerve. The text doesn't explain exactly how this happened, but one could imagine that God confused the drivers of the chariots so that they broke rank and caused collisions with each other. Regardless, they found themselves engulfed with water-walls on both sides, and in the turmoil of battle confusion. They realized immediately that God was still fighting for Israel, and attempted to retreat, but it was too late. The trap was sprung and the waters returned to their place. The Sages, in fanciful midrash, suggest that the waters were created initially with the command that they should split for Israel in the future, and only when they had accomplished this task could they return to the normal, creative order.

Thus the Egyptian army was destroyed by the direct intervention of

God on Israel's behalf. Forever would this miracle be celebrated as the historical salvation of Israel, bringing her from slavery to freedom. It thus would also stand as a paradigm for revealing the ultimate salvation in Messiah's death, for Israel was seen as "baptized into Moses" (1Cor 10:2), a metaphor that would inform that ritual of the *mikvah* as symbolically moving from death to life. Even as Israel "went through the midst of the sea" (14:22), so *mikvah* would become a symbol of just such a "crossing" from death to life.

The Israelites watched as the "great hand of God" (14:31, הַיָּד הַגְּדֹלָה) accomplished His victory over the enemies of His people. A similar expression, usually translated "outstretched arm" (בִּזְרוֹעַ נְטוּיָה) is used throughout the Tanach to describe this kind of sovereign work of salvation by God on behalf of His people (cf. Ex. 6:6; Deut. 4:34; 5:15; 7:19; 9:29; 11:2; 26:8; 1Kings 8:42; 2Kings 17:36; 2Chr. 6:32; Psa. 136:12; Jer. 27:5; 32:17,21; Ezek. 20:33-34). Another similar expression is "with a mighty hand" (בְּיָד חֲזָקָה, cf. Ex. 13:9; 32:11; Num. 20:20; Deut. 4:34; 5:15; 6:21; 7:8; 9:26; 26:8; Jer. 32:21; Ezek. 20:33-34; Psa. 136:12; Dan. 9:15), most often used in connection to the exodus. Peter refers to God's "mighty hand" in 1Pet 5:6, "Therefore humble yourselves under the mighty hand of God, that He may exalt you at the proper time." Similarly, "Your right hand" (יְמִינֶךָ) is used to denote God's power (cf.Ex. 15:6,12; Psa. 16:11; 17:7; 18:35; 21:8; 44:3; 45:4,9; 48:10; 60:5; 63:8; 74:11; 80:15,17; 89:13; 91:7; 108:6; 110:5; 121:5; 138:7; 139:10; Is. 41:13), especially in providing refuge and salvation for His people. The "right hand" in Hebrew usage denotes a place of honor, power, and authority. All of these expression speak of God's sovereign power—His ability to order the affairs of our lives and of this world. Used often in connection with the exodus story, these expressions speak of God's infinite power to accomplish all of His holy will on behalf of His chosen people.

Our *parashah* ends with the "Song at the Sea," (שִׁירַת הַיָּם), the poetic, hymnic expression of praise and joy for God's deliverance. We should note initially the obvious fact that music and songs of praise are the natural expression of praise to God in the Scriptures. Music and poetry allow the human soul to express the deep emotions and thoughts that words alone often cannot convey, and this is true in every human culture. Anthropologists often consider music and dance as one aspect of cultural identification, because music (and the expressions it evokes) signal a bed-rock reality of human expression. In God's infinite wisdom, He gave to human kind the ability to create and use music, and it is therefore most fitting that we utilize music as a mode of praise and worship to express our heartfelt emotions of adoration to our Creator and Savior.

It is not certain how the Song of the Sea was composed. It is clearly one of the oldest pieces of epic poetry contained in the Hebrew Bible, and therefore offers an example of Hebrew in its early stages. Poetry often "freezes" the language in which it is written, since it cannot be updated and retain its poetic structure. Our text notes that "Moses and all the children of Israel sang this song." How did they learn it so quickly! Did Moses compose the song and then teach it to the rest? Or is this an example of a "spiritual song" in which, in some miraculous manner, the Spirit of God gave spontaneous music to the nation as a whole? We are not certain. It may well be that the song was composed after the exodus event as a means of praise, but also as a way to embed within the national conscience of Israel this historical moment of eternal significance. Regardless, this hymn became a national monument forever retained in the history of God's chosen people, having become the eternal word of God written in the Torah.

The structure of the Song is as follows:

vv. 1–10 celebration of God's great victory over the Egyptian foe
vv. 11–13 describe how God is incomparable to other deities
vv. 14–16 describe how the exodus impacted surrounding nations
vv. 17–18 are prophetic and anticipate God's continuing reign

We may note a number of things in the Song by way of explanation:
1. In v. 2 the name of the Lord is יָהּ, *Yah,* used only in poetry and as the theophoric element in names (e.g., *Yirmi-yahu,* "Jeremiah") and has survived in the oft used imperative, *Hallelu-Yah,* "Praise Yah." Also, v. 2 is found in its entirety in Is 12:2 and Ps 118:14, showing its on-going use as a liturgical element. Accordingly, it has been used in the synagogue siddur from ancient times.
2. In v. 2, the Hebrew uses the word זִמְרָה, "song," in the phrase "Yah is my strength and my song." But *zimrah* can also mean "strength," and thus the word is most likely used in a double sense: "Yah is my strength (עָזִּי) and [the theme of] my song."
3. In v. 3 Adonai is called a "man of war" (אִישׁ מִלְחָמָה), and this is followed by "Adonai (יהוה) is His name." Thus, the meaning of יהוה, as the God Who keeps His covenant promises, is connected here with His willingness to fight for His people in order to save them. The Hebrew Bible conveys this concept as God's own sovereign work, not as the work of His people. We may compare David's words (1Sam 17:47), "all this assembly may know that the Lord does not deliver by sword or by spear; for the battle is the Lord's and He will give you into our hands." Zechariah proclaims (4:6), "'Not by might nor by power, but by My Spirit,' says the Lord of hosts." Thus, God as warrior has no connection with "holy war"

as conceived by the Crusaders or by Islamic *jihad,* in which people take into their own hands what the Hebrew Bible ascribes entirely to God's sovereign and miraculous work.

4. In v. 8, "the blast of Your nostrils" is used also in 2Sam 22:16. This is Ancient Near Eastern metaphor for the wind as utilized by God for His purposes.

5. In v. 8, the term "piled up" (נֶעֶרְמוּ) is taken midrashically by the Sages as deriving not from עֲרֵמָה, "a heap, pile," but from עָרְמָה, "cunning, shrewdness." This is taken as an allusion to retributive justice. Even as the Israelite male children were drowned in the Nile because the Egyptians "dealt shrewdly" with the Israelites, now the waters deal with equal shrewdness in drowning Pharaoh's army.

6. V. 13 uses the language of a shepherd: "In Your lovingkindness You have led the people whom You have redeemed." "Lovingkindness" (חֶסֶד) is often in connection to covenant faithfulness. In faithfulness to His word of promise, He leads His chosen ones as a shepherd leads and guards His sheep. Note the parallel in Ps 78:52, "But He led forth His own people like sheep and guided them in the wilderness like a flock."

7. In vv. 14–16, the terror upon the surrounding nations is highlighted. In v. 14, "inhabitants" (יֹשְׁבֵי, *yoshvei*) may be understood as "those who sit," that is, "those who sit on thrones," meaning "rulers." Thus, the peoples fear, and so do their rulers. In v. 15, the Edomites, the descendents of Esau, would become the constant foe of Israel, yet the story of the exodus would forever cause them to tremble in light of how God fights for His people. V. 16 speaks of the people God has "ransomed" (עַם-זוּ קָנִיתָ). The word קָנָה (*qanah*) means "to purchase." Here, as throughout the Scriptures, redemption is cast in economic terms. Israel as a slave in Egypt is given her freedom through the payment of a price. This economic metaphor undergirds the whole concept of divine redemption or ransom.

8. V. 17 uses the unique expression "the mountain of Your inheritance" (בְּהַר נַחֲלָתְךָ). It refers to the city of Jerusalem, and Mt. Zion, upon which the Temple would be built, and the place where God promised to put His Name, heart, and ears forever (cf. 1Ki 9:3; 2Ki 21:7). This "sanctuary," which speaks in one way of the earthly Tabernacle and Temple, is viewed as a replica of the heavenly Sanctuary "not made with hands" (cf. Heb 9:11). Thus, "The sanctuary, O Lord, which Your hands have established."

9. V. 18 closes the Song with the same exultation with which it began: "The Lord shall reign forever and ever" (יהוה יִמְלֹךְ לְעֹלָם וָעֶד). The Kingship of God over all the universe is therefore the primary theme of the Song.

The *haftarah* text chosen for this *parashah* (Jer 49:1–22) is Jeremiah's prophecy against the nations that have sought the destruction of Israel. Edom, in particular, is singled out, for Edom failed to assist Judah when beseiged by Nebuchadnezer, desiring rather to remain silent in hopes of saving himself from being conquered by Babylon. Edom (descendants of Esau) watched as his brother, Jacob, was maliciously beaten and taken into captivity. Thus, even as God fought against Egypt and brought Pharaoh to his knees as his crack troops were drowned in the sea, so God would destroy Edom, meting out their due punishment for their refusal to aid Judah in their day of trouble. Here, once again, we see the prophetic promise of God's utter faithfulness to Israel, bringing the nation back to Himself in repentance and faith, and causing His chosen nation to dwell in the Land in safety.

> "In those days and at that time," declares ADONAI, "the sons of Israel will come, both they and the sons of Judah as well; they will go along weeping as they go, and it will be ADONAI their God they will seek. They will ask for the way to Zion, turning their faces in its direction; they will come that they may join themselves to ADONAI in an everlasting covenant that will not be forgotten. (Jer 50:4–5)

The Apostolic portion (Rom 8:1–14) takes the theme of salvation portrayed in the exodus event and applies it to the salvation of each one who has exercised saving faith in Yeshua. Even as Moses led the children of Israel through the Red Sea to safety and salvation from the Egyptian army that sought their demise, so the believer has died with Messiah and risen to new life in Him. Even as Israel was led by Moses through the Red Sea to safety, so the child of God is led by the Ruach HaKodesh to walk in ways of righteousness as witnesses of God's grace in the Messiah. Indeed, even as the exodus event established Israel as God's covenant nation, so the believer is confirmed in his or her identity in Messiah as their life becomes more and more conformed to Yeshua.

> For all who are being led by the Spirit of God, these are sons of God. (Rom 8:14)

Parashah 57
Triennial Cycle

Exodus 15:19-16:24

Haftarah: Isaiah 45:20-25 | Apostolic: John 6:31-51

The Bread from Heaven

Our text describes the beginnings of the journey of Israel through the Sinai desert on their way to the Promised Land, following their liberation from the slavery of Egypt. One can only imagine the mixed emotions of the people as they left the oppression of more than four generations. All they had known was slavery, and all their parents, grandparents, and many great-grandparents had known was oppression. Slavery had become a way of life, and freedom was an unknown quantity. Venturing out into the wilderness of Sinai undoubtedly presented fears and misgivings. How would they survive? How would they face the challenges of the unknown? As a nation of former slaves, could they really hope to defend themselves against nations with organized armies?

Before we summarily point our fingers at the lack of faith that would be evidenced by the beleaguered nation, we should ask ourselves how we might have acted. When faced with the unknown future, are we resolute in our faith? Even when we are certain of God's favor toward us, do we approach the difficult events of life with a resolute and unwavering faith? In many ways, the story of Israel's grumblings in the desert mirror our own deficiencies.

Our *parashah* begins with an epilogue to the Song at the Sea. Miriam traditionally is identified as the older sister of Moses and Aaron, who was instrumental in saving the infant Moses by intervening when Pharaoh's daughter found him in the waters of the Nile (cf. Num 26:59; 1Chron 6:3). She obviously held a leadership position within the nation (cf. Mic 6:4), for in the course of time, she sided with Aaron against Moses as the sole spokesman of God to the nation (Num 12). In our text, she leads the women in the Song at the Sea in a kind of antiphonal chorus.

Israel enters the "wilderness of Shur (שׁוּר)," a designation for the northwest desert of the Sinai peninsula. They journeyed for three days without finding an oasis that could provide the people and their flocks drinking water. This was no small problem! Three days in the desert without water spelled certain disaster if the problem was not resolved. When they finally arrived at Marah, the water there was brackish, and could not be used. Marah (meaning "bitter") is usually identified with *'Ain Hawarah*, located about 45 miles southeast of the Gulf of Suez. The name Marah is given to the place by Israel in light of her experience of finding that the waters there were bitter. Imagine finally coming upon water after three days in the desert, and then realizing that it cannot be used! The result was that the people complained against (עַל, *'al*) Moses. Our sinful inclination is to complain when natural supplies are exhausted. Faith looks beyond the natural to the supernatural.

Here is the first miracle of preservation given to the people by God, a miracle that also brings with it a testing of the people's faith. Hearing the complaint of the people, Moses cries out to God. He is shown a nearby "tree" (עֵץ, *'eitz*, can refer to anything of wood) which he throws into the water, and the water becomes sweet. *Mechilta* notes that this is a double miracle, for the tree (or wood) itself was most likely bitter, but it turned the waters sweet.

Verse 25 ends with a very important notice: "There He made for them (לוֹ, *lō*) a statute (חֹק, *choq*) and regulation (מִשְׁפָּט, *mishpat*), and there He tested them (נִסָּהוּ, *nisāhu*)." The Sages note that God gave to Israel "statutes and regulations" before ever coming to Sinai and the giving of the Torah. Perhaps this notice is a general summary of all that would transpire at this place, including the giving of manna and quail, and the commandments regarding the gathering and preparation of the manna. But its inclusion here, at the miracle of the bitter waters, tells us that God's miracles on behalf of His people also present a test. Would they accept the work of God as sufficient for their needs, or would they continue to rely upon their own means for self-preservation? Inevitably, when God intervenes in the lives of His children, His hand of provision requires a response of faithful reliance. The purpose of God's miracles, which are with us every day, is to strengthen our faith in Him. Apart from the exercise of faith, the ultimate purpose of miracles is short-circuited. This is the meaning of Matthew 13:58– "And He (Yeshua) did not do many miracles there because of their unbelief."

Generally, the rabbis delineate a difference between a "statute" (חֹק, *choq*) and a "regulation" (מִשְׁפָּט, *mishpat*) in this way: a "statute" is a commandment given by God for which there can be given no rational explanation. In other words, the commandment is to be done simply because it is required, not because we can figure out exactly why we are to do it. In contrast, a "regulation" is something that makes sense rationally. Whether or not such a distinction can be maintained in every usage of these terms, it is true that sometimes God gives us commandments without adding any explanation—He simply expects us to obey because He has commanded us to do so. In other cases, His commandments come with a fuller explanation of why the regulation makes good sense. In either case, the laws of God are received by the heart of faith as those things which our loving Father has given for our good and His glory. Inevitably, obedience is the mark of genuine faith.

It is interesting that this notice regarding God's "statute" and "regulation" comes at the place called Marah ("bitter"). By God's providence, we may be led into times of difficulty—experiences where the water is "bitter" rather than "sweet." It is in these times when His commandments become the proof of our faith. Will we remain faithful to Him in spite of the current trouble? Will we continue to obey His statutes when the way forward seems impossible? What we discover is that within God's commandments there is a divine protection for our souls. The heart of faith lays hold of God's instruction (Torah), lives in accordance with His commandments, and finds in this reliance upon His goodness a path through the troubled times. "Your word is a lamp to my feet and a light to my path" (Ps 119:105). Our natural inclination may be to scurry about to find our own path—to resolve the problem in our own way. But a maturing faith sets itself to seek and obey God's commandments, and finds in them a light showing His divinely ordained path through life's harshest deserts. "Your statutes are my songs in the house of my pilgrimage" (Ps 119:54).

This is the specific message of God's words to the nation in our text (15:26):

> And He said, "If you will give earnest heed to the voice of the Lord your God, and do what is right in His sight, and give ear to His commandments, and keep all His statutes, I will put none of the diseases on you which I have put on the Egyptians; for I, the Lord, am your healer."

God identifies Himself as Israel's "healer" (אֲנִי יְהוָה רֹפְאֶךָ, *'ani Adonai Rof'echa*). When He brings His people into a wasting desert, He does so not with the purpose of simply afflicting them or causing them trouble. Rather, He does so as the miraculous Healer, to demonstrate His greatness to them. But note carefully that such healing comes as His people exercise their faith in Him. Obedience to His commandments is a demonstration of true faith. This verse teaches that if we place our faith in Him, a faith demonstrated by obedience, He will protect us and heal us, that is, transform us into the people He intends for us to be. His purpose for leading us into the desert is that He might heal us. He is "Adonai your healer."

This is demonstrated by the flow of the narrative. Even though the people were given sweet water at Marah, v. 27 immediately notes that the people came to Elim, a name that most likely describes this palm grove—an oasis in the desert. At Elim, twelve springs bubbled forth, one for each of the twelve tribes, signalling the fact that full provision for the nation was given. "God will supply all your needs according to His riches in glory in Messiah Yeshua" (Phil 4:19). The notice that Israel "camped beside the waters" reminds us of the words of the Psalmist (Ps 23:2), "He leads me beside quite waters." Even in the desert, there is a place of quite shalom.

How long Israel camped at Elim is not clear, but they departed from there and came to the wilderness called "Sin" (סִין, *siyn*), not to be confused or connected with our English word for transgressions, nor with the wilderness of Zin (צִן, *tzin*, Num 33:36, which is identified with Kadesh). The wilderness of Sin most likely denotes the central region of the Sinai peninsula. (The etymological similarity between "Sin" and "Sinai" seems inevitable.) A chronological note is given in Ex 16:1 regarding when Israel arrived at this third location: "…on the fifteenth day of the second month after their departure from the land of Egypt." This would mean that Israel had been on her sojourn for exactly one month since the exodus event. What may seem a short time from our perspective had doubtlessly become a long time for the nation. A month of limited provisions and water may have greatly reduced the livestock. Food provisions were becoming increasingly scarce, and the people realized that they were facing starvation in the desert. And once again they gave in to complaining. This may seem disquieting given the fact that Israel had witnessed such great miracles and compassion toward them by the Almighty. Yet it is not surprising, because hunger and the fear that one would not be able to provide for their children can drive people to actions they would never carry out in normal circumstances.

Immediately the people's thoughts turn to comparing the bleak future (as they saw it) with the slavery they endured in Egypt. Neither option was a good one, yet in Egypt they still remained alive (for the most part). Generations had endured the heavy burden of servitude, but here, in the desert, it appeared as though the whole nation would perish. Suddenly the "meat pots" of Egypt seemed very enticing.

It is interesting to note that the people judged the motives of Moses and Aaron (16:3): "… for you have brought us out into this wilderness to kill this whole assembly with hunger." Obviously, it was not Moses and Aaron who had made the decision to leave Egypt. Nor was it their decision to lead Israel into the desert. God was the One who redeemed them from Egypt, and God was the One leading them in the desert. Here we see a tell-tale sign of a lack of faith: the focus has shifted away from God to men. Surely Israel knew that God was the One Who had redeemed them from Egypt, and was leading them on their sojourn. The visible presence of God was evident in the pillar of cloud and fire. Yet when they found themselves in dire straights, they charge Moses and Aaron with malevolent motives. Faith looks to God; the flesh relies upon men.

Furthermore, the grumblings of Israel against Moses and Aaron were, in fact, grumblings against the Lord. Since the Lord had chosen Moses and Aaron, and since they were fulfilling their calling by leading the people, Israel's grumblings were ultimately against God. Note 16:9, "...the Lord hears your grumblings which you grumble against Him. And what are we? Your grumblings are not against us but against the Lord."

God does not immediately rebuke the people for their grumblings. Instead, He reveals to Moses His divine plan for providing them food. But again, His miraculous intervention comes as a means for testing the faith of Israel. He will reign "bread from heaven" (לֶחֶם מִן־הַשָּׁמָיִם) and give to Israel the sustenance she requires. It is this very phrase, "bread from heaven," that is foundational for Yeshua's own *midrash* on our text, in which the manna is a fitting illustration of His own incarnation. And in line with the giving of the manna as a test of faith for Israel, so the coming of the Messiah presents the ultimate test of faith. John 3:36— "He who believes in the Son has eternal life; but he who does not obey the Son will not see life, but the wrath of God abides on him."

The regulations given to Israel in regard to how they should gather and prepare the manna form the test of their faith/obedience. This will show "...whether or not they will walk in My instruction (בְּתוֹרָתִי, *b^etôrāti*)." Here, the English "instruction" is the Hebrew word "Torah," emphasizing that Torah is instruction, not merely law or commandment. The regulations are quite straightforward: every day they were to gather enough manna for that day. They were not to gather for the next day, nor were they to keep manna from one day to the next. Moreover, on the sixth day, they were to gather twice as much as usual, so that on the seventh day they could remain in their place, and not toil to gather their food. On normal weekdays, in the evening, they would gather meat from the quail that were provided, and in the morning they were to gather manna for their bread.

As Aaron was revealing to the people God's plan for providing them food, the glory of the Lord (*Shekinah*) appeared in the cloud (16:10). We should not think that somehow the visible presence of God had ceased at some time. Exodus 13:22 makes this clear. But note the wording of our text (16:10): "It came about as Aaron spoke to the whole congregation of the sons of Israel, that they looked toward the wilderness, and behold, the glory of the Lord appeared in the cloud." The *Shekinah* was always present, but the people were not always looking for Him. Perhaps the constant presence of God had been taken for granted, and had slipped away from the mental consciousness of the people. At this instance, however, they turn to look out at the wilderness and once again see the pillar of cloud. God is ever with His people, but a lack of faith dulls their spiritual vision.

God's provision of food for His people was given so that they might understand and believe in Him as *their* God, not just the God of Moses and Aaron (16:12) "… and you shall know that I am the Lord *your* God." God brings us into times of trouble so that when He makes a way for us, our personal faith in Him increases (James 1:2–4).

So the meat (quail) comes at twilight (בֵּין הָעַרְבַּיִם, *bein ha'arbayim*) and the manna in the morning. This reminds us of the Pesach sacrifice that was also to be slain "at twilight (Ex 12:6)," and of the sacrifices in general that were revealed to Israel as a foreshadow of the "Bread from heaven" Who is Messiah, Yeshua. The one points to the other.

The people were instructed to gather an omer for each person in the tent (16:16). The omer here is a dry measure that is one-tenth of an ephah. The exact measure is debated, but most consider it to be roughly equivalent to what would fill a common eating bowl.

When the manna first appeared, the people looked at it and exclaimed, "What is it?" (מָן הוּא, *man hu'*). The Hebrew word מָן (*man*) is used only in connection with the "manna" in the Tanach, but it is speculated to be an emphatic form of מָה (*mah*), meaning "what." Thus, מָנָה, "what is it?" is a contraction of מָן הוּא. It was unlike anything the people had seen before. (Alternatively, the Hebrew could be translated "it is manna," in which case the people recognized it as food, and Moses confirms this by his statement.) Ps 78:25 describes the manna as the "bread of mighty ones (angels)" (לֶחֶם אַבִּירִים, *lechem 'abirim*) and Neh 9:20 connects the manna with the Spirit: "You gave Your good Spirit to instruct them, Your manna You did not withhold from their mouth, and You gave them water for their thirst."

The notice given in our text about what happened when the people gathered the manna is specific (16:17–18): "The sons of Israel did so, and gathered much and little. When they measured it with an omer, he who had gathered much had no excess, and he who had gathered little had no lack; every man gathered as much as he should eat." This does not mean that those who were lazy (gathering little) ended up with the same amount as those who gathered a full measure. What it means is that the regulation set forth by God, that each should gather an omer, was perfectly suited for each family. A tent that had only a few people had just the right amount, and tent that had many people had just enough. God's regulations work! And wouldn't we expect that they would? After all, He is our Creator—He knows exactly what we need.

The manna would appear each morning, and tradition has it that it would be gone by midday (b. *Yoma* 76a). God gave a far greater abundance than was needed for the nation—the provision was limitless. Everyone's needs were met with plenty left over. We are reminded of the miracle of the loaves and fish, which, when the crowd was satisfied, bushels of leftovers were collected. The needs of God's people never exhaust His infinite supply.

Some of the people, however, did not heed the instructions of Moses, that none was to be kept over for the next day. Those who tried to store up what they had gathered discovered that it bred worms (16:20). This teaches us that both the provision for the six days as well as the provision for the Sabbath was a miracle of God. For on the Sabbath, the double portion gathered on the sixth day remained fresh. Yet on the weekdays, any left over manna became foul. God was carefully providing the daily needs of His people. This phenomenon informs the Disciples' Prayer: "give us the bread we need for today." Trust in the Lord is something that must be exercised constantly. We can not expect that a "spiritual high" will last. Feeding upon the spiritual nourishment of God's presence is the daily privilege of His people. His word is to be our daily food, His Torah our constant nourishment, His Messiah our spiritual staple.

In the same manner, the double portion of manna gathered on the sixth day evidenced a trust in God. Since manna stored up during the week became foul, it would stand to reason that some might have considered gathering twice as much on the sixth day as an exercise in futility. But those who believed what God had said obeyed, and were nourished during their Sabbath rest. God's work was completed in six days, providing all the food the people needed. His finished work thus carried them into and through the seventh day of rest. We rest because He has completed His work.

This Sabbath principle thus came to the Israelite nation as a test, to see if they were willing to put their complete trust in God. The same test confronts us. It is not uncommon to hear that obeying the Torah stands in the way of a livelihood in our diaspora world. Since the commerce of our day seizes the seventh day as one of the most lucrative days of business, for example, it is surmised that following God's Torah commandments simply "doesn't work" in our modern world. But then they didn't appear to "work" for some of the Israelites either (as next week's portion will reveal). Some went out on the Sabbath to gather manna, apparently because they didn't believe gathering a double portion on the sixth day would work, or because they simply failed to plan ahead. Yet it is clear that those who did follow God's commandments had their needs completely met.

Many who have determined to honor the Sabbath in our times can offer the same scenario. While humanly speaking they may have thought that honoring the Sabbath would inevitably result in lose, what they have witnessed time and again, is that honoring God by honoring the Sabbath has resulted in blessing they could have never planned, and in ways they could have never foreseen. Thus, the testing of Israel's faith, presented to us in this *parashah*, is precisely the same for us: will we receive God's word and live accordingly, trusting that He will provide, or will we rationalize that God's word doesn't work in our times, and try to make our own way? The crowd of faithful witnesses who have gone before us (Heb 11) stand as ample proof that trusting God and obeying His commandments is surely the path attended with His blessing.

Interestingly, the *haftarah* portion chosen by the Sages to accompany this *parashah* in the triennial cycle is Is 45:20–25. Here, ADONAI is calling His people Israel back to Himself and away from the idolatry in which they are engaged as "fugitives of the nations." And v. 23 contains the declaration of the Almighty that encapsulates His utter sovereignty:

> I have sworn by Myself, the word has gone forth from My mouth in righteousness and will not turn back, that to Me every knee will bow, every tongue will swear allegiance. (Is 45:23)

This is the very verse Paul quotes and applies to Yeshua in Phil 2:10, "… so that at the name of Yeshua EVERY KNEE WILL BOW…."

And this connects directly to the Apostolic portion for this *parashah* (Jn 6:31–51), for Yeshua refers to Himself as "the bread from heaven," the very sustenance necessary for eternal life:

> Yeshua then said to them, "Truly, truly, I say to you, it is not Moses who has given you the bread out of heaven, but it is My Father who gives you the true bread out of heaven. For the bread of God is that which comes down out of heaven, and gives life to the world." Then they said to Him, "Lord, always give us this bread." Yeshua said to them, "I am the bread of life; he who comes to Me will not hunger, and he who believes in Me will never thirst. (Jn 6:32–34)

Like the meat from sacrifices which became forbidden after a certain period of time, so the manna could not be stored for the next day. This similarity may well point to the fact that the manna was to be seen as similar to a sacrificial offering. The Bread from heaven, Yeshua, was broken as a sacrificial offering so that we might have eternal life.

Parashah 58
Triennial Cycle

Exodus 16:25-17:16

Haftarah: Isaiah 58:13-14 | Apostolic: Mark 2:27-28

The Torah Teaches Faith

One of the often heard complaints against the Torah is that it is not of faith. Paul's statement in Galatians 3:12 that "the Torah is not of faith" has been regularly misinterpreted to mean that true faith and Torah do not mix. (In the context of Gal 3 the meaning most assuredly is that the Torah does not *produce* initial saving faith but rather proves whether faith is present or not.) Our *parashah* today however argues strongly against the notion that the Torah envisioned something different than the life of faith.

Three "stories" are woven together in our section: 1) the whole issue of gathering manna and how manna was to be gathered in view of the Sabbath, 2) the striking of the rock to produce water for the Israelites, and 3) the battle of Amalek against Israel, with Moses' raised hands to give them the victory. It may seem at first that these three stories are arbitrarily chosen and just "pasted" together without any coherent theme. But a closer look reveals something entirely different. What all three have in common is their lessons regarding faith, and the manner in which HaShem expected the ancient Israelites to exercise genuine faith in Him for their daily salvation.

We may first note the obvious parallels with other significant events that pertain to the manna. First, there was sufficient manna for everyone, meaning that there was an "infinite supply" because the manna had come from the hand of God. The manna was gathered לְפִי־אָכְלוֹ לְקָטוּ, "according to what he eats" (16:18) meaning there was always enough manna for everyone. The manna was given to Israel to prove to them that God was able to meet their needs at the individual level. No one need go hungry who has the Almighty as his God. We experience this in our relationship to the Bread from Heaven. He is able to supply every need, no matter how big or small.

Second, we note how clearly all were viewed as equal in terms of their needs, and the manner in which God intended to meet their needs.

The princes or elders had no priority, nor did males, nor adults—everyone ate what they needed, and everyone was filled. As in all generations, God teaches that station in life makes no claim of merit upon God, but all are equally needy in His sight, and all receive from the same hand of His grace the filling of his or her needs. It is all of grace.

Third, the whole issue of gathering the manna was an exercise in faith. Trying to assure tomorrow by gathering more than what was needed for today was futile: the manna bred worms and was spoiled. How then were the Israelites to be content for tomorrow? Only by trusting that God would send the manna as He promised.

This same principle is doubly applied in regard to Shabbat. Every other day the extra manna, left over until morning, spoiled. But on the sixth day the people were instructed to do what on all other days was utterly futile: gather twice as much. That required faith! Would God preserve the manna so that food on the Shabbat would be available? If you thought He would, you gathered twice as much. If you thought He would not (or could not), you obviously would not go to the extra trouble of gathering extra. Those who did gather extra, by their obedience also demonstrated their faith that it would last in this specific situation.

The life of faith is a life lived on a daily basis, trusting God for what one cannot see, and for what is entirely out of one's control. Why else did Yeshua teach us that we should expect God to provide our "daily bread?" Faith lays hold of tomorrow on the basis of God's word today. This was practically demonstrated in Israel through the manna.

Fourth, it seems impossible that Israel could miss the parallels between the manna and the Pesach lamb. Nothing of the lamb could be left over until morning. Whatever was left over had to be burned. The number of people per lamb was determined by לְפִי אכלוֹ, "according to what he eats," the exact same phrase noted in the gathering of the manna. These similarities must have stood out to the people as a pattern: the manna and the Pesach lamb, both prescribed by God, were connected. That Yeshua would claim that He was the "bread from heaven" (John 6:31ff) thus binds the manna and the lamb together in the very Person they both foreshadowed.

We should remember also that the lessons learned from the manna are in connection with Shabbat (before Sinai!). The rest enjoyed on the Shabbat by the Israelites was to be a fitting picture of how their life of faith issued in rest, not only for body but also for soul. Far from a day of "legalistic knit-picking," the Shabbat was given by HaShem to teach us about the shalom for which we all strive. The point? Shalom comes from submission to God—doing life His way.

In that regard, we learn once again that obedience to God (in this case, keeping Shabbat) requires preparation. The people were to bake and prepare in advance of the Shabbat *so that they could rest.* Our rest in HaShem is not something automatic: it requires our obedient participation, an obedience that flows from the faith that has been given to us as an eternal gift of the Almighty. Thus, preparing to obey is just as important as obeying.

It is this important truth that connects the *haftarah* (Is 58:13–14) to our Torah *parashah*. Prophesying about the millennial Temple, Isaiah gives the words of HaShem: "If because of the sabbath, you turn your foot from doing your own pleasure on My holy day… I will make you ride on the heights of the earth…." Obedience to God—following in His precepts—brings lasting success in life. Indeed, keeping the Shabbat is a demonstration of faith in God's promises.

And this links to our Apostolic portion (Mk 2:27–28) in which Yeshua states: "The Sabbath was made for man, and not man for the Sabbath." God has given the Shabbat as a revelation of His grace, not as a burden upon the shoulders of His people. In the Shabbat we learn not only to grow in our faith and trust in Him, but we also are constantly reminded that it is by His finished work that we are redeemed and forgiven so that we may serve Him in spirit and truth.

The second story is that of Meribah. The people are complaining about the lack of water, and even are fearful they will die in the wilderness. In this frame of mind they reason that slavery in Egypt was better. Of course, the story is famous: God instructs Moses to strike a rock with the now famous staff and water flows from it, enough for all the people. Paul midrashically considers this whole story a fitting illustration of the blessings that flow from Yeshua (1Cor 10:4ff).

What is the lesson of faith that binds this story with that of the manna? It is submission to authority. And the ability to submit to God is a function of genuine faith. Note carefully how the text reads: (17:2) "Why do you contend with me (Moses)? Why do you test HaShem?" In other words, when the people were grumbling against Moses (even to the point he thought they might kill him, cf. 17:3) who was clearly God's appointed leader, they were actually grumbling against HaShem!

So how is one able to submit to the leadership of mere humans with all of their own failings? Only by trusting God! If God has appointed leaders, then submitting to them has nothing to do with the obvious fact that sometimes they will make mistakes. Submission to them comes from a settled trust in God that He is the One Who is ultimately in control.

One level at which this is practised is marriage. Husbands, are you submitting to God and to the wisdom of your wife? Wives, are you submitting to your husbands as unto the Lord? If you are, you are demonstrating a faith, not first and ultimately in your spouse, but in the Lord's ability to work in your spouse. Such a submission will prompt your regular prayers for the one to whom you submit.

Learning to submit one to the other is also the "stuff" that builds community. Recognizing God's patterns of authority brings stability and longevity to the various levels of relationship fostered within the *kehilah*. Ultimately, the ability to submit to authority is the product of a growing faith in the Almighty.

The final story in our parashah is about Amalek's attack upon Israel and the fact that the battle was fought on two levels: with Joshua and the military, and with Moses on the mountain. The two spheres of battle, of course, were vitally linked. Amalek could not be defeated without Joshua and his men engaging in battle, but they could not win the battle unless Moses' hands remained faithful (note v. 12, וַיְהִי יָדָיו אֱמוּנָה עַד־בֹּא הַשֶּׁמֶשׁ, "and so it was that his hands were faithful until the going of the sun.")

What is the picture here? It is a portrayal of the necessary function of intercession. Moses, as the mediator between God and Israel, intercedes on her behalf. When he does, Israel wins. When he ceases, Israel fails. Israel's success in battle depends upon the mediator, but the mediator does not fight the battle. Here we see a wonderful picture of the divine/human cooperative. God is the One who wins the battle, but He does so through the efforts of those who engage the enemy in His Name. If we apply this picture to the process of sanctification, we recognize that our own growth in holiness is ultimately secure because God has promised that He will make us holy, and Yeshua is interceding for us. We believe His prayers will surely be answered. Yet this process of sanctification requires our own engagement in the battle. We must walk, run, wrestle, fight, and put to death the deeds of the flesh. In short, the process of sanctification requires our active participation in living a disciplined life of obedience to God, resting secure in the work of Yeshua on our behalf.

Faith therefore recognizes that the battle is fought on two levels: at the sphere of my existence as well as in the heavenly sphere. The spiritual battles in which we are engaged have a direct connection to those being fought in the heavenlies (Eph 6). Moreover, faith recognizes that victory in this world is the result of the faithful intercession of our Master, who "always lives to make intercession" for us (Heb 7:25). "…as He is, so also are we in this world" (1Jn 4:17).

Parashah Seventeen
יִתְרוֹ – Yitro

"Jethro"
Exodus 18:1-20:26

In the Triennial Cycle there one Parashah

18:1-20:26

Parashah 59
Triennial Cycle

Exodus 18:1–20:26

Haftarah: Isaiah 61:1–6 | Apostolic: Luke 4:16–30

Amalekites vs. Kenites

As is typical of Hebrew narrative, our Torah section this Shabbat, if read without thought, might appear to be out of order. 18:5 speaks of Jethro coming to the wilderness, at the mount of God, while 19:1 gives the indication that the camping at the mount of God came later. In fact, the order of the narrative is not strictly chronological, and this is instructive. The order is given to highlight the differences between Amalek, the eternal enemy of Israel, and the Kenites, who befriended God's chosen people (1 Sam 15:6). Jethro, you see, was a Kenite (Judges 4:11). Note the contrasts:

Chapter 17	Chapter 18
Amalek came & fought	Jethro came and brought peace
Chose men (for war)	Chose men to settle disputes
Moses sat on a rock	Moses sits to judge
Moses' hands heavy	Moses' responsibilities heavy
War from generation to generation	All people will go in peace

What is more, when Jethro comes, the elders along with Aaron come to offer sacrifices together and to eat a covenant meal.

What is the point? God extends His covenant blessings, as He promised, to those who bless Abraham's seed, but curses those who curse him. In other words, Moses, by arranging the events of the story in the order he does, emphasizes that the Abrahamic covenant is alive and well, being fulfilled because of God's faithfulness to His own word.

Furthermore, the fact that our *parashah* goes through the giving of the Ten Words (ch. 20) shows the desire of the ancient community of Israel to tie the giving of the Torah at Sinai with the Abrahamic promise. Rather than contrasting the two as has often been done by theologians, the biblical text goes to great lengths to show that the two covenants are actually parts of a single whole. To those who participate in Abraham's faith in God, the Torah is given as a light for one's path, a loving *halachah* by which life is to be lived. To those who curse God and His people, however, the Torah is a letter holding a guilty verdict and sentence of condemnation. Subtly, our Torah section brings this contrast before us by the juxtaposition of the Amalekites and Kenites.

Ordered Leadership

The obvious message of the chapter revolves around the issue of leadership. Moses, in attempting to do God's bidding in leading the people, was actually doing a bad thing (18:17), for unwittingly he was depriving the people of entering into the *mitzvot* of serving. Leadership, however, could not be given out willy-nilly. It was on the basis of personal integrity and demonstrated wisdom that leaders were chosen. "Select ... able men who fear God, men of truth, those who hate dishonest gain ...." Compare the list of qualifications for an overseer or deacon in Paul's epistle to Timothy (1 Tim 3). Leadership requires humility, spiritual strength, and personal integrity. And these qualities cannot be tested in a day, or a week, or a month. This is why leaders should come from within the community, not outside of it. The qualities necessary for leaders are seen in the way they personally live out what they believe and teach, and this can only be discerned in knowing them in the context of life.

It was this issue of what qualified leaders that brought about such a great change in the emerging Christian Church of the 2nd and 3rd Centuries. From a Hebrew perspective, leaders were known through their personal application of Torah. The Greek mindset was different, however. For the Greek society, the realm of ideas could be viewed as disconnected from actions. What one thought or reasoned was not necessarily connected with one's life. One could "believe" something without this "belief" changing the way he or she lived. As the emerging Christian Church became more and more populated by Gentiles, this Platonic perspective became the norm for selecting leaders and teachers. Those who were educated in the Greek academies were naturally put forward as the leading teachers on the basis of their education. This meant that those with credentials were sought after, regardless of whether they were known within the community. The key issue was that the criteria for leaders had shifted from a demonstration of wisdom in life, to the amount of time one had studied in the academies.

This does not negate that much can be learned from teachers and preachers outside of the community. But one ought to be very careful about making significant decisions and changes in life based upon what an unknown leader says or teaches. One of the fundamental qualities of

Jewish community is that one's teacher is part of one's life. This is what is meant by the saying in *Perkei Avot:*

> Joshua ben Perachiah and Nittai the Arbelite received the tradition from them (Jose ben Joezer and Jose ben Jochanan). Joshua ben Perachiah said, Procure yourself a teacher, acquire unto yourself an associate, and judge all men in the scale of merit. (1.6).

The Giving of the Torah

Chapter 19 begins with a reference to the time: "In the third month (new moon)... on that very day." Nisan was the month of the exodus, Iyar the intervening month, and now Sivan had arrived, the third month. The Hebrew text begins with בַּחֹדֶשׁ, emphasizing that what comes now in the narrative is to be seen as significant, as highlighted by a new beginning. As Cassuto writes: "The words *on that day*, which parallel *On the third new moon,* re-emphasize that the Israelites came to this place at the commencement of a new period of time, as though to indicate that the event that is due to take place there was so important that no other happening could precede it in that interval of time. Had this event been second chronologically, it might have been regarded as of secondary importance."

We know that, as far as faith is concerned, a mixed multitude stood at the foot of Sinai. Some came with the faith of Abraham, a faith in the promised Messiah, while others clearly did not. Yet, when Moses announces the covenant words of Adonai, they all respond with "all that the Lord has spoken we will do." Always, until Messiah returns, there remains a mixture of belief and unbelief, of the righteous and the unrighteous, of those who believe in truth and those who confess with the mouth but lack genuine faith.

And so it was at Sinai, proven by the fact that God warned repeatedly that the people and priests not "break through" to see His glory, lest He "break through" to destroy them. Doesn't covenant result in fellowship? Why the harsh warnings to keep the covenant people separate from their covenant God? Because not all Israel is Israel—not all who have a physical standing in the community have a spiritual reality in faith. And God separates on the basis of His Messiah—He is the dividing mark, the touchstone of all righteousness—"He who believes in the Son has eternal life; but he who does not obey the Son shall not see life, but the wrath of God abides on him" (Jn 3:36). Though the community was to purify itself in a ceremonial way (as indicated by abstaining from sexual relations), only the Lord sees the heart. As long as the people remained sinners, they must approach God through His chosen representative—no other way is possible.

The Fear of God

Why the awesome display at the giving of the Torah? 20:20 gives the answer: "Do not be afraid; for God has come in order to test you, and in order that the fear of Him may remain with you, so that you may not sin." In our modern world of pluralism we have become convinced that fear is fundamentally bad. Yet the Torah teaches us that sometimes God's methods of revelation are chosen to incite fear—a fear that remains—a fear that offers the fruit of peace. Fearing God is simply recognizing who I am in light of who He is, and recognizing this in the realm of what He has said, not what I feel or wish He had said. Fearing God means loving Him because of Who He is and what He has done.

It is not as though the fear of God is exactly equated with the common emotion of fear alone, as though the "fear of God" could equally be understood as "being afraid of God." There is, of course, an element of "being afraid" in the whole concept of fearing God, but the fear of God exists in a different realm. While being afraid of someone causes one to distance one's self from the object of fear, the fear of God does just the opposite. It draws one closer to God. Some theologians have therefore opted for the idea of "reverence" or "being filled with awe" to explain what the "fear of God" is.

But defining the "fear of God" as "reverence" or "being filled with awe" is not entirely sufficient. One can be in awe of a mountain range, or have great reverence for a president or king. Yet in both of these examples there results no necessary relationship. The "fear of God" exists within the confines of a covenant relationship—one in which the greater the fear, the closer the relationship. Rather than separating, the fear of God draws the worshipper closer to Him. Yet in this drawing closer, the realization of His greatness increases, and one's respect and love grows proportionately greater. And in turn, as one lives life in the realm of a growing and maturing fear of Him, one is inclined to find life more and more lived in accordance with His righteousness. What appears to be opposites actually adhere in the realm of the fear of God. It is in this apparent antinomy that knowledge and wisdom are to be found. For the fear of God is the beginning of both of these (Prov 1:7; 9:10). This reality informs the meaning of Qohelet's conclusion:

> *The conclusion, when all has been heard, is:*
> *fear God and keep His commandments,*
> *because this applies to every person.*
> Qohelet (Ecclesiastes) 12:13

The Ten Words

Traditionally, in Christian circles, the Ten Words are called the "Ten Commandments." However, the biblical text uses the expression עֲשֶׂרֶת הַדְּבָרִים, *'aseret hadevarim*, "Ten Words" when referring to what God inscribed on the two tablets which Moses brought down from Mt. Sinai. In fact, referring to these as Ten Words allows a more accurate enumeration of the Ten since the first Word is not a commandment at all, but the necessary titulature or authoritative title of the One making the covenant, of which the Ten Words is the written document.

This is because the Torah as a whole, and the Ten Words in particular, are patterned after the Suzerain-Vassal treaties or covenants common in the Ancient Near East. Such covenants were enacted between a Great King and a Vassal king who would rule a given region for and on behalf of the Great King. This type of covenant required obedience and allegiance from the Vassal king for which he would receive support and protection from the Great King. Included in the treaty or covenant, however, were clear and decisive penalties if ever the Vassal were to renege on his duties or even rebel against the authority of the Great King in hopes of establishing himself as his own sovereign.

Characteristic of these Suzerain-Vassal treaties of the Ancient Near East was that the Great King, who was enacting the treaty or covenant, would first give his own title along with a short history of his relationship to the Vassal king. Thus, in our biblical text, the Ten Words begin, not with a commandment, but with the identification of the Great King: *I am Adonai your God, who brought you out of the land of Egypt, out of the house of slavery.* Here we see the name of the Great King as well as the decisive event by which He and the Vassal (the nation of Israel) have come into relationship.

The fact that these Ten Words became traditionally known as the Ten Commandments also figured into various enumerations of the Ten. Since generally the Christian Church considered the Ten to be commandments, it became common to find ten commandments, thus skipping past the opening titulature. The following table shows the traditional Jewish, Roman Catholic, and Protestant variations in how the Ten are numbered.

Jewish	Roman Catholic	Protestant
1. I am the ADONAI…	1. No other gods / Don't make idols	1. No other gods
2. No other gods / Don't make idols	2. Don't use God's name in a false oath	2. Don't make idols
3. Don't use God's name in a false oath	3. Keep the Sabbath	3. Don't use God's name in a false oath
4. Keep the Sabbath	4. Honor parents	4. Keep the Sabbath
5. Honor parents	5. Don't murder	5. Honor parents
6. Don't murder	6. Don't commit adultery	6. Don't murder
7. Don't commit adultery	7. Don't steal	7. Don't commit adultery
8. Don't steal	8. Don't give a false witness	8. Don't steal
9. Don't give a false witness	9. Don't covet your neighbor's house	9. Don't give a false witness
10. Don't covet	10. Don't covet your neighbor's wife, servant, etc.	10. Don't covet

The differences are easy to spot: the Jewish list begins with "I am ADONAI…" as the first Word, and then combines "no other gods" and "don't make idols" together as the second Word. The Protestant list is the same as the Jewish, except that it does not begin with "I am ADONAI" and therefore separates "No other gods" and "Don't make idols" to form Words one and two. The Roman Catholic list combines "No other gods" and "Don't make idols" to form the first Word, but separates "Don't covet your neighbor's house" from "Don't covet your neighbor's wife, servant, etc." in order to fill the ninth and tenth Words.

Regardless, the structure of the Ten Words is clear: the first half of the Ten relate to how one loves God while the second half relates to how one loves one's neighbor. Thus, when Yeshua was asked about the greatest of the commandments, He answered by saying:

> YOU SHALL LOVE THE LORD YOUR GOD WITH ALL YOUR HEART, AND WITH ALL YOUR SOUL, AND WITH ALL YOUR MIND. This is the great and foremost commandment. The second is like it, 'YOU SHALL LOVE YOUR NEIGHBOR AS YOURSELF.' On these two commandments depend the whole Law and the Prophets." (Matt 22:37–40)

Thus, loving God and loving one's neighbor answers to the basic structure of the Ten Words.

Note that it is the fifth Word, the one which commands to honor one's parents, that is the "bridge" between the two halves. That is, as a child grows and is taught to honor his or her parents, they are in a much better position to understand what it means to willfully submit to God as their heavenly Father as well as to treat neighbors with the respect they deserve as bearing the image of God.

In fact, it seems clear by the structure of the Ten Words that one builds upon another. Thus, being redeemed from Egypt shows that Israel belongs to God Who redeemed His firstborn. This means Israel is to have allegiance to no other gods, for there are no other gods. The exodus event proved this conclusively. Since, therefore, the God of Israel is the one and only God, it becomes the duty of His redeemed people to sanctify His Name. Honoring God as the One and only Divine King leads to obeying His commandments, which begins by acknowledging the covenant He has made with us, the sign of which is the Shabbat. Then, once we have bowed in submission to God, we recognize that we must love our neighbors, for they bear the image of God Whom we serve.

The point is simple: as we work our way down the list of these Ten Words, we see how they are all bound together and how each one leads to the next. We might diagram this concept like this:

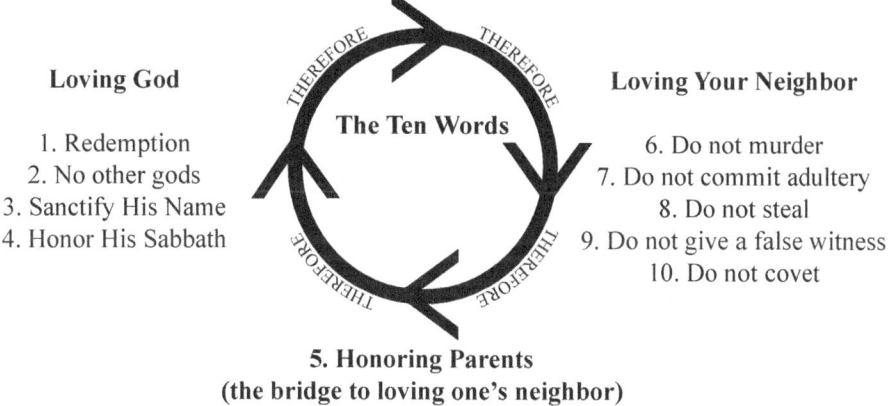

1. *"I am ADONAI your God, who brought you out of the land of Egypt, out of the house of slavery."*

The opening word of the Ten makes it clear that there is a prior relationship between God and those to whom He is writing, for the Ten Words are inscribed upon the stones by the very finger of God (Ex 31:18). This relationship is one of redemption, of being delivered out of the "house of slavery." This is a crucial point in understanding the Ten Words as a whole, as well as the entire Sinai covenant: we obey God, not to achieve or forge a relationship with Him, but because He has already chosen us and redeemed us for Himself. Thus, our desire to obey God is out of a heart of gratitude, not motivated by fear.

Moreover, this being the case, the covenant established through the Torah, and summarized in the Ten Words, is not a call to believe or confess that ADONAI is God, but a clear declaration of what we already know and confess to be true, that He is the One and only God and there is none other (Is 45:21–22). Thus, we bow before Him as our Savior, our King, and our Father, confessing from hearts of gratitude that what He commands, we will do.

2. *"You shall have no other gods before Me. You shall not make for yourself an idol, or any likeness of what is in heaven above or on the earth beneath or in the water under the earth. You shall not worship them or serve them; for I, ADONAI your God, am a jealous God, visiting the iniquity of the fathers on the children, on the third and the fourth generations of those who hate Me, but showing lovingkindness to thousands, to those who love Me and keep My commandments.*

This common translation, "…no other gods <u>before</u> <u>me</u>" follows the Vulgate (*coram me*) and is incorrect. The Hebrew עַל פָּנָי, *'al panaiy*, can be literally taken as "beyond Me" (as the use of עַל, *'al*, in Gen 48:22, "give you one portion <u>more</u> <u>than</u> your brothers…"), or עַל פָּנָי, *'al panaiy* can mean "in addition to Me" (as the use of עַל, *'al*, in Gen 31:50, "… if you take wives <u>besides</u> my daughters…."). Regardless of the precise nuance of the prepositional phrase, the second word absolutely prohibits any form of polytheism or the worship of idols, whether in thought, word, or deed.

The negative likewise demands the positive, which is that God and God alone deserves the fear, love, and worship of all that He has created. Thus, to fail to worship God in truth is likewise to transgress this commandment.

Further, the second Word does not in any manner suggest that other gods actually exist, even though fallen mankind has believed there are other gods and have given themselves to serve them. In reality, all other "gods" are demons (1Cor 10:19–20). As Isaiah affirms:

> Declare and set forth your case; indeed, let them consult together. Who has announced this from of old? Who has long since declared it? Is it not I, ADONAI? And there is no other God besides Me, a righteous God and a Savior; there is none except Me. Turn to Me and be saved, all the ends of the earth; for I am God, and there is no other. (Is 45:21–22)

In summary, this second Word of the Ten forbids the use of:
 a. objects as a focus of worship
 b. rituals as an attempt to control Him, or which are done with the idea that the ritual itself obligates God to some action

From a positive standpoint, this means we must:
 a. teach the truth about God's character
 b. guard against those things which inevitably lead to or are equal with idolatry
   • rebellion / insubordination, 1 Sam 15:23
   • greed, Col 3:5
 c. Commit ourselves to worship God as He has instructed us, and not by our own designs.

3. *You shall not take the name of* ADONAI *your God in vain, for* ADONAI *will not leave him unpunished who takes His name in vain.*

The Hebrew of this third Word is not easily conveyed in our English translations. The line is לֹא תִשָּׂא אֶת־שֵׁם־יְהוָה אֱלֹהֶיךָ לַשָּׁוְא, literally, "You shall not lift up the name of ADONAI your God to waste/vanity."

First, the verb נָשָׂא, *nasa'*, never means to "utter" or "speak" but always has the sense of "lift up," "take up," "raise," and so forth. Thus, *nasa'* is used to "take up (or raise) a proverb" (Num 23:7; Job 27:1) or to "lift up a song" (Ps 81:3), or a prayer (Is 37:4). Note as well Ps 24:4 which has the phrase "lift up his soul to vanity," the very language of our text.

Second, the word translated "vanity," שָׁוְה, *shav'h*, does not mean "to lie" but rather denotes that which is "worthless," "a waste," or "in disorder."

Thus, to "lift up the Name of God to that which is worthless or a waste is to evoke the Name of God in a false oath or in an attempt to make a falsehood appear as true. Likewise, evoking the Name of God in false worship is to profane the Name of God, i.e., to incorporate the Name into that which is worthless.

In Summary:
 How is this commandment broken?
  • By claiming God agrees to something that is evil (e.g., taking an oath in God's Name which you never intend to honor)
  • By attempting to control God by chanting His Name (e.g., believing that speaking the Name has some magical power)
  • By making the Name common as any other word (e.g., using God's name as "filler" in prayer or speech, or using it as a

thoughtless explicative.)
- By using the Name in a vulgar way (e.g., cursing, lewd or base speech)

How is this commandment honored?
- By using God's name in a manner which proves that I fear and love Him. (e.g., in praise of His character, in honoring His ways and thoughts)
- By taking seriously the times I call upon God as a witness.

"[this commandment] does not condemn those who fail to believe; it condemns those who believe and do nothing about it.... What is dangerous is not intellectual atheism, which is unpopular, but mild religion, which is very popular indeed.... The real enemy is not irreligion but vague religiosity." (E. Trueblood)

4. *"Remember the sabbath day, to keep it holy. Six days you shall labor and do all your work, but the seventh day is a sabbath of* ADONAI *your God; in it you shall not do any work, you or your son or your daughter, your male or your female servant or your cattle or your sojourner who stays with you. For in six days* ADONAI *made the heavens and the earth, the sea and all that is in them, and rested on the seventh day; therefore* ADONAI *blessed the sabbath day and made it holy.*

The first imperative in this fourth Word is the command to "remember" (זָכוֹר, *zāchôr*). Too often people misunderstand the Hebraic concept of "remember," taking it simply to mean to "think about" or "to recall to one's mind." But we should first consider that the text under investigation is a covenant text. When covenant texts from the Ancient Near East are studied, we find the word "remember" used in a technical sense, meaning "to act in loyalty to the covenant." Conversely, "to forget" is used in covenant contexts to denote "disloyalty to or rebellion against the covenant."

In this light, note for instance Ex 2:24: "So God heard their groaning; and God remembered His covenant with Abraham, Isaac, and Jacob." This does not mean that God had forgotten the covenant for a time and then suddenly recalled it when He heard the groaning of the Israelites! Rather, the meaning is that God acted in faithfulness to the covenant He had made with the patriarchs, the result being that He acted on behalf of His people and delivered them from the slavery of Egypt.

Let us consider, then, the use of the word "remember" as the opening command in this, the fourth Word. To "remember" the Sabbath means to guard and keep it as the sign of the covenant God has made with Israel and thus with all who join themselves to the covenant people through faith in God and His Messiah, Yeshua.

Moreover, the Shabbat is not a day given to mark Jewish identity but the day that functions as the sign of the covenant God enacted with His people at Sinai.

> So the sons of Israel shall observe the sabbath, to celebrate the sabbath throughout their generations as a perpetual covenant. It is a sign between Me and the sons of Israel forever; for in six days ADONAI made heaven and earth, but on the seventh day He ceased from labor, and was refreshed. (Ex 31:16–17)

As we know, a mixed multitude stood at Sinai to receive the covenant (Ex 12:38), so the Sinai covenant as a whole, revealed in its fulness in the Torah, was not given to establish Jewish identity either. In fact, the Sinai covenant is partner with the earlier Abrahamic covenant as the vehicle by which the promise made to Abraham would be realized: "in you all the families of the earth will be blessed" (Gen 12:3, cf. 18:18; 22:18; 26:4; 28:14). This promise, referred to as "the Gospel" by Paul (Gal 3:8), was central in David's mind when, having been given the eternal covenant of kingship he exclaimed, "and this is the Torah for mankind" (2Sam 7:19, Hebrew). David understood that it was through the covenant promise of his unending dynasty that the Torah would come to all of the families of the earth, for Yeshua is the final and ultimate King in David's royal dynasty (Acts 2:30–31), and He proclaimed that He came to establish the Torah, not to abolish it (Matt 5:17–21). This is why Yeshua stated regarding the Shabbat, the sign of the covenant, that "the Shabbat was made for mankind" (Mk 2:27). He does not say the Shabbat was made for the Jews.

Therefore, the idea that this fourth Word pertains only to Jewish people finds no basis in the Scriptures themselves. On the contrary, the Shabbat remains a sign of the covenant in which all the believing remnant are members, whether Jewish or non-Jewish. What is more, as Isaiah writes, God promises blessings upon those who honor God by keeping the Sabbath.

> For thus says ADONAI, "To the eunuchs who keep My sabbaths, And choose what pleases Me, and hold fast My covenant, to them I will give in My house and within My walls a memorial, and a name better than that of sons and daughters; I will give them an everlasting name which will not be cut off. Also the foreigners who join themselves to ADONAI, to minister to Him, and to love the name of ADONAI, to be His servants, every one who keeps from profaning the sabbath and holds fast My covenant; even those I will bring to My holy mountain and make them joy-

ful in My house of prayer. Their burnt offerings and their sacrifices will be acceptable on My altar; for My house will be called a house of prayer for all the peoples." (Is 56:4–7)

In Summary:
How is this command broken?
- by treating the Shabbat (seventh day of the week) as the same as the other six days of work, i.e., by continuing one's normal work on the Shabbat.
- by deliberately causing others to work for me on the Shabbat so that I gain monetarily by their labors.
- by failing to use the Shabbat as a time of rest in which I am afforded time to gather with other believers, worship God in the context of community, and openly honor God for all of His kindness and mercy to me in Yeshua. The Sabbath is called a *"mikra kodesh,"* a "holy gathering" in Lev 23:2-3. As disciples of Yeshua, we should follow His example of gathering with others on the Shabbat: "And He came to Nazareth, where He had been brought up; and as was His custom, He entered the synagogue on the Sabbath, and stood up to read." (Lk 4:16)
- by engaging in commercial enterprise on the Shabbat (buying and selling, cf. Jer 17:19–27; Neh 13:19–22).
- by failing to work during the other six days of the week so that I can cease my labors on the Shabbat.

How is this command honored?
- by stopping my normal daily work and using the Shabbat as a day to gather with other believers in order to:
  - share the Scriptures and pray together
  - to worship God for all of His blessings in Yeshua and the work of His Ruach HaKodesh
  - to encourage and lift up each other by bearing each other's burdens and thus fulfilling the Torah of Messiah (Gal 6:2)
- by living according to God's calendar, and thus preparing for the Shabbat so that I am able to keep it. This means preparing for and observing all of the Shabbats (both the weekly as well as the festival Shabbats).
- by refusing to be lazy and instead, regularly working six days each week to provide for my own needs and for the needs of others (my family; the poor; etc., cf. 1Tim 5:8; Eph 4:28).
- by recognizing that the primary lesson of Shabbat is to teach me about the eternal rest which I have in Messiah, and my need to rest in His finished work.

A Final Thought:

Yeshua gave us a very important lesson about Shabbat, which is recorded in Matt 12:11–12.

> And He said to them, "What man is there among you who has a sheep, and if it falls into a pit on the Sabbath, will he not take hold of it and lift it out? How much more valuable then is a man than a sheep! So then, it is lawful to do good on the Sabbath." (Matt 12:11–12)

We should remember that throughout the centuries, rabbinic Judaism has added a myriad of laws to the observance of Shabbat, laws which greatly expanded the simple, straightforward commandments given in the fourth Word. These man-made laws are not one-and-the-same with God's Torah, and should therefore not be forced upon the conscience of anyone. While some may choose to follow such rabbinic traditions, and may find value in them, they are not to be given equal authority with the Torah itself. Thus, there may be times on Shabbat where, following the teaching of Yeshua, we would engage in an activity on Shabbat which rabbinic Judaism would forbid.

Likewise, as followers of Yeshua, we should take seriously His statement that "it is lawful to do good on the Shabbat." We must use wisdom in this, but there may be times when aiding a fellow believer in his or her need, and doing so on the Shabbat, may take precedence over our normal Shabbat activities. Further, this may apply particularly to those whose occupation involves the saving of life (fire fighters, police officers, doctors, nurses, EMTs, etc.). For Yeshua, using a *qal v'chomer* (a fortiori) argument, reasons that if it is lawful to care for the life of one's animal on Shabbat, then most certainly it is lawful to care for the life of another person. For mankind, not the animals, are bearers of God's image and therefore people have even greater value than animals. Thus, for those whose work involves saving human life, doing so on the Shabbat would clearly be lawful and necessary.

5. *"Honor your father and your mother, that your days may be prolonged in the land which ADONAI your God gives you."*

The commandment contained in this fifth Word is "to honor" (כָּבֵד, *kaveid*), which has the sense of "putting one's praise or honor upon someone," to "weigh them down with praise." (The basic sense of the verb *kaveid* is "to be heavy.")

Perhaps the first question we must ask when considering how to obey this fifth Word is: "Who are my parents?" As the family unit in our society continues to break down, an increasing number of children maintain relationships with not only birth parents, but also with step-parents, foster parents, or live-in partners. How does this commandment apply in these cases?

Even in those situations which are far less than the norm as God has ordained for the family, we must foster a spirit of submission and respect. We must learn to confront what is wrong with an attitude that maintains a respect for what is right. How sorrowful it is that many children in our society grow up in an environment which is patently immoral. The sin of our society may make it nearly impossible for some children to ever honor their "parents," for all they have every seen are parents who seem to be entirely without honor.

The terms used in the 5th Word, אָב ('āv) "father" and אֵם ('eim) "mother," are broader in scope than the English words imply. "Father" in the Hebrew may refer to one's actual father, or to any male blood relative. The same word may refer to one in authority, as a king (1 Sa 24:11) or a teacher (cf. 2Ki 2:12). "Mother" may stand likewise for any female in authority (Judges 5:7). This being the case, "father and mother" in our text should be understood to refer to those who have primary authority over us as children. Thus, honoring father and mother extends to step-parents or foster parents, or to others who complete the role of a parent.

For orphans and those who have been adopted, this commandment is fulfilled by honoring those who function in a parental role. If, at some stage, it is deemed wise to initiate a relationship with birth parents who were previously unknown, such a relationship ought also to be characterized as giving honor as much as possible. The overarching principle in this fifth Word is that we honor parents and those who fulfill a parental role in our lives because they are, by God's good providence, those He has placed over us.

A second, and more difficult question, is how children are to honor parents who, in general, have lived lives of dishonor. The first thing to establish is that it is by God's hand of providence that we were born to our parents. Thus, honoring our parents is first and foremost a conscious desire to honor God.

Second, we may honor our parents even if they appear to be dishonorable, by not engaging in gossip against them. The natural tendency is to tell others of our parents' faults and to diminish them in the eyes of our friends and acquaintances. But this is *lashon hara'* (evil speech) and is something God hates (Prov 6:16–17). Honoring our parents mean keeping ourselves from speaking evil against them to others. Further, we honor parents whose lives are less than honorable by respecting the fact that God has placed them in authority over us. If they ask of us that which is contrary to God's ways, then we should first appeal to them for a different outcome, and if such is not forthcoming, then we should decline but do so in a respectful manner. Whatever the case, we should seek as much as possible to submit to their authority in all matters which do not violate the clear teaching of God's word. In doing so, we would hope to show them the ways of God and in so doing, to open their eyes and hearts to the Gospel.

A third consideration on the fifth Word is that, by logical extension, it also applies to parents. That is, we are to help others obey God, not put barriers in their way from walking as God has instructed. Thus, for parents to make it difficult for their children to honor them is contrary to the Ten Words. Paul hints at this when he writes: "Fathers, do not exasperate your children, so that they will not lose heart. " (Col 3:21). Therefore, this fifth Word of the Ten is directed toward parents as well as children. Parents must seek to live in an honorable fashion so as to make it easy for their children to obey this commandment.

In Summary:

How is this fifth Word broken?
- By failing to give your parents the honor they deserve as God's appointed source of life and authority. (i.e., if parents are viewed as God's servants, to despise the servant is to equally despise the one who sends the servant.)
- By acting as a tyrant toward your children and failing to live in a manner which fosters their respect. (To the extent that parents fail to honor God they make it equally difficult for their children to obey this commandment.)
- By giving into the natural tendencies to rebel. (i.e., a submissive spirit is an essential element in honoring those whom God has placed as authorities over us.)

How is this fifth Word honored?
- By first submitting to God, and as a result, honoring the authorities He appoints over us. (We must view our responsibility to honor parents as a means of honoring God.)
- By establishing godly integrity and compassion in our lives so as to gain the respect of our children. (As our children see us honoring those in authority over us, and living out integrity with compassion, honoring us as their parents will be a far easier duty.)

6. *"You shall not murder."*

Since the King James Version (KJV) became the authorized English translation within the Protestant Church for nearly 450 years, it is understandable why its translation has greatly affected Christian theology. And this influence is seen in the manner in which the sixth Word has been interpreted by some denominations within the wider Christian Church.

The KJV translates the sixth Word as: "Thou shalt not kill." Given this translation, one understands why some took this Word of the Ten to require a complete passivism—no taking of human life whatsoever, regardless of the situation.

But the KJV, in this instance, is a very poor translation. The Hebrew word used in the sixth Word is not the word usually translated "to kill" (הָרַג, *harag*). The word used here is רָצָה, *ratzach*, "to wrongly take a person's life." Some have taught that this particular word describes premeditated murder, but this conclusion cannot be sustained. Numbers 35, which deals with the "cities of refuge," employs the word in connection with the "man-slayer," someone who accidently kills another person (defined as "manslaughter" in our times). In this context, the killing of an individual is clearly accidental and therefore the one who committed manslaughter is given refuge in one of the designated cities. The fact that our word *ratzach* is used in this context shows that it cannot be narrowed to mean "premeditated murder." Yet the word itself is much narrower in its scope than the broader and more inclusive term *harag* ("to kill"). This narrower meaning emphasizes the unwarranted taking of a person's life. Thus, the death penalty, clearly prescribed in Gen 9:6, is not controverted by the sixth Word, nor does the taking of life in self-defense run counter to its meaning.

As in all of the Ten Words, even those which are cast in a "you shall not" form, there is both a positive and negative aspect to each, and the same is true for the sixth Word. Thus, helping to prevent murder is likewise enjoined upon us by this commandment. This means that to stand by idly and do nothing when we see someone's life in danger is to disregard and break the sixth Word. This obviously applies to murder by abortion and all other situations in which defenseless children are at risk of losing their lives. In obedience to this Word, we must do all in our power to preserve life and rescue those who are in danger of being murdered.

Finally, we guard ourselves against breaking this commandment by keeping our hearts from bitterness and anger which leads to hatred. Yeshua taught us that hating one's neighbor is like murder (Matt 5:21–22), for hatred may in fact lead to murder, even as Cain became angry against his brother Abel and sought to kill him (Gen 4:5–8).

In Summary:

How is the sixth Word broken?
- By taking a person's life unjustly (murder is an attribute of Satan [Jn 8:44] and characteristic of fallen mankind's disposition [Cain murdered Abel]).
- By taking one's own life (Suicide is as much or more a disregard for the value of God's image than is homicide.)
- By failing to carefully protect life (if failing to protect the unborn child is wrong, how much more the brutal taking of his or her life! Cf. Ex 21:22ff)
- By allowing the sin of hatred in our lives. (Hatred is displayed by slander, gossip, character defamation, or abuse, and often is the first step in the course of murder.)

How can the sixth Word be honored?
- By growing in our ability to love others
- By doing all in our power to protect life
- By loving and promoting justice

7. *"You shall not commit adultery."*

Once again, we must define our terms, and so the first question to be answered is "What is the biblical definition of adultery?"

Two words in the Tanach generally represent the idea of "immorality." One is זָנָה, *zanah*, usually translated "to commit fornication" or "to be a harlot." The Greek word which usually translates Hebrew *zanah* is πορνεία, *porneia*, from which we derive the English word "pornography." The second word is the one in our text, נָאַף, *na'af*, usually translated "to commit adultery." The Greek word which usually translates this Hebrew term is μοιχεία, *moicheia*.

Zanah/porneia is the broader term, encompassing all illicit sexual activity. *Na'af /moicheia* is a subset of *zanah/porneia*, narrowing the definition to the meaning "marital infidelity." The Biblical text, however, does not necessarily keep such a fine distinction. *Zanah* and *na'af* are often used together to describe sexual sin in general, and when they are so used, they form a literary unit, shading their individual distinctions. They are likewise used metaphorically of spiritual infidelity, especially in the prophets' judgment of the nation of Israel (Cf. Is 57:3; Jer 3:1-3; 13:27; Hos 2:2).

While a case can be made that *na'af* in the Ten Words refers specifically to marital infidelity, many scholars have seen in the word a broader prohibition of all illicit sexual activity.

Walking in the truth of the seventh Word means both to abstain from sexual sin as well as to guard oneself from that which would lead to such transgressions. This means that we must guard our eyes, ears, and thoughts so as not to be inundated with the immorality of our era and culture. This also means that we must fill our heart or minds with that which is righteous, and particularly with the word of God, so that we will be strong to withstand the *zeitgeist* (spirit of the time).

For those who are married, we honor this seventh Word by carefully and continually strengthening our love and care for our spouse. This means practicing the biblical doctrine of forgiving and not allowing disagreements and offenses to become deeply rooted within our marriage. For single adults, honoring this Word means guarding one's heart in all relationships with the opposite sex and not allowing emotions or fleshly desires to override what we know is God's will.

Finally, Yeshua makes it clear that divorcing one's spouse may cause them to commit adultery by marrying another person. The only exception to this is when the divorce results from one of the spouses committing fornication or when an unbelieving spouse abandons a believing spouse. Thus, divorce may often lead to breaking this seventh Word.

In Summary:

How is the seventh Word broken?
- By engaging in sexual relations with someone other than your spouse. (Such a sin begins inwardly as a sin of the mind and heart.)
- By causing someone else to commit adultery (Divorce may have this consequence, cf. Matt 5:32.)
- By allowing immorality to become an accepted thing in home and society. (Note Yeshua's warning against lust, Matt 5:27-28)

How is the seventh Word honored?
- By agreeing with God that marriage is honorable (of high importance in God's community are wedding ceremonies, celebration of wedding anniversaries, and vibrant marriages)
- By actively guarding against the flood of immorality which flows in our society (pornography, sexually explicit lyrics, sexually oriented media, immodest fashions, homosexuality, etc. must be opposed by God's people)
- By engaging in godly discipline of mind and heart (We inevitably become like that at which we most often gaze.)

8. *"You shall not steal."*

The eighth Word is predicated upon a general Torah axiom, which is that private ownership of real and tangible property is a God-given right. As far as the individual is concerned, he or she must treat all possessions as still belonging to God, and given to the individual for their use, but since God has given all things, it becomes the responsibility of the one to whom He has given, to be a faithful guardian and steward of the property. Moreover, that which is owned is to be used for the glory of God, and the owner is responsible to make this a reality.

Indeed, all civilized societies are based upon this foundational principle, that individuals within the society have the right to exclusive ownership of private property. Any individual or collective, including a government, which seeks to uproot this basic right, is in violation of the eighth Word.

Moreover, theft is wrong because of the fact that God owns everything.

> The earth is ADONAI's, and all it contains, the world, and those who dwell in it. (Ps 24:1)

> The heavens are Yours, the earth also is Yours; the world and all it contains, You have founded them. (Ps 89:11)

Therefore, to take something that He has not given is, as it were, to steal from Him. In the same manner, to acquire property of any sort in an illegal fashion is theft. Thus, to purchase something that one knows is stolen is in violation of the eighth Word. Likewise, failing or refusing to attempt to find the owner of lost property and instead, taking it unto oneself, is theft and violates this Word.

In a positive vein, then, to uphold this eighth Word requires that we seek to find the rightful owner of any item we may find or happen upon. Further, we should make every effort to make certain that items we buy are being sold by their rightful owner. And we should do all in our power to prevent theft. If we see a theft in progress, we should alert the proper authorities in hopes of apprehending the thief.

A guard against breaking this commandment contained in the eighth Word is to guard our hearts against covetousness. Covetousness, the inappropriate desire for property of whatever sort, can lead to theft. And the antidote against covetousness is learning to be content and thankful for what God has provided. In this regard, note Prov 30:8–9,

> Keep deception and lies far from me, give me neither poverty nor riches; feed me with the food that is my portion, that I not be full and deny You

and say, "Who is ADONAI?" Or that I not be in want and steal, and profane the name of my God. (Prov 30:8–9)

To this we may also highlight the exhortation of Paul:

He who steals must steal no longer; but rather he must labor, performing with his own hands what is good, so that he will have something to share with one who has need. (Eph 4:28)

We may derive from Paul's words that stealing is a double crime, for it not only transgresses the eighth Word specifically, but also negates the entire second half of the Ten Words which are summed up in "love your neighbor as yourself."

Finally, theft may also occur in a non-physical realm. For instance, to withhold honor from someone to whom honor is due is to rob them of what is rightfully theirs. Likewise, to withdraw our support for someone we have promised to support is also a type of theft.

In Summary:

How is the eighth Word broken?
- By claiming ownership of something which rightfully belongs to someone else. (The value of the object is of no matter. When something is found, it still has a rightful owner, and this command is broken when no attempt is made to find the owner.)
- By failing to give to someone what they rightfully deserve. (Stealing may apply to the non-physical realm as well as the physical. We may rob others of honor, support, sustenance, etc.)
- By failing to protect what rightfully belongs to my neighbor (Failing to warn one's neighbor of possible theft, or refusing to help identify a thief, or neglecting to do all in one's power to prevent theft—any of these may be classed as theft and break the eighth Word.)

How is the eighth Word honored?
- By carefully guarding the ownership rights of each other. (Doing all in our power to help guard our neighbor from being robbed and doing all we can to return found items to their rightful owner.)
- By learning to be content with what God has given us (stealing begins with a spirit of discontentment, that is, not being satisfied with the portions God has allotted to us.)

9. *"You shall not bear false witness against your neighbor."*

The Hebrew that lies behind this English translation is: לֹא־תַעֲנֶה בְרֵעֲךָ עֵד שָׁקֶר, literally "You shall not answer against your neighbor a lying testimony." The meaning is obvious: when called upon to be a witness of an event, one is prohibited by the ninth Word to construct a lie and present it as what is true. Leviticus 19:11 may have the same situation in mind: "You shall not steal, nor deal falsely, nor lie to one another."

It is interesting that the term "neighbor" (רֵעַ, *rei-a'*) is used here rather than "brother" (אָח, *'ach*). If "brother" had been used, then this commandment would have possibly been narrowed to one's clan or family. Indeed, there are instances where "brother" and "neighbor" are clearly delineated in respect to various laws (cf. Deut 15:2, 3). But the use of the word *rei-a'* suggests that this commandment was intended to encompass one's relationship with any person, regardless of whether or not that person was a part of one's family or clan. "Neighbor," then, could be understood as "fellowman"—as anyone who, created in God's image, bears the marks of his or her Creator. Thus, to "love one's neighbor as oneself" is to treat all human beings with the respect that their image-bearing deserves. To demean another person on the grounds that he or she is not part of a certain clan or race is thus to fly in the face of God Who has given us this Word to obey.

While this Word seems to primarily to envision the situation where a person has been summoned to give witness before judges, it also encompasses giving a false witness in general. Thus, it prohibits gossip or *lashon hara'* in which a person's reputation is damaged by spreading lies or unfounded accusations.

In the same vein, we can fail to uphold this commandment by remaining silent when we hear a falsehood being spread, or a false witness being given. If we have the ability to correct a false report or witness, we are obligated to do so. Once again, this comes under the broad heading of loving one's neighbor as oneself (Lev 19:18).

In Summary:

How is the ninth Word broken?
- By lying or failing to tell the truth in a court of law. (A society unable to uphold justice is doomed to failure.)
- By damaging another person's reputation through unconfirmed reports and evil gossip. (We should engage in conversations about the failings of others only when we are sure the information is true and we are actively involved in helping

bring a godly solution to the problem).
- By remaining silent when we know a falsehood is being spread. (Failing to correct a false witness when we are able to do so is equal to giving a false witness.)

How is the ninth Word honored?
- By a firm commitment to speak the truth. (This involves both expressing what we know to be true, and shunning false pretenses.)
- By actively guarding the reputation of others. (The damage done by false accusations is often irreparable.)

10. *"You shall not covet your neighbor's house; you shall not covet your neighbor's wife or his male servant or his female servant or his ox or his donkey or anything that belongs to your neighbor."*

What is the definition of the word "covet"? The Hebrew verb for "covet" is חָמַד, *chamad*, and has a basic meaning of "desire," or "take pleasure in." It is used in a good sense, as in the desirability of the Torah being more than fine gold (Ps 19:11; cp. Is 53:3; Ps 39:12). It is, however, often used of an evil desire, of an inordinate and ungoverned, selfish desire. The word is also found in connection with idolatry (cf. Is 1:29; 44:9; Prov 1:22) in the sense of people delighting to worship false gods.

The Greek word underlying the concept of "covet" is ἐπιθυμέω, *epithumeō*, which follows the same basic pattern of the Hebrew term, meaning "to desire, long for, lust after, covet"

Coveting, then, begins with the desire of the heart but comes to fruition when this desire remains unchecked. Such undisciplined desire inevitably leads to an evil longing for things or position without a humble submission to the will of God in one's life. In a very real way, the sin of coveting is at the root of all other sin.

In this light, we may now see the overall structure of the Ten Words in this way:

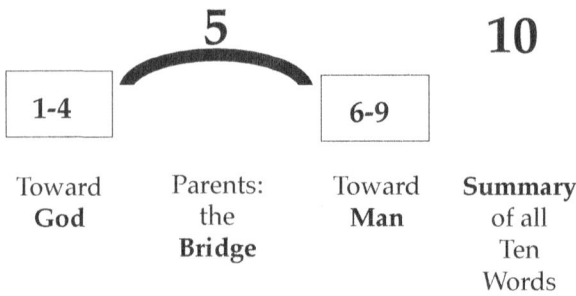

How is the tenth Word broken?
- By allowing uncontrolled desires for things, position, or pleasure to dwell in our hearts. (There is nothing wrong in seeking the best. This commandment is broken when desire controls rather than being controlled. We must strive to desire God's will, and only when this is a reality will we find lasting satisfaction in life.)
- By failing to be satisfied with God's provision. (Are those things which please God my greatest desire and joy?)

How is this commandment honored?
- By fostering genuine thankfulness. (The antidote to covetousness is contentment. And, being truly thankful is the path to contentment.)
- By learning the spiritual discipline of controlling one's thoughts and intentions.

Contentment is wanting what you already have!" The primary issue may be in honestly assessing the value of what you already have!

> "Woe to those who scheme iniquity, who work out evil on their beds! When morning comes, they do it. For it is in the power of their hands. They covet fields and then seize them, and houses, and take them away. They rob a man and his house, a man and his inheritance." Mic 2:1,2

> "But each one is tempted when he is carried away and enticed by his own lust (ἐπιθυμία, the same root word used for "covetousness"). Then when lust has conceived, it gives birth to sin; and when sin is accomplished, it brings forth death." James 1:14-15

> "Watch over your heart with all diligence, for from it flow the springs of life." Prov 4:23

> "For the word of God is living and active and sharper than any two-edged sword, and piercing as far as the division of soul and spirit, of both joints and marrow, and able to judge the thoughts and intentions of the heart." Heb 4:12

The Ten Words & the New Covenant

> Behold, days are coming, declares Adonai, when I will make a new covenant with the house of Israel and with the house of Judah, not like the covenant which I made with their fathers in the day I took them by the hand to bring them out of the land of Egypt, My covenant which they broke, although I was a husband to them, declares Adonai.
> But this is the covenant which I will make with the house of Israel after those days, declares Adonai, I will put My torah within them, and on their heart I will write it; and I will be their God, and they shall be My people. And they shall not teach again, each man his neighbor and each man his brother, saying, 'Know Adonai,' for they shall all know Me, from the least of them to the greatest of them, declares Adonai, for I will forgive their iniquity, and their sin I will remember no more.
> Jeremiah 31:31-34

The characteristic of those who are part of the New Covenant is that they keep the Torah, for it has been written on their hearts.

1	**I am Adonai your God, who brought you out of the land of Egypt, out of the house of slavery.**
2	**You shall have no other gods before Me** **You shall not make for yourself an idol . . .**
3	**You shall not take the name of Adonai your God in vain . . .**
4	**Remember the Sabbath day, to keep it holy. . .**
5	**Honor your father and your mother . . .**
6	**You shall not murder.**
7	**You shall not commit adultery.**
8	**You shall not steal.**
9	**You shall not bear false witness against your neighbor.**
10	**You shall not covet . . .**

Parashah Eighteen
מִשְׁפָּטִים – Mishpatim
"ordinances"
Exodus 21:1–24:18

In the Triennial Cycle
there are Three Parashot

21:1–22:24 | 22:25-23:33 | 24:1-18

Parashah 60
Triennial Cycle

Exodus 21:1–22:24

Haftarah: Jeremiah 34:1–14 | Apostolic: 1Corinthians 6:9–11

Relationships

The cycle of life we so highly prize within the Torah community causes us often to reflect on the past, and to consider the future. As parents, we dedicate ourselves to the important task of preparing our children for adulthood, and particularly that, by God's grace, they would carry the life-message of God's greatness into their generation. The presence of the Yartzeit Board in our synagogue is a constant reminder that one generation gives way to the next. I have often remarked that one day my name will be on that board, and it will be left to my sons, daughters and grandchildren to pray the *kaddish* as they remember me. Then it will be the responsibility of their generation to be leaders in the community and to hand the message, both in word and deed, to their generation and the next.

This highlights the supreme importance of community and the relationships that are the building blocks of community. It is only when we apply the biblical standards of righteousness that relationships will flourish as God intends, and we will be able to disciple the next generation to carry on the important task of sanctifying His Name in our world.

Unfortunately, in our modern society, personal feelings reign supreme in matters relating to relationships, and this phenomenon surely has its affect upon us as well. As a result, God's standards for relationships are viewed as archaic and unworkable in our modern times. When God's instructions conflict with our feelings, we find ways to "reinterpret" what God has said so that we can follow our feelings and believe we're obeying God. In this way, relationships based upon personal feelings have replaced objective, biblical standards and "feelings" have eclipsed the bedrock of obedience. "What *should* I do" has been replaced by "what does my *heart tell me* to do." Little wonder the ears of many have grown deaf to the Torah, because the hearts of many no longer feel the need to listen to that unchangeable standard that regulates the lives of all people in all eras. Why should they? They have come to "understand" and even been encouraged from the pulpit to believe that one's own thoughts and feelings are in many ways paramount to knowing what is right "for me." "How can one eternal, standard fit the infinite variety of psychological profiles found in humankind"? And so, unwittingly, Freud has led the Christian community into a most subtle relativism, not based upon the pluralism of philosophies (something the apologist can critique), but upon the uncharted waters of individualism. Each person, so we are told, must find his or her way to the truth, sifting life's messages through the psyche of one's own self-realization. This, by-and-large, has become the church's answer to the so-called dilemma of "finding one's self," a condition applied to teenagers in the 60's and 70's, but now applicable for many adults who, during "mid-life crises" are still in the business of "finding themselves."

In the midst of such humanistic thinking, it would be easy to "throw the baby out with the bath water," to neglect talking about "relationships" because the term has lost its value in an era where its use is so encumbered by humanistic psychology. But to neglect the pivotal importance of relationships would be just as grave an error as to impose the humanistic psychology of the day upon the scriptural teaching about relationships. Let us never forget, *the relationships which God created among humankind reflect the relationship He longs to have with His people.* And this is so because *the relationships which He created among humankind can reflect the relationship between the Father, the Son, and the Spirit.* In other words, God's will is that human relationships should reflect the relationships extant with the Godhead, for mankind was created in the image of God. Therefore, to the extent that our relationships with one another reflect the relationship enjoyed between Father, Son, and Spirit, to this extent we make known the image of God in us.

This is one reason why God spends so much time telling us how our relationships ought to be, and how they are to be regulated. In our Torah section, we have a great many laws which either regulate relationships or prescribe payment or restitution for restoring relationships. Furthermore, in some instances our *parashah* notes relationships which are prohibited. "Do not let a sorcerer live" pretty much makes a relationship with such a person an impossibility!

Our *parashah* begins with the words "these are the ordinances" (וְאֵלֶּה הַמִּשְׁפָּטִים, *v'eileh hamishpatim*). *Mishpat,* translated "ordinance," literally means "judgment." In other words, these are God's assessments—His judgments in terms of how relationships within the Torah community are to be lived out. We are faced, therefore, with a clear and simple decision: will we accept God's assessments regarding proper relationships, or will we set them aside for our own? Will we trust His way or lean upon our own understanding?

The opening paragraph deals with how a slave or servant was to be treated in terms of the economics of his or her service to the master. The way the English reads, it might appear cruel and uncaring, but we need to read more carefully. The situation is this: if a male servant or slave enters his time of service already having a wife, then at the shᵉmittah or sabbatical year both he and his wife and their children are free to go without having to pay any redemption price for any member of the family. If, however, a male servant or slave enters his service alone, and is given a wife during the six years he serves his master, then at the sabbatical year, he does not have to pay a redemption price for his freedom, but some reimbursement for his wife and children (if they have had children) must be made to his master. The English reads: "…he shall go out alone" (21:4). However, the issue being dealt with here is one of economics, as the wider context makes clear (e.g., damages and restitution). Often in the ancient world, a person became a slave or servant in order to repay a debt for which he or she did not have the ability to pay. In Israel, however, six years was the maximum for such an arrangement—the sabbatical year marked the release of all slaves.

When our text states "he shall go out alone," the Hebrew translated "alone" is בְּגַפּוֹ (vᵉgapô), which is the preposition ב (b) followed by גַף (gaf), with the third masculine singular possessive suffix וֹ (ô). The question is the meaning of גַף (gaf), a word used only here. Most commentators take this word to be from גּוּף (guf), "body," and thus meaning "in [or with] his own body," that is, he is free to go as he came. But again, in the context, the issue is monetary. Since a slave did not earn wages, when the time of release came, he legally could only take with him what he had initially brought. So we should understand the phrase "he shall go out alone" to mean "he does not have to pay a redemption price for himself." This meaning is confirmed by the parallel of the next verse (21:5), in which the word חָפְשִׁי, chofshi, "free" is used: "I will not go out free."

It seems obvious that if he had the means, he could pay the redemption price for his wife (money he acquired during his time of servitude) and children. Such a scenario is not entirely out of the question: other family members or friends could have come to his aid in supplying the necessary redemption price for his newly acquired family.

But even if he did not have the means to redeem his wife and children, he had the option to remain with them as an indentured slave. It appears as though the owner was not given the option of refusing such a request. He would take the man "to God" (אֶל־הָאֱלֹהִים), meaning "to the place where God's judgment was made known," i.e., the recognized court (note that אֱלֹהִים, *Elohim,* is also used of judges in 22:8, 9) in order to establish that the slave or servant, who had the legal right to go free, had given up this right in order to remain with his wife and children.

A major question now arises in such a scenario: is the man to be counted as a purchased slave or as a freeman? Has he given up his freedom so that he remains in the status of a slave, or is his master obligated to compensate him for his work? A crux in answering this question is the word עֹלָם, *'olam* in 21:6, "…he shall serve him permanently (עֹלָם, *'olam*). If this means "for the rest of his life," then how are the laws of the *sh^emittah* and *yovel* (the Sabbatical and Jubilee years) to be observed? For our text begins by noting that the slave in question is a Hebrew, and Lev 25:40–41 makes it clear that all Hebrew slaves were to return to their families at the Jubilee.

This being the case, the Sages understood our text to mean that the slave who puts his ear to the doorpost remains a slave to his master only until the Jubilee (cf. Ramban on Ex 21:6; Ibn Ezra on Lev 25:40–41; *Mechilta* on Ex 21:6). At that time, he and his family go free. Thus, the slave who remains with his master in order to remain with his family is working for the release of his wife and children. His labor is compensated by purchasing the redemption of his family at the Jubilee.

The matter of a Hebrew daughter sold as a maidservant (אָמָה, *'āmāh*) is different than that of a male slave (21:7–11). She does not obtain release at the *sh^emittah* year since she was obtained with a view to marriage. If, after obtaining the young lady, the owner is not pleased with her in terms of being suitable as his wife, she is given the right of redemption. He has no right to sell her as a slave to someone else. If the man who initially acquired her has a son who desires to take her as his wife, then she is to be treated as a free woman (not a slave), meaning that she has the right to refuse the offer, and to obtain a dowry if she does agree to the marriage.

But 21:10 seems to talk of polygamy. It appears to describe the scenario in which the man who initially obtained the young woman as a slave took her as his wife and then later is displeased with her. As a result, he marries another woman. Then 21:10 indicates that, in regard to the slave woman whom he initially married, he must maintain "her food, her clothing, and her conjugal rights." So on a surface reading, it appears that the man is required by the Torah to maintain both women as wives.

We should first step back and consider the wider teaching of Scripture. Paul teaches us clearly that the relationship between husband and wife is a divinely painted picture of Yeshua's relationship with the His *kehilah* or "congregation" (*ekklesia*, Eph 5:25ff). In the same manner as Yeshua loves His *kehilah* as His bride, so every husband is to love his wife. This type of love has, at its heart, a quality of uniqueness. To give to others what should be reserved only for a spouse is the quickest way to damage this most important relationship. Yeshua has one bride, one people, one wife. The picture of polygamy just does not work to describe what the Bible clearly teaches about Yeshua and His *kehilah*.

What is more, the Scriptures are replete with the teaching of monogamy, from the earliest description of marriage (Gen 2:24) through the wisdom literature ("the heart of her husband trusts in her," Prov 31:11) and even in the words of Yeshua (Mt 19:4ff) and the Apostles (Eph 5:33). All of these pictures and admonitions fall if polygamy is actually God's plan for marriage. But what then of our portion that appears to assume the rightful existence of polygamy?

The pivotal turning point in this passage is something hidden to all but those reading the Hebrew text. For in order to accommodate the long-standing position on polygamy by the Rabbinical authorities, the Hebrew text, while not changed, has nonetheless been interpreted to condone polygamy, and all English translations have followed without exception. This pivotal point is in 21:8, where the text has the word לֹא (*lō'*), "no" or "not," but which the Masoretes wrote in the margin should be read a לוֹ (*lô*), "for himself." Since the two words are pronounced exactly the same, it was an ingenious way to make the text say what it actually does not. Taking 21:8 as written it would read like this: "If she is displeasing in the eyes of her master who did not designate her (אִם־רָעָה בְּעֵינֵי אֲדֹנֶיהָ אֲשֶׁר־לֹא יְעָדָהּ), then he shall let her be redeemed. He does not have authority to sell her to a foreign people because he has dealt unfairly with her." Now this entirely changes the meaning from what the English translations have. What the text now says is that the man who bought her, originally intending to marry her, but did not, in the end, take her as his wife—then he may designate her as wife for a son (if she is so willing), or else allow her to be redeemed, but he may not sell her to foreigners because he has failed to meet the expectations given when he first indicated to her that he desired to marry her.

But there is one more translation blunder which must be corrected, for 21:10 seems still to have polygamy in mind: "If he takes to himself another woman, he may not reduce her food, her clothing, or her conjugal rights." What this seems to imply is that if he decides not to marry her after all, does not designate her as wife for a son, and she is not redeemed by anyone, and he marries another woman, he still must treat her as a wife, for he must maintain conjugal relations with her. The Hebrew word translated by all the English versions as "conjugal rights" or equivalent is עֹנָתָהּ (*'ānātāh*), a word found only here in all of the Tanach. As a result, the meaning of the word is uncertain, and the translators have given it the sense of "conjugal rights" based upon the context as they interpret it.

But documents from other ancient Near Eastern cultures (such as those found in the Akkadian language) have similar laws, with this wording: "food, clothing, and oil" or "food, clothing, and shelter." The Hebrew word עֹנָה (*'onāh*) could easily be cognate to the Akkadian terms used for "oil" or "shelter." Thus, the meaning of the text would simply be that if, after purchasing the woman for a bride, then deciding not to marry her but marrying another, the man must maintain her welfare—he cannot simply turn her out to a life of poverty. Moreover, if he fails to deal with her properly, she is to be set free without the need to pay any redemption price.

With this understanding of the text, based squarely upon the words themselves, rather than supporting polygamy it sustains the virtue of monogamy, and furthermore shows the requirement to take the marriage relationship seriously. As husbands, the treatment of our wives is to be accepted as a sacred privilege given by God Himself. We are to care for her, respect her, and in every way edify her as a picture of how Yeshua Himself cares for, respects, and builds up His bride, the *kehilah*. Our love for her cannot be shared or divided, but must be singular, faithful, and enduring. This is one of the highest *mitzvot* we can fulfill, as this picture is the only one in the universe endowed with such clear brush strokes of Yeshua's love for His bride.

Another passage within this *parashah* which deserves our special attention is 21:22-25, perhaps the most clear Torah teaching on the issue of abortion. Once again, we must look carefully at the text if we expect to navigate through the murky waters of the English translations.

The core terms in this passage are in v. 22, translated by the NASB as "so that she has a miscarriage." This is a translation of וְיָצְאוּ יְלָדֶיהָ, which literally means "and her child comes forth." "Miscarriage" means "to give birth prematurely to a fetus, so that it does not live." But there is a perfectly good word for this in the Hebrew, שָׁכֹל, *shākāl* (cf. 2 Ki 2:19; Mal 3:11; Gen 31:38; Jb 21:10; 2 Ki 2:21). What our text indicates is not that the child is stillborn, but simply that the trauma causes the child to be birthed prematurely. The issue of injury to the woman and to the baby are taken up separately in the following context. If the woman is injured but the baby is fine, then the restitution is determined by the woman's husband. If, however, there is further injury (v. 23) which, in the context, must be interpreted as injury to the baby (since injury to the woman has been dealt with in v. 22), then the child is treated as fully viable and penalty is meted out accordingly, life for life, etc.

Why is this passage put here, in these particular laws? I think the reason is clear, for these laws generally are dealing with manslaughter and negligent homicide. The laws which immediately follow describe death by a bull which, known to be dangerous, is nonetheless not sufficiently restrained by its owner. This describes a situation of negligent homicide. In the same way, men who fight in the presence of a pregnant woman *have neglected to take into consideration the high value of the child she carries.* As such, injury to her child falls within the context of negligence, and if the child is killed as a result, then there is a clear case of negligent homicide.

What lessons we can learn from this passage? Rather than supporting abortion (as some would have us think), this text accredits to the baby in the womb the status of a living soul. But this text, rightly understood, also gives us a glimpse into the heart of God and His view of life. Indeed, He sanctifies life—He sets it apart as valuable in all respects. It must therefore be cared for, nurtured, and protected. Not only must the life of a child within the womb of his or her mother be guarded, but the mother also must be cared for with special attention, for she is the very instrument of God to bring into His creation yet another soul, a soul created in His image, and breathing the breath of life from His very nostrils.

Abortion, then, is nothing less than spitting in the face of God. It is a hideous idolatry where mankind has put his own selfish interests and pleasures ahead of the clear commands of God. Living by feelings and not by Torah has opened the way for even "religious" people to find an excuse for snuffing out the life of the unborn. The scourge of "partial-birth abortions" should horrify us all, and launch us into action against it in every legal and God honoring way. If the life of the unborn is of no value, then surely our understanding of God has changed, and we have created Him in our image. No wonder the words of Scripture seem to have such little power in our society, for we have found effective ways to make them subservient to the whims of psychology. The pleasures of life have eclipsed the Giver of life, and we have cast His words behind us (Ps 50:17).

Let us resolve, then, by His grace and power, to walk in His ways and to sanctify His Name through righteous, biblical relationships. Let us resolve once again to make our marriages a living testimony of God's love for His own, of Yeshua's relationship with His bride. Let us covenant once again before HaShem to love life as He loves it, to guard and protect it as a supreme gift from His hand, and not to waste it or devalue it, but to agree with Him that life is sacred. Let us, in our relationships, be the canvas upon which He may paint the glory of His own person and the majesty of His salvation.

We may conclude with just a few remarks on the *haftarah* and Apostolic portions which accompany this *parashah*.

It is clear why the ancient authorities chose the Jer 34:1–14 as the *haftarah* for this triennial portion. At the end of the *haftarah* reading, the freeing of Hebrew slaves/servants in the *Sh{e}mittah* year is mentioned:

> At the end of seven years each of you shall set free his Hebrew brother who has been sold to you and has served you six years, you shall send him out free from you; but your forefathers did not obey Me or incline their ear to Me. (Jer 34:14)

Quite often, the selection of the *haftarah* was done merely on the inclusion of a similar theme or similar verbiage since the *haftarah* function simply as a reminder or mnemonic device for the Torah portion.

We have chosen 1Cor 6:9–11 to accompany this triennial portion, for in this portion of Paul's epistle, he speaks of the unrighteous who will not inherit the kingdom of God, and he includes some categories that are enumerated in the Torah portion.

> Do not be deceived; neither fornicators, nor idolaters, nor adulterers, nor effeminate, nor homosexuals, nor thieves, nor the covetous, nor drunkards, nor revilers, nor swindlers, will inherit the kingdom of God. (1Cor 6:9–10)

Note that Paul is writing of those whose lives are characterized by these sins, for he goes on to write:

> Such were some of you; but you were washed, but you were sanctified, but you were justified in the name of the Lord Yeshua Messiah and in the Ruach of our God. (1Cor 6:11)

Here is the glorious reality of the Gospel, which is the power of God resulting in salvation to Jew and Gentile (Rom 1:16)! Lives dominated by sin, and by all manner of destructive behaviors, can be redeemed and transformed by the saving power of the Almighty. Note carefully that Paul writes "Such *were* some of you...." The old has been taken away and in its place a life of righteousness has been planted. This is the work of the Almighty, giving a new heart and drawing His chosen ones to Himself, to become like His Son, Yeshua.

> *For by grace you have been saved through faith; and that not of yourselves, it is the gift of God; not as a result of works, so that no one may boast. For we are His workmanship, created in Messiah Yeshua for good works, which God prepared beforehand so that we would walk in them.*
> Eph 2:8–10

Parashah 61
Triennial Cycle

Exodus 22:25–23:33

HAFTARAH: ISAIAH 49:1–6 | APOSTOLIC: JAMES 1:26–2:4

These are the Ordinances (con't.)

Our last *parashah* began with the notice that "these are ordinances" given by God to Moses, which he in turn was to give to the people of Israel. Whereas the Ten Words were given as a convenient summary or index of the ordinances, in these *parashot* we see the beginnings of their explanations and applications.

The purpose of the ordinances given by God in the Torah are essentially twofold. First, they were given in order to set God's people apart from those who trust in false gods (Deut 4:5–7). As the ways of God are lived out by His people, they are set apart unto Him, and from the paganism of the nations. Secondly, the ordinances of God are given to His people in order to establish a firm and wise foundation for interpersonal relationships. Lasting relationships at all levels, whether within the primary unit of the family, or in the extended community family, are maintained and enhanced when one is careful to obey the principles given to us by our Master and Creator.

The first ordinance mentioned in our *parashah* relates to lending money to a fellow covenant member, designated as עַמִּי, *'ami*, "My people." One is not to charge interest when loaning money to someone in need. The word for "interest" is נֶשֶׁךְ, *neshech*, which literally means "to bite." The Mishnah refers this to advance interest that is initially "bitten off" or deducted from the amount of the loan (cf. b.*Bava Metzia* 60b). It may also refer to accrued or compounded interest. This prohibition is very practical: if a poor person is in need of a loan, to charge interest only makes his burden heavier, and increases the possibility that he would not be able to repay the loan, putting him in even further poverty. Thus, loaning money without interest flows from a love for one's neighbor (Lev 19:18). In Deut 23:20–21 it is specifically permitted to charge interest (תַשִּׁיךְ, *tashich*) to a *nochri* (נָכְרִי), that is, to a foreigner who is passing through (as distinguished from a גֵּר, *ger*, a foreigner who has taken up residence within Israel). This most likely denotes a foreign merchant who seeks a loan to further his business. Since he may leave and thus present a situation where the loan could not be recovered, charging interest allows the lender to recover his original loan amount more quickly. Moreover, since an Israelite who might be doing business in a foreign country, and who seeks a loan from a foreigner would surely be charged interest, this allowance is based upon the principle of reciprocity.

The principles related to taking a neighbor's cloak, coming as it does within the context of loaning money, should be understood as taking a cloak as a pledge or collateral for a loan (cf. Amos 2:8; Prov 20:16; 27:13; Job 22:6). The cloak (כְּסוּתָה, *kesutah*) was a large piece of cloth used not only as a garment, but also as one's blanket for sleeping. In this case, the poor person has given what might be his only valuable possession, and something he needed for maintaining daily life. The pledge or collateral is given as a symbolic intention to repay the loan. But since the dignity and freedom of the poor is not to be violated, the cloak must be returned before the day is over (sunset). The Almighty Himself has a special care for the poor, and thus He will carefully look after their needs (cf. Deut 24:12–13). God's own compassion for the poor is to be the pattern followed by the creditor. It is from this principle that even in our own modern jurisprudence, the necessities of life cannot be extracted from a debtor, even in the worst case scenario, i.e., bankruptcy.

This idea that God's own compassion is to set the standard for one's actions, as well as the willingness to submit to judges in civil matters, flows easily into the next section of our *parashah,* namely, one's duties toward God (22:28–31, Hebrew 22:27–30). V. 28–"You shall not curse God, nor curse a ruler of your people." Here the Sages understand אֱלֹהִים, *Elohim* as referring to judges who speak on God's behalf (cf. Ex 21:6; 22:8–9), since the parallel line has "nor curse a ruler of your people." Paul quotes this verse after realizing that he had spoken against the High Priest (Acts 23:5). Apparently he was unaware that the High Priest was presiding over the council at his trial. Was his eyesight poor enough that he could not see all who were in attendance? Regardless, realizing his error, he submits to the "ruler" on the basis of our Torah text, which teaches that insubordination against God-appointed rulers is equivalent to insubordination against God Himself.

Honoring God and His appointed leaders is now linked to the giving of the first fruits of the crops, herds, and even the first born of one's children (who were redeemed, e.g., Ex 34:20). Our verse indicates that the first fruits are the choicest portion of the crop. The wording is somewhat ambiguous, but Sarna (*JPS Torah Commentary*) translates "your crop, in full bloom, namely, the best part of it." God, speaking in the first-person, instructs that one is to give the first fruits "to Me." This was understood to mean that first fruits were given to the priesthood who served "before the Lord." In the replacement theology of the emerging Christian Church (2nd Century CE), the "bishops" became the "priests," and it therefore became the requirement to bring first fruits and tithes to the bishops, of whom the archbishop was designated as the "High Priest" (cf. *Apostolic Traditions* 31). But our *parashah* specifically commands that first fruits be "brought into the House of Adonai your God" (23:19), meaning that they were to be given to the priests who served in the Tabernacle and eventually in the Temple.

The subject of giving the first fruits, that is, the best of one's produce and flocks to the Lord, connects with the prohibition of eating the meat of animals killed by predators (i.e., "torn," טְרֵפָה, *t'reifah*). To do so rendered the person unclean (Lev 17:15). We should note carefully that eating in accordance with God's ordinances is considered an aspect of being "holy people to Me" (22:31). From God's perspective, the whole matter of *kashrut* is one of sanctification unto Him, first and foremost. While there may be clear health benefits in eating a kosher diet, the primary purpose is to set us apart to God (cf. Lev 11:44-45; Deut 14:21).

Chapter 23 of our *parashah* begins by stressing the need for justice to prevail within the covenant community. Not only does justice require wise and honest judges (specifically detailed in the previous *parashah*), but it likewise requires honest witnesses. 23:1-3 offer five prohibitions: 1) one cannot give unfounded hearsay testimony in judicial proceedings; 2) collusion on the part of a witness with one of the parties for a fraudulent or deceitful purpose is prohibited; 3) no consideration is to be given to the social standing of the litigants; 4) one is not to pervert justice by deferring to the majority view if one is convinced that it is erroneous; 5) even though the Torah regularly enjoins compassion for the poor, one is not to allow their emotions, however noble, to color one's judgment.

The stress upon preserving justice is now extended to one's enemy (23:4–5). The early rabbinic commentary on Exodus (*Mekhilta*) suggests that all the following could be the intended meaning of the term "enemy": 1) gentile idolater, 2) convert to Judaism who has relapsed into idolatry, 3) a Jewish apostate, and 4) a Jew who exhibits enmity toward a fellow Jew. Clearly, regardless of how we might define "enemy" in this context, the situation envisions life within a common community. It seems highly likely that Yeshua had this text (and those similar to it, e.g., Prov 25:21) in mind when He taught us to love our enemy (Matt 5:43ff). As those who are created in the image of God, we must not allow our hostile and vindictive emotions to overcome our humanity. We are to exhibit the same kind of compassion that the Creator shows for those who are in need, even if they have been hostile toward us in the past. "Doing good to those who hate you" (Lk 6:27) is demonstrated in our *parashah* by helping in the common issues of life, like helping to return an animal that has strayed, or helping to unload a too-heavy burden from an animal. By extension, we might translate these ancient examples for our modern times as returning lost items and helping in an emergency (like changing a flat tire on the roadside).

Justice (the primary topic of this paragraph) is dependent upon honest judges. The desire of the judges that a criminal not go unpunished is not to override their decision making and thus bring about a miscarriage of justice. The phrase "do not kill the innocent or the righteous, for I will not acquit the guilty" of 23:7 was understood by the Sages to mean that once a person has been declared innocent and "not guilty" (=righteous), he could not be tried again for the same offence. It is upon this understanding of our text that double jeopardy was outlawed in our own justice system. That is, once a person has been declared guilty and punished for a crime, a second person cannot be so punished for the same crime, even if the original verdict was found to be faulty (cf. b.*San* 33b; cp. 5th Amendment, US Constitution).

In distinction to the judges' desire that criminals be brought to justice, there is also the possibility that judges could be bribed. Since they held in their power the judicial outcome, they were likewise targets for bribery. Since God, as the final Judge, "shows no favor and takes no bribe" (Deut 10:17; 2Chron 19:7), earthly judges who serve in His court, are to follow suit. The Sages extended "bribery" to "verbal bribery," so that it was prohibited for a litigant to laud the judge with verbal niceties (b.*Ketubbot* 105b).

Likewise, the judge is not to look down upon a stranger (גֵּר, *ger*), that is, one who is a foreigner but has most likely taken up residence within the nation of Israel. Whereas before (Ex 22:21[22]) the similar injunction was given to all Israelites, here it is specifically enjoined upon judges. In addition, a motive clause is added: "since you yourselves know the feelings of a stranger." The judges should consider that they, or their forefathers, felt the tyranny of injustice in Egypt, being treated as foreigners without legal recourse. As such, the judges should have an additional personal motive for seeing that a foreigner be given the same justice as a native born.

The next section of our *parashah* deals with agricultural laws, which naturally coincide with the cycle of the year and thus the festivals. The agricultural laws also connect with the fair and kind treatment of the poor and those within the society that were at a disadvantage (such as orphans, widows, and foreigners).

In the sabbatical year (שְׁמִטָּה, *sh'mitah*, from the verb שמט, "to let drop," "to release") or the seventh year in a seven year cycle, it was prohibited to sow or reap crops (the fuller explanation is given Lev 25:1–7, 18–22; Deut 15:1–10), "so that the needy of your people may eat" (Ex 23:10). In the overall scheme of things, the *sh'mitah* was a matter of conservation. Arable land that is continuously cultivated is soon depleted of its nutrients and thus becomes less productive. However, these laws extend to orchards and vineyards as well, so that the annual fruit which appeared during the sabbatical year was considered "ownerless," meaning it was available to all. Moreover, since grain fields were harvested by hand, a good amount of the grain fell in the fields, and was capable of producing volunteer crops the next year. It seems likely, therefore, that even in the sabbatical year, there was some standing grain in the fields.

The mention of the *sh'mitah* year now is tied to the other appointed times, namely, the weekly Sabbath, and the three pilgrimage festivals (each referred to as חַג, *chag*, "procession," "round dance," "festival" and cognate to Arabic *haj*), all three of which are closely tied to agricultural events. Passover Day, Yom Teruah (Rosh HaShanah), and Yom Kippur are not mentioned since they are not festivals that are rooted in the soil. Pesach and the Feast of Unleavened Bread were viewed as a single festival (e.g., Mk 14:12; Lk 22:7).

The Sabbath is to the weekly cycle what the *sh'mitah* is to the yearly cycle. On it all are given the opportunity of rest, but our verse (23:12) specifically mentions beasts of burden, and the son of a female slave, along with the "stranger" or *ger*. By *qal v'chomer* (an argument comparing the "light" with the "heavy"), it is reasoned that if the most disadvantaged of society are afforded rest on the Shabbat, then surely this applies to all others. It is interesting that the animals are said to have "rest" (נוּחַ, *nuach*) but the people are said to be "refreshed" (נָפַשׁ, *naphash*). Thus, the rest that comes to mankind is of both a physical and a spiritual nature.

Ex 23:13, which prohibits evoking the names of pagan gods, may seem intrusive, but actually it fits perfectly into the flow of this passage. The pagan world of the Ancient Near East knew many festivals, most of which centered around an invocation of the gods to renew the soil and to invigorate the flocks in order to be fertile. These were accompanied by magical rites aimed at propitiating divine powers and enlisting their aid in bringing produce and offspring in the coming year. Thus, we should understand the prohibition of not "mentioning the name of pagan gods," or letting them be "heard from your mouth" to be connected with such pagan rituals, which apparently were attractive to Israel throughout her history. This is further emphasized in the next verse (23:14) by the command to celebrate the feasts of Israel "to Me," that is, to God exclusively.

The same emphasis is found in v. 17: "Three times a year all your males shall appear before the Lord ADONAI."

The Feast of Unleavened Bread (חַג־הַמַּצּוֹת, *chag hamatzot*) occurred at the time of the barley harvest (Abib was the Cannanite name of the month in which the grain ripened) and is commanded in Ex 12:14–20. The requirement of eating only unleavened bread is tied to the exodus event when the hasty departure from Egypt left no time for the dough to raise. But unleavened bread may have also been a reminder that bread in its most desired form (i.e., fully raised) was possible only as God blessed Israel with yet another harvest. Eating unleavened bread may have symbolized how bleak life would be if God did not continually bring nourishment to His chosen nation. The offerings that were brought at the festival served as a reminder that God was the giver of all food (which we regularly acknowledge by the blessing of the *hamotzi*). Thus, none were to appear at the festival "empty handed," that is, without the appropriate offering.

The Feast of the Harvest (חַג־הַקָּצִיר, *chag haqatzir*) is better known as the Feast of Weeks (Shavuot) or Pentecost (the term used by Greek speaking Jews) since it occurs fifty days from "the day after the Sabbath" of Passover. It is also called the "day of the first fruits" (Num 28:26) since the first fruits of the wheat harvest were brought to the priests. From ancient times Shavuot was celebrated as the commemoration of the giving of the Torah (cf. 2Chron 15:10–13 where King Asa called a great assembly of the people in the third month for a national ceremony of covenant renewal; cf. Jubilees 6:17).

The Feast of Ingathering (חַג־הָאָסִף, *chag ha'asiph*) is better known as the Festival of Booths (Tabernacles) or Sukkot. Again, this festival is tied to the exodus event, for when the people of Israel came out of Egypt, they lived in temporary booths or *sukkot* (plural of *sukkah*, "booth"). It was common during the harvest of vegetables and fruit that temporary booths were constructed in the fields for protection and for sleeping. Thus, the final harvest of the year is likewise part of the Sukkot celebration. Decorating the *sukkah* with various fruits and vegetables carries forth this theme. In biblical and rabbinic literature, Sukkot took on such an importance that it was called "the Festival" (הֶחָג, *he-chag*, cf. 1Ki 8:2[3], 65; 12:32; Ezek 45:23; Neh 8:14; 2Chron 5:3; 7:8–9; cp. John 7:2f). The Feast of Ingathering is noted to occur "at the end of the year," meaning the end of the agricultural year. The parallel phrase in Ex 34:22, "at the turn of the year," likewise means the transition from one agricultural season to the other.

23:18–19 append some general rules governing the sacrifices that would take place on the aforementioned festivals. Offering the "blood of

My sacrifice with leavened bread" pertains particularly to the sacrifices offered at the Feast of Unleavened Bread. The Sages derive from this that the Pesach sacrifice could not be offered until all the leaven of the Land had been disposed of. Thus, the time set for removal of all leaven was noon on the 14th of Nisan, the time when the offering was made in the Temple. But in order to safeguard the prohibition of not offering the sacrifice while leaven remained, the time was pushed back two hours (m.*Pes* 5:4; t.*Pes* 3:3).

It is also prohibited for "the fat of My feast to remain overnight until morning." 34:25 reads "nor is the sacrifice of the Feast of the Passover to be left over until morning." In like manner, the consumption of the Pesach lamb was to be finished during the night hours (the rabbis set midnight as the time after which no meat of the Pesach could be eaten), and any that was left over had to be destroyed by burning.

The third statute relates to bringing the choicest of the wheat harvest at the Feast of Shavuot (the word רֵאשִׁית, *reishit* obviously means "choicest" here, cf. Num 18:12; Deut 33:21 1Sa 15:21; Ezek 44:30; Amos 6:6).

The final prohibition, "You are not to boil a young goat in the milk of its mother" has been notoriously difficult to interpret. Being grouped as it is with regulations clearly connected to festivals, many ancient interpreters understood it to refer to some kind of pagan ritual, engaged in at the pagan festivals, which Israel was to shun. Thus, Maimonides understood this prohibition as relating to a pagan rite, while other rabbinic commentators (Rashbam, Ibn Ezra, etc.) understand it simply on humanitarian grounds, that it was intrinsically inhumane to use the mother's milk to boil her kid, parallel to the prohibition of taking the mother bird with her young (Deut 22:6). Philo, in the 1st Century CE, held that the prohibition, while pertaining to "the flesh of lambs or kids or any other young animal," only prohibited boiling such in the milk from the animal's mother and not milk in general. In time, the rabbis interpret this verse (and its parallels in Ex 34:26 and Deut 14:21) to prohibit eating any meat with milk, including meat of fowls.

Initially, a line from the Ugaritic literature (*KTU* 1.23) was thought to include a reference to "boiling a kid in milk." Line 14 of that text entitled "The gods pleasant and beautiful," was translated: "boil a kid in milk, a lamb in butter." This appeared to give credence to the idea that our biblical text related to a pagan sacrificial ritual. However, more recently, Ugaritic scholars have reassessed the cuneiform characters, and decided that this original translation has no basis (see Robert Ratner, "'A Kid in Milk?': New Photographs of *KTU* 1.23, line 14", *HUCA* 1986, pp. 15–46). Though the exact translation remains uncertain, current scholarship almost universally denies that the Ugaritic text can be used to posit a pagan, sacrificial ritual, which would inform our current text.

Given these data, perhaps the best we can do in interpreting this prohibition is to suggest that humanitarian concerns are primary. During festivals when so many animals were slaughtered and sacrificed, there was still to be a recognition that the life of the animal is important to God and must be properly appreciated. More directly, the relationship between mother and offspring is not to be violated. (For further study on the "meat & milk" issue, see my paper, "You Shall Not Boil a Kid in its Mother's Milk: The Interpretive History of a Curious Commandment," available at www.torahresource.com).

Our *parashah* ends with a most remarkable description of the Angel of the Lord (23:20–23) and the exhortation to Israel that they should be wholly given over to the worship of God alone, and not give way to any of the pagan practices that surrounded them. The description of the Angel is intriguing, for the attributes of God Himself are ascribed to Him. We may note three commands, and two attributes that undergird His authority.

Commands: **1)** be on guard before Him (הִשָּׁמֶר מִפָּנָיו). The point is that Israel, by the presence of the Angel, is to reckon with the fact that God is in her midst. Eben Ezra writes regarding this phrase: "All which the Angel does is a thing of HaShem. Do not add to it, nor take away from it." **2)** obey His voice (שְׁמַע קֹלוֹ). This is the positive aspect, the next command will encompass the negative. The Angel comes with the authority of God Himself. **3)** Do not rebel against Him (אַל־תַּמֵּר בּוֹ). Disobedience in regard to His instructions will be considered as rebellion against God Himself.

Attributes: (the basis for the commands) **1)** He is completely just: "He will not pardon your transgression," meaning that He will not overlook sin to sweep it away without consequence. **2)** "Since My Name is in Him" (כִּי שְׁמִי בְּקִרְבּוֹ). This gives the reason why He cannot overlook sin—He is endowed with the same infinite character as HaShem. Yet Is 42:8 teaches us: "I am Adonai, that is My name; I will not give My glory to another, nor My praise to graven images." How could the very Name (i.e., the exact character of the Almighty) be within the Angel? Here, early in the Torah, we are once again confronted with the mystery of the Godhead. The One God reveals Himself in plurality. He could just as easily have said "I will go with you, etc." but He does not. Instead, the Angel He sends comes with the fullness of His presence—the Name is within Him.

In the final analysis, then, the ordinances that are given have as their ultimate purpose the preparation of God's people as His dwelling place. He desires to dwell among His people, and for this reason, He requires that they be sanctified unto Him. He makes His people righteous in order that He might dwell with them.

Parashah 62
Triennial Cycle

Exodus 24:1–18

Haftarah: Isaiah 60:16–61:19 | Apostolic: Matthew 26:27–28

The Covenant at Sinai

The section before us on this Shabbat contains the wonderful and mysterious account of the actual enactment of the covenant made between God and Israel at Sinai. It is wonderful because it relates the dwelling of God with man in a tangible manner. God and man sit at table together and commune in the context of holiness. Here we see the goal of redemption, the very purpose for which Israel was redeemed from Egypt. Even as the exodus forever forged the paradigm for redemption, so this covenant ceremony establishes the paradigm for the very purpose of redemption, that is, the re-established fellowship of God with His image bearers. From the point of his banishment from the Garden of Eden, an estrangement existed between God and man. Granted, the covenants made with Noah and the patriarchs Abraham, Isaac, and Jacob, strongly indicated that God's purpose was to repair the breach which sin had caused, and to restore fellowship with mankind. Yet it is here, in the enactment of the covenant with Israel, that the means of such restoration is revealed.

Obviously, God remains holy and unchanged by the sinfulness of man. How then can fellowship be restored, seeing that man had become unholy through willful disobedience and the sin that had pervaded the race? The answer is found in the cleansing of sin through the death of an innocent sacrifice on behalf of man, and through the mediation of this atonement by a mediator. All of this is dramatized in the awesome events of our *parashah*.

The events of our *parashah* clearly portray Mt. Sinai as the model after which the Tabernacle or *mishkan* (and eventually the Temple or *heikal, beit hamichdash* in rabbinic language) would be constructed. There are three distinct "zones" in our story: the foot of the mountain, an intermediate ascent upon the mountain, and the top of the mountain where the glory of God resided, covered by a thick cloud. The people remain at the foot of the mountain, while representatives of the people ascend to the intermediate area. Moses alone continues up to the top of the mountain where he alone speaks with God. These three "zones" correspond exactly to the courtyard of the Tabernacle, where the people came; the Holy Place, where the representatives of the people, the priests, served; and the Most Holy Place, where only the High Priest was allowed to enter once a year. It was in the Most Holy Place, like the top of the mountain, where the Glory of God dwelt over the cherubim of the Ark of the Covenant. Thus, the initial enactment of the covenant became the pattern for the Tabernacle, and thus the pattern that revealed the means by which God would effect atonement, which in turn resulted in the restoration of fellowship between Himself and His people.

This general picture of the Sinai events is very important in understanding the overall perspective of the covenant, embodied in the giving of the Torah. It is all intertwined with God's gracious intention to bring about atonement and the restoration of fellowship with sinners. Whereas the theology of the emerging Christian Church often pitted the giving of the "Law" as opposed to grace, we discover that just the opposite is the case. The Sinai covenant stands as the very paradigm for God's way of atonement, the very means for cleansing sinners and restoring them to His favor and communion.

This is precisely Paul's point in his often misunderstood words of Galatians 3:19 – "Why the Torah then? It was added because of transgressions, having been ordained through angels by the agency of a mediator, until the seed would come to whom the promise had been made." The words "because of transgressions" (τῶν παραβάσεως χάριν προσετέθη) have been misunderstood as meaning "to punish transgressions," but this is not only short-sighted, but misses the thrust of Paul's argument at this point. The Torah covenant was given "with regard to transgressions," that is, as the revelation of God's way of dealing with transgressions, all with a view to the ultimate sacrifice that would be made by Yeshua ("the Seed") to Whom the promise (beginning with Gen 3:15) had been made. In the covenant at Sinai, we are given a fuller picture of how God would effect atonement, overcome the breach that transgressions had caused, and ultimately bring about eternal restoration through the sacrifice and mediation of His Messiah, Yeshua.

We may also note, by way of the general picture presented in our portion, that God brings man to Him. We are struck with the fact that our story contains a number of ascents and descents. His initial instruction to Moses is "come up to Adonai" (v. 1). The majestic summit of Sinai pictures the holy abode of the Almighty. He does not diminish His holiness in order to dwell with man. On the contrary, He elevates man to His own level of holiness in order to effect the fellowship for which his was created. In a very real sense, then, Moses' ascent to the very presence of

God foreshadows the final and ultimate dwelling of God in the world to come. Even as Yeshua's ascension to the right hand of God means that there is a man in heaven today, so His ascension is a kind of "first fruits" that guarantees the ingathering of the complete harvest. If He dwells in the very presence of the Father, then so will all those who are "in Him."

This reality constitutes one of His purposes in His present intercession as High Priest for His people, as noted in His priestly prayer: John 17:24 "Father, I desire that they also, whom You have given Me, be with Me where I am, so that they may see My glory which You have given Me, for You loved Me before the foundation of the world." While the picture presented in our *parashah* only has Moses ascending to the very presence of God, the ultimate goal is that all of God's people should be there as well. Yeshua's work on our behalf assures us that this will be the case in the world to come, where mortal will be transformed to immortal, and where the "Lord God the Almighty and the Lamb are its temple" (Rev 21:22). No more will there be a need for various "zones" (courtyard, Holy Place, Most Holy Place) but all will dwell in the very presence of the Holy One. The fellowship of Gan Eden will be the eternal reality.

The initial command for Moses, Aaron, Nadab and Abihu, and the seventy elders to ascend the mountain offers a threefold division: Moses is the mediator *par excellence*, Aaron and his sons are the second level of mediators, and the seventy elders represent the nation of Israel. In this regard, Moses acts as the High Priest, Aaron and his sons as the priests, and the seventy elders as the people. The symbolism of "seventy" is doubtless that of a complete representation (cf. Num 11:16, 24; Ezek 8:11): all the people of Israel (including those foreigners who had joined themselves to Israel in the exodus) were represented as covenant members. Moreover, Aaron and his sons, along with Joshua, the servant of Moses, represented the people in the covenant meal that was to take place upon the mountain. And ultimately, Moses represented the entire nation as he functioned in the capacity of mediator before God. Thus, the covenant had individual as well as corporate dimensions.

It is not certain how many times Moses ascends and descends the mountain. The opening verses of our *parashah* may be a general heading for the pericope, signalling the overall purpose, that is, the giving of the covenant to Moses through his ascension to the top of the mountain. Liberal scholarship has used this portion (and others) to suggest that various accounts of the Sinai covenant have been woven together in a tangled "mess," so much so that one is now unable to decide exactly what happened. It is more likely, however, that the narrative is simply compacted around the essential information, and all of the details regarding just when Moses ascended and descended are not given in their entirety.

Verse 3 says that "Moses came and recounted to the people…," not giving us a clear indication of the chronology of these events. He relates "all the words and all the ordinances (מִשְׁפָּטִים, *mishpatim*)" of the covenant. This most likely included the Ten Words and their expanded meaning and application as we saw in the previous two *parashot*. It may be that "words" (הַדְּבָרִים, *had^evarim*) denote the apodictic ("you shall not") commands represented in the Ten Words, while "ordinances" relate to those matters that would need to be determined on a case by case basis by the jurisdiction of the law courts, i.e., judges.

The people (perhaps represented by the seventy elders) respond in one accord (קוֹל אֶחָד, *qôl 'echad*): "All the words that Adonai has spoken we will do." This should not be construed as a "rash" response of those who had not understood the immensity of the Torah, or who, in pride, considered their ability to obey God without reckoning with their weakness. On the contrary, this affirmation to obey construed the clear intent of the people. They fully accepted the covenant as it was given, which included means for restoration when one failed to obey.

Verse 4 indicates that Moses wrote down all the words of Adonai. This document is called the "book of the covenant" (סֵפֶר הַבְּרִית, *sepher hab^erit*) in v. 7, which is generally understood to be the material we have in Ex 21:1–24:18. In so doing, Moses sets the template for all subsequent prophets who would hear the word of Adonai through revelation or vision, and then write it down to be delivered to the people. While the Ten Words, written by the finger of God, were directly from Him, the words written by Moses and subsequent prophets bore no less authority. Though God used human agents to give the full revelation of His word, He nonetheless superintended their work through the agency of the Ruach HaKodesh (Holy Spirit). Thus, "all the words of Adonai," to which the people refer, include those written down by Moses as well.

Next, Moses arises early in morning and builds an altar at the foot of Mt. Sinai, which included twelve "pillars" (מַצֵּבָה, *matzeivah*) representing the twelve tribes of Israel. These "standing stones" were viewed as enduring witnesses to the covenant, not unlike boundary markers of the Ancient Near East. Note Josh 24:27 where a similar stone so functions: "Behold, this stone shall be for a witness against us, for it has heard all the words of Adonai which He spoke to us; thus it shall be for a witness against you, so that you do not deny your God." These are to be distinguished from the "sacred pillars" erected by pagan peoples as representations of their gods (cf. Ex 23:24; 34:13).

After constructing the altar, young men are commissioned to offer bulls upon the altar. These were chosen, not only because the task was arduous, and required the energy of young men, but also perhaps because they represented the firstborn of the nation who had been spared in the exodus. Ultimately, the priests of the tribe of Levi would be symbolic of the firstborn of Israel (Num 3:12). They offered burnt offerings (עֹלָה, *'olah*) and peace offerings (שֶׁלֶם, *shelem*), two types of sacrifices that fit the awesome occasion. The burnt offering, consumed entirely upon the altar, represented the complete dedication of the people to God. The peace offerings, part of which was consumed on the altar, and part eaten by those offering the sacrifices, symbolized the covenant meal of communion between God and His people. In both cases, however, the blood is dashed upon the altar, for the life of the animal was viewed as contained in the blood (Lev 17:11), and this belonged entirely to the Life Giver.

Moses also takes half of the blood and sprinkles it upon the people, or perhaps, upon the twelve standing stones (pillars) that represented the people. We are not told what this represented, but it is clearly a part of the covenant ritual. One cannot escape the parallel to the blood that was put on the doorposts of each Israelite house in the exodus. Like the blood that covered and thus protected the Israelites from the plague of death, so the blood sprinkled upon the people represented the taking of the life from the innocent sacrifice and applying it to the people as God's covenant partner. Their transgressions, though grievous, would be wiped clean by the atonement afforded through sacrifice, pointing to Yeshua the ultimate sacrifice which alone could pay for sins (cf. Heb 10:4).

Having completed the sacrifices, Moses now reads what he had written in the book of the covenant, in the hearing of the people. Once again they respond by accepting the covenant upon themselves, but this time there is an added dimension: "All that Adonai has spoken we will do, and we will be obedient!" (כֹּל אֲשֶׁר־דִּבֶּר יְהוָה נַעֲשֶׂה וְנִשְׁמָע). The additional "and we will be obedient (literally, we will hear)" most likely means that the people promised to continue to await God's instructions. They were willing to obey what God had said so far, and were also committing themselves to what He might reveal yet in the future. This has been a hallmark of Jewish response to the Torah: even before one knows what exactly the Torah may contain, they are willing to commit themselves to obedience because they know that the Law Giver is none other than the holy, benevolent Almighty. We say "yes" to God even before we understand what He wants us to do. The Talmud (b.*Shabbat* 88a-b) contains an interesting interchange between a Sadducee and a student of Torah (most likely a Gentile, for the Talmud has "Raba," but no Sadducees remained in the days of Raba, and this convention is often used to substitute for a Gentile) who was engrossed in his study:

> 'You rash people,' he [the Sadducee] exclaimed, 'who gave precedence to your

mouth over your ears: you still persist in your rashness. First you should have listened, if within your powers, accept; if not, you should not have accepted.' Said he to him, 'We who walked in integrity, of us it is written, The integrity of the upright shall guide them. But of others, who walked in perversity, it is written, but the perverseness of the treacherous shall destroy them. (Prov 11:3)

I think it is interesting that the same argument is often heard in our day, that unless one is able fully to obey the Torah, one should simply reject it. But the ability to be *perfect* in obedience is not the prerequisite of a desire to be obedient. How foolish it would be if our children were to inform us that they really couldn't accept our authority and rules because they realized they could never perfectly obey us! What any father longs to hear is not a retort of ability or inability, but a genuine expression of desire to be obedient. We demonstrate our love for God in that we desire to obey Him, whatever He commands.

While sprinkling the blood upon the people, Moses says: "Behold the blood of the covenant, which ADONAI has made with you in accordance with all these words." It is striking how parallel the words of our Master are to this text: "for this is My blood of the covenant, which is poured out for many for forgiveness of sins" (Matt 26:28). His words here are connected to the whole Sinai event, where the covenant is ratified through the sprinkling (giving, pouring out) of blood. In Luke's account (Lk 22:20) we have: "This cup which is poured out for you is the new covenant in My blood." Here the covenant is specifically identified as the "new covenant" (cf. Jer 31:31-34), but this is not at odds with the covenant ratification at Sinai. For the new covenant envisions that time when the Sinai covenant (the Torah) will become the life of Israel, as they obey God from a heart of faith, having had their sins and transgressions removed forever.

Verses 9–11 contain a remarkable scene: Moses, Aaron and his sons, and the seventy elders ascend the mountain and "see the God of Israel." We should also include Joshua in this group, as the plural of v. 14 indicates. Ex 32:17 also relates that Joshua was on the mountain, and high enough so that though he could not see the people, he could hear them. The idea that the chosen entourage "saw the God of Israel" has been variously explained. Generally, the rabbis suggest that they saw the glory of God (the *Shekinah*), or some vision of God, like that which the prophets saw in their visions. Others suggest that by "see" we should understand "gain a revelation of" or "come to understand," much like our English word "see" is sometimes used. The Lxx felt the tension of the text, which plainly suggests that the invisible God is somehow corporeal, and translates "and they saw the place where the God of Israel stood." The Targum has "and they saw the Glory of the God of Israel, and under the throne of His glory was the work of a precious stone." The Samaritan Targum reads ירא (*yara'*, "to fear") rather than ראה (*ra'ah*, "to see") and renders the phrase: "And they feared the God of Israel, and there, where they met him, the ground was like a Sapphire." All of these are attempts at explaining the unexplainable: God is a spirit, and "no one has seen God at any time" (John 1:18, cf. Col 1:15; 1Tim 1:17).

Yet the Hebrew seems straightforward. Not only does it say that they "saw the God Israel" (וַיִּרְאוּ אֵת אֱלֹהֵי יִשְׂרָאֵל), it says further in v. 11 that they "saw God" (וַיֶּחֱזוּ אֶת־הָאֱלֹהִים), utilizing a heightened verb (חָזָה) describing not only visions, but also used for seeing with one's eyes (Ps 11:7; 17:15; 58:9, 11; Prov 22:9; 29:20; Is 33:20; 57:8; Jb 19:26, 27). Moreover, the text indicates that they saw His feet under which were tiles of blue (lapis lazuli) forming a clear (טָהֹר, *tahor*) pavement. And like other instances were people came into the presence of God, and were amazed that they remained alive, so v. 11 emphasizes that "He did not stretch out His hand against the nobles of the sons of Israel." They came into the very presence of the Almighty and remained alive. Furthermore, "they ate and drank." They participated in a covenant meal with the God of Israel.

But it does not seem far fetched at all to be reminded that the mediator of the covenant was none other than Yeshua, for He is consistently the agent of God's enactments with mankind. Here, like the often repeated scenes in which the Angel of the Lord appears in the history of Israel, and is reckoned as one with יהוה, both in attributes and actions, Moses and his company see the Divine One in His pre-incarnate manifestation. Ultimately, it is the glory of Yeshua that shines in the face of Moses as he descends the mountain.

Our *parashah* ends with the ascent of Moses into the cloud, and the actual writing of the Ten Words upon the two stone tablets that had been prepared by Moses. He instructs the rest to remain at their intermediate location, and that given any matters of judgement, Aaron and Hur were "in charge" (v. 14). The plural "we will go" must include Joshua, though it is clear that only Moses eventually enters the thick cloud that encompassed the glory of God. Like the Ruach, Who aided Yeshua in His work upon the earth, so Joshua accompanies the "mediator of Israel" as he ascends to the top of the mountain.

The motif of the six days followed by the seventh is once again encountered at this pivotal juncture. Apparently Moses awaits a specific invitation from the Almighty before entering the cloud. This he does for six days, and the voice of God bids him enter on the seventh. We can imagine that Moses used the six days for preparation of heart and mind as he contemplated the awesome or even dreadful task he was about to undertake. Who could imagine entering into such close proximity with the Creator, seen as a "consuming fire" (cf. Heb 12:29) and remaining alive? Yet, like the creation week, the seventh day brought the anticipated invitation, and ultimately the rest that would come from hearing the very words of God.

Moses remained there for forty days and forty nights, meaning that he was sustained by God's power, not by common food. And ultimately, he would return to Israel with the very words of God, which would be spiritual food for them as well. God has spoken to man, and in His words are the way of life. In this regard we remember the words of Peter when asked by Yeshua if he and the disciples would abandon Him as the others had: "Master, to whom shall we go? You have words of eternal life" (John 6:68).

The *haftarah* (Is 60:17–61:9) was no doubt chosen because it envisions that full restoration of Israel, living in accordance with Torah and thus experiencing all of the blessings of HaShem in eternal, unending joy and shalom.

The Apostolic portion (Matt 26:27–28) is added in order to emphasize that fact that the prophecy of Isaiah is dependent upon the completion of Yeshua's work, though Whom alone are sins forgiven and the New Covenant (Jer 31:31–34) established and brought to fruition.

Thus, in the completed work of Yeshua, the grand picture presented first at Sinai, and then prophesied by Israel's prophets, is made complete.

Parashah Nineteen
תְּרוּמָה – Terumah
"contribution offering"
Exodus 25:1–27:19

In the Triennial Cycle there are two Parashot

25:1-26:30 | 26:31-27:19

Parashah 63
Triennial Cycle

Exodus 25:1-26:30

Haftarah: Isaiah 66:1–13 | Apostolic: 1Corinthians 6:12–20

God Among His People

The phenomenal scene of chapter 24, with Moses and company ascending Mt. Sinai, is really beyond comprehension. Even more difficult to grasp is what must have been the awesome and in many ways terrible feelings Moses encountered as he left the rest and headed into the cloud, there to converse with God. Perhaps no other chapter in the Torah captures the essence of worship as this one does—man and God, conversing together in the realm of His infinite holiness.

Equally remarkable and important is the manner in which the text continues. Our *parashah*, following immediately upon the heels of the mountain experience, begins to describe in detail the מִשְׁכָּן, (*Mishkan*), its precise layout, and the articles of furniture that were to be built for it. The message is an obvious one: God intends to dwell with His people, giving to them the same kind of communion that Moses enjoyed on the mountain. God in all of His glory would dwell among the people of Israel.

Here we find a truly remarkable revelation about God: He will descend to dwell with His people. It is not that He would somehow give each and every one of His children the experience of climbing the mountain as Moses and the others had done, but that He would Himself descend from the mountain and reveal His presence among the people in the very place where they were dwelling. Here we find the progressive revelation of the incarnational reality: God dwelling with mankind.

But we find another important truth in the arrangement of these *parashot*—God's dwelling among His people could not in any way diminish His holiness. If He were to dwell among His people, then there would be required a separation between His holiness and the unholy character of the people. Thus, the *Mishkan* represents not only the locus of His revealed presence, but also the boundaries dividing between the holy and the profane.

And thus the purity laws became a necessary reality. No one unclean may enter the region of the *Mishkan*, and only those specifically sanctified (set apart) for the holy work of intercession could enter the *Mishkan* proper, and only one, the כֹּהֵן הַגָּדוֹל (high priest), could enter the Most Holy Place, the very place where the שְׁכִינָה (*Shekinah*), the glorious presence of God, was manifested. The *Mishkan* is Mt. Sinai at the people's level, a Mt. Sinai that would move with them!

Thus, the entire sacrificial system, the priestly activities, the elaborate laws of purities, the structure of the *Mishkan* itself—all of this was given for one purpose—that God and man might have friendship and communion—that the Creator and His creatures might converse together and enjoy each other's company. In a very real sense, the *Mishkan* foreshadowed the Incarnate One Himself, Who would dwell among men as Immanuel, "God with us."

The first request in the process of building the *Mishkan* was for the people to gather the necessary materials to complete the construction: וְיִקְחוּ־לִי תְּרוּמָה, "and they shall take for Me a portion." We see that the word translated "portion" is *terumah*, a word built upon the root רוּם, "to lift up," "make high" and often translated "contribution." Note that this was not a requirement but is stated to be מֵאֵת כָּל־אִישׁ אֲשֶׁר יִדְּבֶנּוּ לִבּוֹ, "from each one whose heart moves him." The word translated "moves" is נָדַב, *nadav*, "to urge on" (*qal*) and "to volunteer" (*hitp.*). (It is interesting that this verb contains the exact letters of Aaron's son's name, Nadav, who would later be slain in the very *Mishkan* which was built by *volunteer* contributions!) Contrary to those who attempt to explain the ancient experience of God's people as primarily *external*, we see once again that the Torah teaches us about the *inward* reality of a spiritual dimension. The giving of these materials was specifically to be by the "moving of one's heart"—responding to the gracious call of God and His desire to dwell among the people. In short, we have here every indication that God's dwelling among His people necessitated their preparing a place for Him in advance of His coming. Their "redemption" had already taken place—a singular, powerful work of God without any request or need for their help. But the purpose of the exodus was not only to rescue them from the evils of Egypt—it was also so that they might worship HaShem. The *Mishkan*, therefore, is an absolute necessity for the realization of God's purpose in the exodus, and the construction of the *Mishkan* is a joint effort between God and Israel.

This emphasizes a crucial truth about our redemption in Yeshua: we were redeemed *so that we might worship HaShem, and this worship requires that we, together with Him, make a place appropriate for His dwelling.* Our Apostolic section reminds us that today, in a primary sense, that dwelling place is none other than our own beings—our bodies in which the Ruach is pleased to dwell, and our communities, in which the power of the Risen Messiah is manifest. The sanctification for which we must strive is a co-operation between our renewed spirits and the Spirit of God. How intent are we in making this dwelling place all that God has instructed that it should be?

Put yourself back into Israel's place as Moses comes asking for contributions. How would you have responded to the request to bring materials for the *Mishkan*? I think any of us would have gladly offered whatever we could to make the *Mishkan* a reality. We would, I think, have given the best we had, and not even considered donating materials which were torn, worn out, or tarnished. Yet God has always looked for the heart of His people to be the place of His dwelling, and we tend to forget that the heart requires ever as much preparation as did the *Mishkan* of old. Do we prepare our hearts with the best which we have, or do we take the leftovers, that which is worn out, tarnished, etc., and attempt to construct a place for His glory to reside? Note well our *Haftarah* (Is 66:1-2)! How is it that we may construct a *Mishkan* fit for God's dwelling? God's dwelling in heaven is all glorious, and the earth is His footstool. But if we should build Him a place where He might rest—where He comes willingly to reside, what is it? "But to this one I will look, to him who is humble and contrite of spirit, and who trembles at My word."

We see in this "*Mishkan* preparation" a two fold character. The first is described by the pair of words "humble" (עָנִי, *'oni*) and "contrite" (נְכֵה, *nᵉcheih*, lit. "smitten") as characterizing one's spirit (רוּחַ, *ruach*). What is a humble and contrite spirit? One who has come to realize that "in me, that is in my flesh, there dwells no good thing" (Rom 7:18), and who has admitted his poverty (עָנִי, *'oni* has as a root meaning "poor" or "impoverished") and thus an inability to "buy" favor with God.

But there is a second characteristic: "who trembles (חָרֵד, *chareid*) at My word." חָרֵד (*chareid*) literally means "to be frightened," "afraid," and is so used in Judg 7:3; 1Sa 4:13; Is 66:5; Ezra 9:4; 10:3 (these are the only other times the verb is used in the Tanach). This word is different than the word often used in combination with God's name (יָרֵא, *yara'*, to "fear God", etc.). This word conveys a genuine fear or fright, and in this verse, in regard to (note the use of עַל, *'al*, "on, upon") God's word. The application is obvious: God desires that we prepare a *Mishkan* of His dwelling in our very beings, a *Mishkan* (soul) that is humble and contrite—a soul that has a genuine fear or fright to transgress or disregard His word.

Now the willingness to observe outward signs of worship is far easier to muster than the heart-felt resolve to worship God in spirit and truth—in fulfilling the mitzvot of love and forgiveness, or of refraining from לְשׁוֹן הָרַע (*leshon hara'*=evil speech or gossip), of remaining faithful to what we know is true, and having a firm resolve to accomplish those tasks to which we have been called, regardless of the personal sacrifice it may entail. Trembling at His word means taking it seriously and acting upon it, utilizing the strength He gives to obey what He commands. It means coming to His word with a humble and contrite spirit, ready to learn—to listen. Not coming with one's mind and heart already certain that nothing more can be learned, but admitting that in all of our knowledge we possess only a fraction of the wealth God has placed in His word! And knowing that the word of God is given, not as an end in itself, but as a means to communion with Him. His word is not the pieces of a game by which, if properly "played," one might defeat his opponent. His word contains the very instructions by which He intends us to construct for Him a Mishkan in which He will dwell, a place where we will commune with Him.

So important is this *Mishkan* that we must constantly be building it—preparing it and making it fit for His rest. Anything that soils it or makes it inappropriate for His presence must be jettisoned from our lives and repudiated as unbecoming a child of God whose primary goal in life is to have on-going communion and friendship with the Creator. May it be so in our lives!

The Articles of the Mishkan

Moses is specifically instructed to make the *Mishkan* and its furniture (כְּלִי, *kᵉli*) according to the pattern (תַּבְנִית, *tabnit*, based on the root בָּנָה, *banah*, "to build," thus "model" or "architectural plan") that was shown to him on Mt. Sinai. We should derive from this that the articles that were to be constructed were specific revelations of God's purpose for the *Mishkan*. It is not far-fetched, then, to seek to understand more precisely how the form of the articles in the *Mishkan* might reveal more fully God's plan of atonement as it created a place for His dwelling.

It seems significant to me that the first article of furniture described is the Ark (אֲרוֹן, *'arôn*, in v. 22 אֲרֹן הָעֵדֻת, *'aron ha'eidut* "Ark of the Testimony") and its top or "mercy seat" (כַּפֹּרֶת, *kapporet*). Thus, the order in which the furniture is described begins in the Most Holy Place, and works its way outward, indicating that the primary goal of the whole *Mishkan* was the activity that would take place in the inner sanctum.

The Ark was to be 1.5 cubits wide, 1.5 cubits deep, and 2.5 cubits long. Many scholars have attempted to demonstrate a precise measurement for the cubit of the Ancient Near East, but none of the studies have been conclusive. Most would put the length of a cubit between 18 and 25 inches. The so-called "royal cubit" is not found in the Tanach, and its mention in texts from Mesopotamia and Egypt indicate that there was a varying standard for this as well. Most scholars today accept a length of 50 c. for the Mesopotamian cubit, and 52.5 c. for the Egyptian cubit (cf. *ABD*, 6:897f). If we accept the 50 c. length (approx. 19.5 inches), then the

Ark would have been 29 1/4 inches wide and deep, and 48 3/4 inches long.

Perhaps most significant is the measurement of its breadth (as if one were to wrap a string around its width and length), the total being eight. Eight becomes a significant number in light of the use of seven throughout the Tanach. The system of sabbatical years is concluded by the Jubilee (*Yovel*), which is the year following the completion of a cycle of seven groups of seven years. Likewise, *Shemini Atzeret,* or the eighth day following the festival of Sukkot, functions as the final conclusion of the Torah festival cycle. Thus, the number eight may well function as a symbol of finality. If so, it reminds us that the Ark is symbolic of the place where atonement is made on Yom Kippur, the one time within the festival cycle when full atonement is portrayed.

The Ark was to be made of *acacia* (שִׁטִּים, *shittim*), a tree attested in the Mediterranean regions in four varieties, and was known for its strength and durability. The Ark was to be overlaid inside and out with pure gold (זָהָב טָהוֹר, *zāhāv tāhôr*), that is, gold without any admixture of other metals. Its purity symbolized the complete holiness of the One Who would manifest His presence there. Rings into which poles (overlaid with gold) were placed were attached permanently to the Ark, and the poles were to remain in their place. This emphasized the mobility of the Ark, for God would travel in the midst of Israel as they journeyed.

The covering for the Ark is regularly called the "mercy seat" in our English translations. The Hebrew כַּפֹּרֶת, *kapporet*, is built upon the verb כָּפַר, *kaphar,* "to cover," "to wipe clean," "to atone." The manner in which "covering" came to mean "atone" is not entirely clear, but a Hebrew idiom that uses our word may be of help in explaining this. In Gen 32:20[21] Jacob, in sending gifts ahead to his approaching brother Esau, says "I will appease him with the present." The Hebrew translated by "I will appease him" is אֲכַפְּרָה פָנָיו, "I will cover his face." Here, the basic meaning of *kaphar*, "to cover," is combined with the idea of "appease." In the perspective of Jacob, to "cover the face" of Esau with gifts means to give him favor so as to cause him not to "turn his face" toward the former transgressions, i.e., his entire attention would be given over to the gifts. But how could the Almighty be "appeased" in regard to sinners? Here, the verb כָּפַר also retains its meaning of "wipe clean," for the blood applied to the "mercy seat" acts as a cleaning agent to wipe away sin.

This helps us understand the use of *kaphar* in relationship to the Ark. God, Who is enthroned upon the cherubim, is entirely satisfied with the life of the sacrifice, symbolized by the blood put upon the *kapporet*. In this way, the transgressions of Israel are "wiped clean" by the blood of the sacrifice, a life for a life.

The manner in which the Lxx translated כַּפֹּרֶת is significant for the fact that the same word is used of Yeshua in the Apostolic Scriptures. The Lxx used ἱλαστήριον, *hilasterion,* "place of expiation," "place of propitiation," to translate כַּפֹּרֶת, *kapporet,* wherever it is found in the Tanach, which Luther translated as "throne of mercy" or "mercy seat," which became the standard translation in the later English Bibles. Since the Ark was considered the throne of the Almighty (cf. 2Sam. 6:2; 2Ki. 19:15; 1Chr. 13:6; Ps. 80:1; 99:1; Is. 37:16), this translation is fitting, for it is here that He dispenses His mercy toward sinners.

With the Lxx consistently translating כַּפֹּרֶת, *kapporet* by ἱλαστήριον (*hilastērion*), the fact that we find this same Greek word used by Paul is significant.

> whom [i.e., Yeshua] God displayed publicly as a propitiation (*hilastērion*) in His blood through faith. This was to demonstrate His righteousness, because in the forbearance of God He passed over the sins previously committed; (Rom 3:25)

Here the Apostle essentially describes Yeshua as the כַּפֹּרֶת, *kapporet,* the very place where, for millennia, the dramatization of atonement was acted out year after year on Yom Kippur. Thus, the Ark, containing as it did the tablets of the Ten Words, stood as the representation of the covenant between God and Israel. And it was in connection with this covenant that the atonement for the sins of the nation was made. In whatever measure the nation had not lived in accordance with the covenant, the sacrifice made on her behalf made atonement.

It was not as though the animal sacrifice "covered" the sins, awaiting the time when Yeshua's sacrifice would remove them. Rather, the animal sacrifice on Yom Kippur constantly represented the ultimate and final sacrifice of Yeshua. As such, God reckoned the sacrifice of Yeshua to all those who, by faith, accepted God's means of atonement. Their faith, like ours, was in the redemption that God Himself would provide.

To the כַּפֹּרֶת, *kapporet,* were attached two figures representing cherubim (כְּרֻבִים, *keruvim*), with wings arching over the Ark, facing each other, but with their faces looking down upon the Ark. The first mention of cherubim in the Tanach is in the Genesis narrative, where, after Adam and Chavah are expelled from Gan Eden, cherubim are stationed at the entrance of the garden to guard it with flaming swords, and particularly to guard the Tree of Life that was in the garden (Gen 3:24). This role of guarding seems fitting for their symbolic representation over the Ark. As ministers of the Most High, they guard (as it were) His throne room. The story of Nadav and Avihu, who were struck dead by a "fire that came out from the presence of Adonai" (Lev 10:2), gives a fitting illustration of what would happen to anyone who approached the throne room of the Almighty in an unworthy manner. Thus, the sanctum of the Ark is guarded by the ministering angels.

The concluding verse of these initial instructions regarding the Ark and its covering is most interesting (25:22):

> There I will meet with you; and from above the mercy seat, from between the two cherubim which are upon the ark of the testimony, I will speak to you about all that I will give you in commandment for the sons of Israel.

It is certain that subsequent revelation would prohibit anyone coming into the Most Holy Place except the Cohen Gadol, and then only on Yom Kippur. Yet this concluding verse seems to indicate that Moses himself enters the Most Holy Place to receive commandments directly from God, which he would then transmit to the people of Israel. Rashi, sensing this problem, suggests that the voice of God emanated from the mercy seat, and came directly to Moses as he stood in the outer sanctum. This may be a correct interpretation, but it may also be that before the institution of the High Priesthood and the ceremonies of the *Mishkan*, Moses did approach the Ark directly. We know from Ex 34:33ff that when Moses would enter the *Mishkan* "to speak with Adonai," that he would remove the veil from his face, and afterward, when he came forth from the tent, his face would be shining as it was when he descended from Mt. Sinai. In other words, Moses would talk with God in the *Mishkan* in the same manner as he did on the mountain. It is from this text, which emphasized the "meeting" of God with Moses, that the *Mishkan* became known as the "tent of meeting" (אֹהֶל מוֹעֵד, *'ohel mô'eid*).

I do not think it too far fetched to suggest that this arrangement foreshadowed the work of our Messiah Yeshua and His presence before the Father as the High Priest of His people. For as we know, the priesthood would be attached to the family of Aaron, not that of Moses, and thus Moses acts as a "high priest," not on the basis of physical lineage, but by direct appointment of God Himself. Yet Moses enters the *Mishkan* and the Most Holy Place, there to speak directly to God Who manifests His visible presence over the Ark, between the cherubim. Moreover, when Moses comes forth from the *Mishkan*, his face shown with the glory of God even as it did when he descended from Mt. Sinai. Likewise, Yeshua, Who does not have His high priestly office on the basis of physical lineage but by divine appointment (Heb 8:4), now "appears in the presence of God for us" (Heb 9:24). And Paul, comparing our Messiah to Moses, speaks of the "glory of God shining in the face of Yeshua" (2Cor 4:6), once again paralleling Moses.

But why would Moses need to enter the tent of meeting to receive further instructions from God? Had not God given the Torah to Moses on the mountain? Most likely, what was needed were instructions and commandments for the application of the Torah in various life settings. We see Moses petitioning Adonai regarding the inheritance of the daughters of Zelophehad (Num 27), as well as what to do with the man who was gathering wood on the Sabbath (Num 15). In each of these cases, Moses receives direct communication from God as to the application of various Torah commandments. Thus, once Moses received further specifics from God, explicating the application of the Torah already given, these became part of the written Torah for future generations.

The *Mishkan*, then, was to function in its primary duty of creating a place where God and Israel could meet (through Israel's chosen representatives)—where God's holiness remained unblemished, and where atonement was made for Israel's sins. The table of the bread of presence, the altar of incense, and the golden menorah, all add to the symbolism of the *Mishkan* as a moveable Mt. Sinai. Like the elders who ascended the mountain, so the representatives of Israel (the priests) would maintain a "covenant meal" with God. Like the cloud on Sinai, so the altar of incense would create a cloud. And like the fire of Sinai, so the menorah would give forth its light. In all of these, the very glory of God, first seen on the mountain, would dwell among men. Here, as we shall see in the coming *parashot*, is the continuing revelation of Immanuel.

Parashah 64
Triennial Cycle

Exodus 26:31–27:19

Haftarah: Ezekiel 16:10–19 | Apostolic: Hebrew 8:1–6

… that I May Dwell Among Them

The previous *parashah* contains the statement of HaShem upon which the entire meaning and purpose of the *Mishkan* (Tabernacle) rests: Exodus 25:8, "Let them construct a sanctuary for Me, that I may dwell among them." In contrast to all of the pagan gods who dwelt in seclusion, far away from mortal man, HaShem, known as the God of Abraham, Isaac, and Jacob, has as His eternal purpose to dwell in the midst of His people. The reason the pagan gods do not want much to do with mankind, and will come close only when enticed by offerings, etc., is that they fear common man will make them common. Rather than soil their reputation with the lowly domain of mortals, the demon gods live in seclusion (or so the myth goes) maintaining their "grandeur" unsoiled.

But the God of Israel has no fear of being changed: He is the Unchanged One, and the One who brings about change. He comes to dwell with His people not for His own advantage, for He is in need of nothing, but for the sake of mankind. He comes to bring to them the ability to fulfill their created purpose—to know Him, and to be known of Him. He comes to give them not only salvation from their foes, but eternal salvation for their souls, offering unparalleled joys in this world and in the world to come.

But His coming to dwell with man requires that man prepare Him a place—a sanctuary (מִקְדָּשׁ, *miqdash*), a place set apart—a "holy" place, for His coming. In all of His eternal love, He is never diminished in His infinite holiness. Here, in the dwelling of God with man, is the focal point of all the Torah. Every regulation, every clean and unclean stipulation, the Shabbat and all the Moedim—all of these focus inevitably upon this one thing: creating a holy place for God to dwell in our midst.

Yet even the *Miqdash*, the *Mishkan* constructed according to God's plan—even this is not the end in itself. For the dwelling of God with man will not be seen in all of its fulness until sin is no more, and the *'olam haba* (world to come) is a reality. There, in the new heavens and earth, there will no longer be the need for a *Mishkan* or a *Heichal* (Temple). No more will there be levels of holiness so clearly delineated in the Tabernacle and subsequent Temples. In the *'olam haba* all will be holy as He is holy; all will be sanctified and fully set apart to Him. There will be no need for separation, because there will be no uncleanness. John alerts us to this when, in describing the new Jerusalem, he says: " I saw no temple in it, for ADONAI El Elyon and the Lamb are its temple" (Rev 21:22).

But until that time, if God is to dwell among His people, sinners as they are, there must be a place of holiness, a *Miqdash*, for His dwelling. This is pictured first in the *Mishkan* (Tabernacle), then in the *Heichal* (Temple) and finally in Yeshua in Whom the fullness of God dwelt in bodily form (Col 2:9). In the incarnation this mystery of the dwelling of God with man took on the most profound measures, for in His humanity He yet remained one with HaShem, and in this mystery demonstrated in the most awesome of ways the purpose of God to dwell among His people.

But how is God dwelling with us now? How can His presence be in our midst if their is no *Miqdash*? On the one hand, He dwells with us as He has always dwelt with His people, in His Ruach (Spirit). Again, mysteriously, the presence of God is evident in the indwelling Spirit of God. Urging, comforting, leading, convicting, illuminating—all of these activities of the Spirit are the inevitable result of God's presence with us. But His presence with us in the Spirit of Messiah (by whom Yeshua is also present with us, Matt 28:19-20), is not in the same measure as His presence will be in our midst when the *Miqdash* is re-established. And His presence in the coming *Miqdash* is not as full as in the *'olam haba*. In each case, the one hastens to the other, and we therefore all await the final victory in the world to come, and the complete, unhindered presence of the Almighty.

If then the Tabernacle and Temple are given to teach us about the presence of God among His people, and therefore are foreshadows of Yeshua Himself (Who embodied the presence of God with man), how are we to "unpack" the message God intends? First, we should be cautioned away from the idea that every minute detail of the Tabernacle must have some reference to the person or work of Yeshua. Some, believing this to be true, have resorted to silly interpretations of the Tabernacle and its furnishings to find a link to Yeshua. More than likely, the specific descriptions of the Tabernacle, and its ornate furnishings, were simply to teach that the place of God's dwelling among men is unique—unlike any other. This, perhaps more than anything, points to the uniqueness of Yeshua as the "only begotten Son of God."

But there is another "big picture" lesson to learn as well: that God dwells with His people, but He does so only according to His terms and not theirs. The precise detail required in the *Mishkan* should remind us that God, not man, has designed the manner in which He will dwell with His people. All too often we fall into thinking that as long as we do "our best" or build His dwelling "with honest intentions," this will be acceptable. If there is an overarching lesson we learn from the *Mishkan*, it is that God defines His dwelling place, not man. We must therefore seek to conform to His ways if we intend to make a place for Him to dwell with us.

Likewise, we learn that He actually provides His people with the means to follow His instructions to build Him a dwelling place. He reveals to them His exact instructions and inspires craftsmen (such as Bezalel) by His Ruach in order that the *Mishkan* might be built as He required. Thus, the building of the Tabernacle was a cooperation between God and His redeemed ones. In similar manner, our own growth in holiness is a partnership with God. He has recreated us, and empowered us by His Spirit for holiness, but He commands us to engage in the disciplines of holiness in order to grow spiritually. We are to "grow in the grace and knowledge" of our Master (2Pet 3:18). This involves regular study and application of the Scriptures, consistent prayer and worship, yielding ourselves to the will of God, serving Him through obedience by doing the *mitzvot*, and guarding our hearts from the entanglements of the world.

It is instructive to note that commands given to Moses regarding the construction of the *Mishkan* (which began in the previous *parashah* and continue in the present one) are done so from the perspective of God Himself. That is, the instructions begin with the Ark, proceed to the veil (כַּפֹּרֶת, *kepporet*), then to the Holy Place and its furnishing, then to the doorway and coverings of the *Mishkan* itself, and finally to the altar of sacrifice in the courtyard and the barrier of pillars and hangings that separated the entire structure from the common space of the Israelite camp. The instructions start in the Most Holy Place, where the presence of God dwelt over the Cherubim, and work their way out to the courtyard where the people would congregate. This, once again, emphasizes the method of God's self-revelation: man does not find God, but God reveals Himself to man.

Thus, in our *parashah*, we are specifically instructed about the veil that would separate the Holy Place from the Most Holy Place, the Altar of Sacrifice, and the manner in which the courtyard would be separated by a surrounding "fence" made of pillars draped with linen cloth.

The altar was to be 5 cubits square, thus measuring about 7.5 feet on each side. It was 3 cubits high, making it about 4.5 feet high. The wood (*acacia*, very strong) was overlaid with bronze. Bronze was used extensively in the Ancient Near East, being easily alloyed and able to withstand higher temperatures. Some take the bronze netting to describe a kind of "grating" for the fire box, while others (mostly rabbinic) take it to be decorative on the outside of the Altar. Whatever the case, it is clear that the Altar could be disassembled, making it easier to carry.

The placement of the Altar is clear: it is to be just inside the opening of the courtyard, that is, the first thing encountered by the worshipers. This emphasizes the centrality of the Altar, and thus of sacrifice in the whole scheme of Israelite worship. That the laver is put further inside the courtyard, and not in front of the Altar shows that the washing required was connected with taking the sacrifice (symbolized by the blood) into the *Mishkan*, not for preparation to offer the sacrifice. That is, the laver is not for the Israelite, but for the priest. Thus, sacrifice precedes cleansing in the Israelite *Mishkan* and not *visa versa*.

That the *Mishkan* itself is divided into two compartments is seen to be very important in the whole outline of Exodus and the Torah. The veil that separated the two areas is described in detail, being woven of the same materials as the other inner tapestries, and having the design of cherubim woven into it. It was to be hung upon four pillars which were placed so that the veil would hang immediately under the clasps which joined the coverings of the *Mishkan*. There is no indication that the veil itself was in any way divided, so entrance into the Most Holy Place must have been at the side.

When Solomon built the first Temple, he did not divide the Holy Place from the Most Holy Place with a veil, but with a solid wall one cubit thick, into which were hung doors as an entrance into the Most Holy Place. The exact method of hanging the doors and their style is debated (cf. 1Kings 6:31-32), but they were of such a value that Hezekiah was compelled to give them as tribute to the King of Assyria (2Kings 18:16). They may have been 20-30 feet tall. Being overlaid with gold meant they rivalled any doors of any temple in the Ancient Near East, and would have been very heavy.

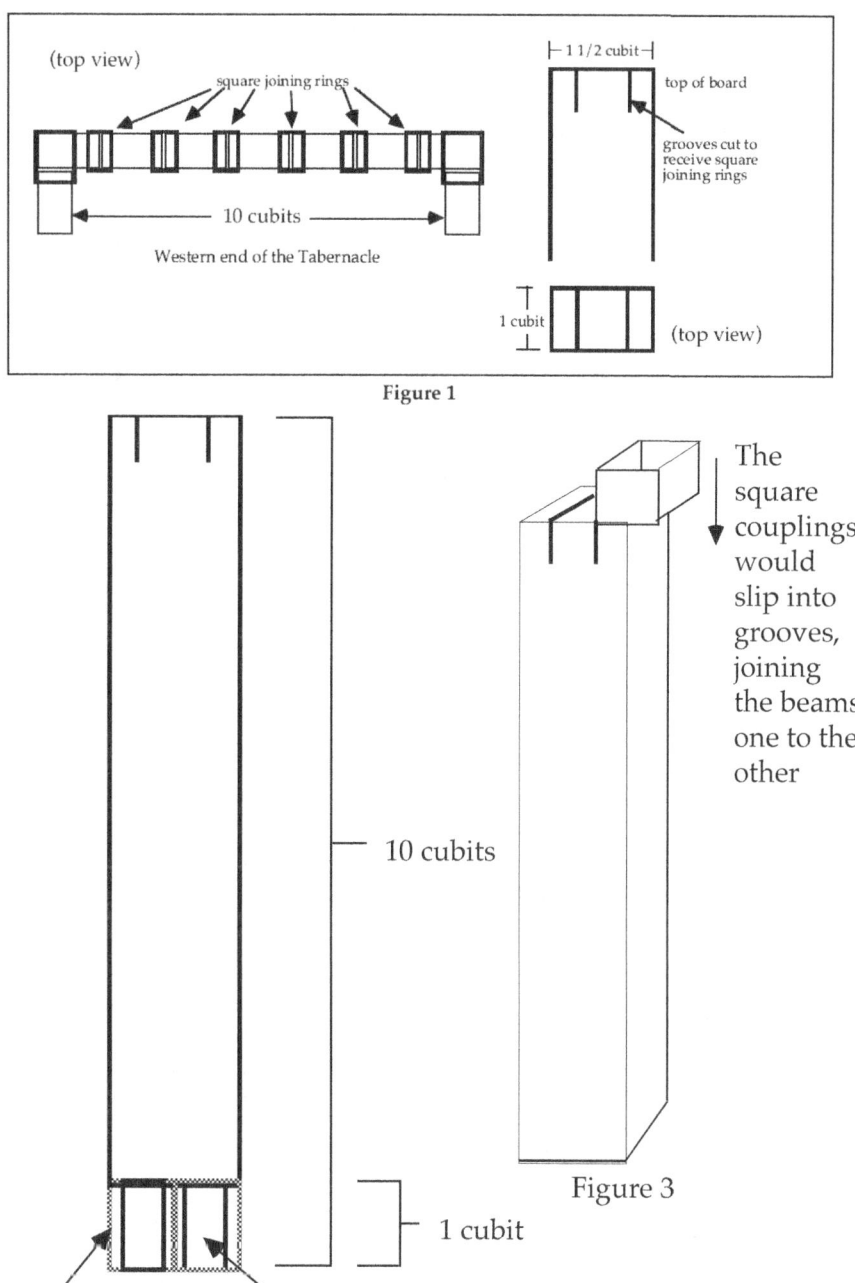

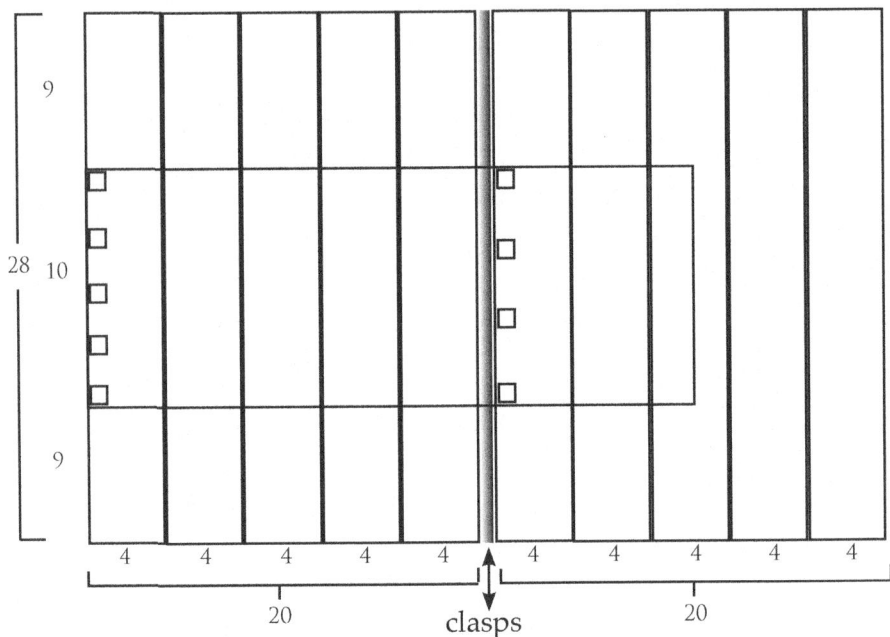

Figure 4
Coverings (Tapestries) of the Mishkan

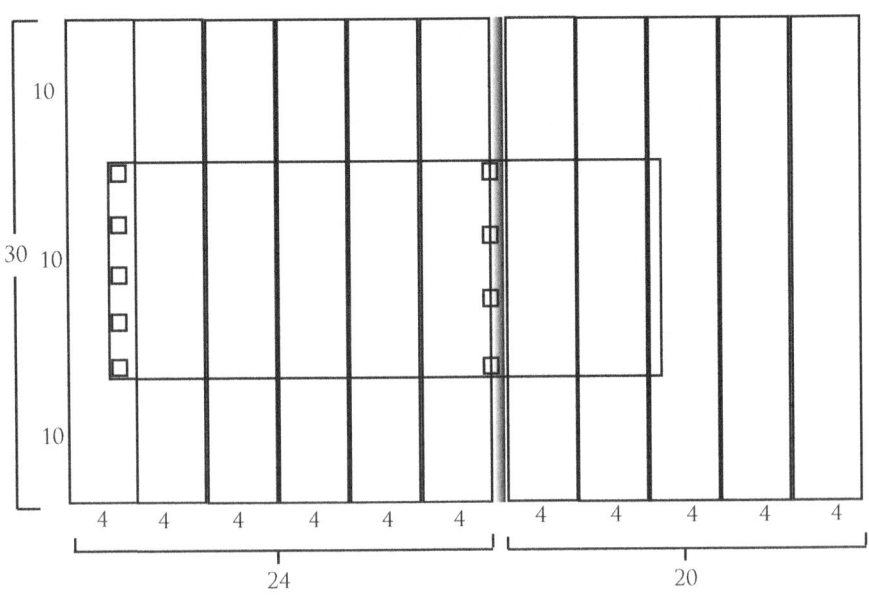

Figure 5
Outer (woolen) Coverings of the Mishkan

Figure 6

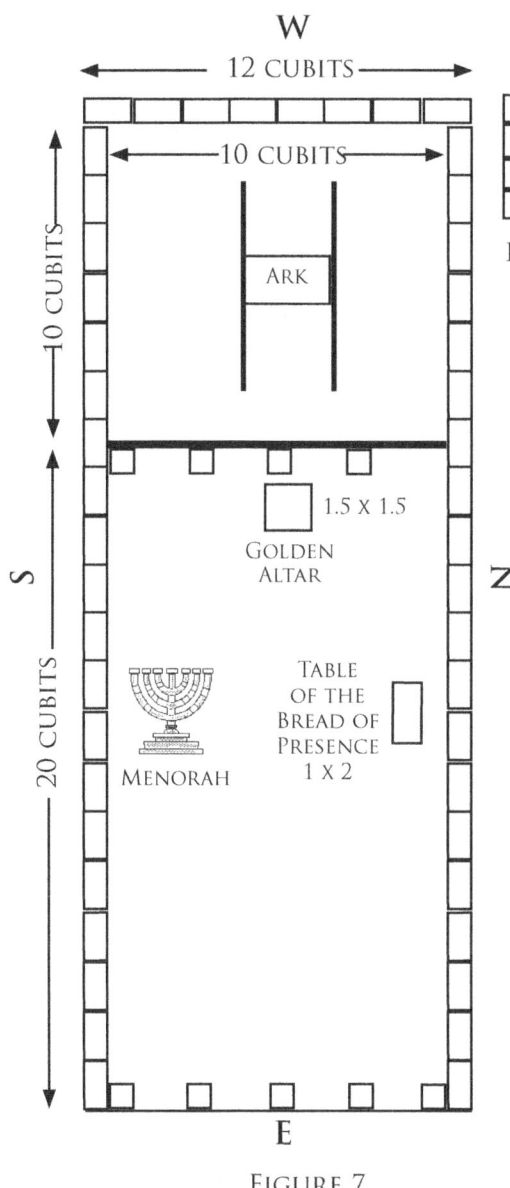

Possible arrangement of the bars (בְּרִיחִם) that held the wall beams

Figure 7

There are a number of issues that confront us when we attempt to understand all of the construction details given to Moses. It seems clear, however, that those things about which we cannot be certain were made clear to Moses by having seen the model of the Tabernacle on the mountain.

First, the idea that there was some type of interwoven frames to secure the top of each of the beams is speculative, but seems to be implied by 26:24 where it states regarding the corner beams that they were "joined together at the top" with a ring (טַבַּעַת, tabba'at). The special notice regarding the corners must be that the corner beams had a special mortise at the top for connecting the two walls.

Second, it is never stated whether the pillars that hold the *perochet* separating the Holy and Most Holy are inside or outside of the veil. Figure 6 has them on the outside, but others think they were on the inside. The arrangement of the tapestries and the outer woollen covers were such that the clasps of each did not fall directly upon each other. The outer coverings consisted of 11 panels, while the tapestries were only 10 panels. The eleventh panel of the outer covering folded in half over the front of the *mishkan*. This shifted the entire covering two cubits, so that the clasps of the outer coverings were two cubits offset from the inner tapestries. The exact reason for this is not stated, but it would have kept light from coming in through the seam, making the only light in the Most Holy Place that of the *Shekinah*, and in the Holy Place that of the *menorah*.

Third, for the arrangement of the pillars holding the *perochet* and the outer veil or curtain there are given no specific details. Were they an equal distance apart? It is clear that the *perochet* was not divided (as is typical of a modern-day stage curtain), so the *cohen gadol* would have entered from the side rather than from the middle. It may have been that the pillars were arranged to accommodate this, and they are so arranged in Figure 6. The pillars at the opening of the *Mishkan* may have been evenly arranged, since there were five in a 10 cubit span.

The silver sockets into which the beams were placed to form the walls of the *Mishkan* were one talent of silver each (Ex 38:27). A talent was approximately 150 lbs., and calculating the size of the beam (1 x 1.5 cubits), and presuming the sockets were the same width and half the length (since there were two per beam), it is clear that they were hollow in order to receive the tendons of the beams. If the dimensions were 1x1x1.5 cubits, the walls of the sockets would have been approximately .9 cm thick. Rashi taught that they were 1/4 cubit thick, which would mean that the walls of the socket would also need to be hollow, for solid walls 1/4 cubit thick would result in the base weighing nine talents (or 1382 lbs.).

As we study the specific instructions given for the construction of the *Mishkan*, we are struck with how detailed they were, how costly the construction was, and how the whole arrangement was marked by ornate beauty befitting a King. In the middle of the desert, where the arid conditions made life difficult, a "palace" was erected, for the King desired to go with His people and to turn the desert into a place of joy and fellowship. And the palace was not simply for His dwelling, but a place where He welcomed the people in, meeting with them (as symbolized in the priesthood, the Bread of the Presence, and the sweet smell of incense), offering them the assurance of His faithful protection.

Parashah Twenty
תְּצַוֶּה – T'TZAVEH

"YOU SHALL COMMAND"
Exodus 27:20–30:10

In the Triennial Cycle
there are three Parashot

27:20-28:43 | 29:1-46 | 30:1-10

Parashah 65
Triennial Cycle

Exodus 27:20–28:43

Haftarah: Hosea 14:4–9 | Apostolic: Hebrews 4:14–16

The Garments of the High Priest

Our Torah portion this Shabbat deals almost exclusively with the garments of the High Priest—Aaron and his sons. Described in detail, there is every reason to believe that the garments worn by the High Priest are used by God to reveal both the purpose of the High Priest's intercession, as well as the manner in which this intercession would be made. It seems most clear that the details given are ultimately to help describe and define the work of the final High Priest Who, from the priesthood of Melchizedek, would bring about the redemption of which Aaron and his sons were types.

But the opening paragraph describes the oil for the menorah, and the duty of Aaron and his sons to maintain the menorah, keeping it lit as a constant light before HaShem. The oil, provided by the people, was used to keep the lights burning "from evening until morning," a phrase well known from the opening story of creation. Since the text indicates that the lamps are to burn "continually," the phrase "from evening to morning" must indicate "every day."

The menorah was the only light in the Holy Place aside from the burning coals of the altar of incense. That the people brought the oil for the lamp shows that they participated in making the priestly service possible, for apart from the menorah the Holy Place would be dark. Since the menorah was fashioned after a living almond branch, it symbolized life. Indeed, in the Ancient Near East, "light" speaks of life, while "darkness" speaks of death. The same is true in the Tanach (cf. Job 28:30, 33; Is 9:1, cp. Lk 1:79; Ps 23:4; Is 53:10-11 in Lxx and Qumran). While the work of the priests regularly included death (sacrifice), the purpose was ultimately for life.

We know that the High Priest foreshadowed Yeshua—this is clear from the Apostolic Writings (particularly Hebrews). How much the people of Ancient Israel recognized that the High Priest was a foreshadowing of Messiah and His priestly work is not certain, but it would seem very likely that some, and perhaps more than we think, recognized in the ornate garments and regulations of the High Priest that he stood as a picture of the final redemption that would be effected by Messiah. Indeed, "Messiah," meaning "anointed one," figures in very closely to the consecration of the High Priest through anointing oil. That this anointing was significant is clear by its mention in Psalm 133.

The garments prescribed for the High Priest are said to be given "for glory and for beauty" (28:2 לְכָבוֹד וּלְתִפְאָרֶת, l*chavôd ul*tifaret*). The first word, כָּבוֹד, *kavôd*, has as much the sense of "honor" as "glory." The office of High Priest was to have a special honor, accorded to it by the unique garments worn. The second word, תִּפְאֶרֶת, *tiferet*, means "beauty," "ornate," and describes something of extra-ordinary splendor. Clearly the High Priest was set apart from all the other priests by these designations.

It can hardly be missed that such designations set the High Priest apart as well for the duties he would perform for the people. They, dependent upon him for the intercessory work he would do, had to rest assured that God would be pleased with him, and by His pleasure forgive their sins. He acted independent of them: he did not take their sacrifices but concerned himself entirely with sacrifices which he alone brought, particularly on Yom HaKippurim. Indeed, he prefigured the coming Promised One Who would deal with sin in a final and complete fashion.

It should also be noted that three times the High Priest is said to function as a priest "for Me," (לְכַהֲנוֹ־לִי, l*chahanô-li* and similar constructions) that is, to minister before God (28:3–4, 41). Thus, we may presume that the garments herein described function both to set the High Priest apart as well as to reveal the character of holiness required for his special and unique duties.

What might each of the garments suggest regarding the office and service of the High Priest? The turban and crown upon it (on which was written קֹדֶשׁ לַיהוה, *kodesh la'donai*), like the colors of the outer garments, bespeak "royalty" and give the High Priest the look of a King.

The Ephod marks the High Priest out as the one who carried the people of Israel before the Lord, for to the Ephod was attached the breastplate upon which precious stones were mounted, each representing one of the Twelve tribes of Israel, being engraved as a signet or seal (cf. Song of Songs 8:6). The word itself (אֵפֹד, '*eiphod*) is derived from the verb אפד, '*apad,* meaning "to fit closely," "to secure an outer garment," "to gird" (cf. Ex 29:5; Lev 8:7). Two shoulder stones, also engraved with the names of the tribes, are attached to the Ephod and carried upon the shoulders. Thus, Israel is borne by the High Priest upon his shoulders (strength) and upon his heart (covenant loyalty).

Likewise, the Urim and Tummim are contained in the breastplate, indicating that the High Priest was the one through whom God's direct revelation would come. The outer Tunic was made entirely of wool dyed with *techeilet*. It therefore marked the High Priest as connected with the "heavenly" realm (for the *techeilet* was the color of the sky). The linen tunic, made of pure white linen, was indicative of the purity of the High Priest, as were the linen breaches worn as an under garment. This emphasizes the personal purity needed to accomplish the priestly intercession for the people. That he wore no shoes teaches that his duties were performed on "holy ground." The sacred nature of his priestly work is thus "before HaShem." In the High Priest, and in him alone, could the people approach the Most High. Consider how this informs Paul's phrase, "in Messiah."

The foreshadowing of Yeshua as the heavenly High Priest is obvious: He is both a King and a Priest (cf. Zech 6:13); He came from the Father; He is man, yet one with the Father: eternal, without beginning. He is therefore sinless while at the same time bearing our sins. He alone carries us before the Father, and only in Him may we have access to God's grace. He is the direct revelation of the Father, and in Him all things are confirmed and established (2Cor 1:20). Apart from His high priestly work, there is no atonement and no forgiveness of sins.

The choice of the *haftarah* for the triennial cycle, Hosea 14:4–9, is not immediately apparent. The connection is based upon v. 6 (v. 7 in the Hebrew), "His shoots will sprout, and his beauty will be like the olive tree and his fragrance like the cedars of Lebanon." Since the Torah *parashah* begins with the commandment for the children of Israel to bring olive oil (שֶׁמֶן זַיִת, *shemen zayit*) for the menorah, the mention of the olive tree (זַיִת, *zayit*) in the Hosea *haftarah* formed the necessary verbal linkage. Beyond that, the beauty ascribed to the garments of the High Priest, and the fact that he represents the tribes of Israel before Adonai, are paralleled in the *haftarah* by the beauty of Israel in the messianic age as they return to Adonai and walk in His ways. Moreover, v. 9 (v. 10 in the Hebrew) contains an admonition to "understand" and to "know them," speaking of the *mitzvot* of the Torah. "For the ways of Adonai (דַּרְכֵי יְהוָה, *darchei* ADONAI) are right (יְשָׁרִים, *y*ᵉ*sharim*), and the righteous will walk in them, but transgressors will stumble in them." Such a command "to know them" was taken by the Sages to mean that even the laws of the Tabernacle and Temple, along with all of the regulations for the sacrifices and priestly service, were to be studied and understood. Thus, we have yet another connection to our Torah *parashah*.

The reason for our choice of Hebrews 4:14–16 is also obvious: from the early chapters of this epistle, Yeshua is seen to be the heavenly High Priest, the One foreshadowed by the earthly High Priest and his service (cf. 2:17; 3:1). But in this text, we see that Yeshua, as our heavenly High Priest, is capable of representing us before the Father because He is Himself one of us. In the mystery of His incarnation, He took on real humanity so that He could fully represent us both in His death as well as in His life. He was "tempted in all things as we are, yet without sin," which though difficult to explain, is nonetheless true. If ever we are tempted to think that Yeshua does not understand our weaknesses, or is somehow unsympathetic to the woes of this fallen world, His incarnation immediately proves otherwise. As "the man Messiah Yeshua" (1Tim 2:5), now at the right hand of the Majesty on high (Heb 1:3), He always lives to make intercession for us (Heb 7:25). Knowing that His work is fully accepted by the Father (Is 53:10–12; Matt 17:5), we may therefore enter into the very presence of the Father with full confidence that we are accepted in the Beloved One (Eph 1:3–5; 2:18; 3:12). This being the case, "let us hold fast our confession!"

Tetzaveh • תצוה

מִצְנֶפֶת, *mitznefet*, "turban" (cf. מִגְבָּעוֹת, *migbaot*, 28:40)

צִיץ, *tzitz*, "crown"

מְעִיל, *m'il*, "linen robe"

חֹשֶׁן מִשְׁפָּט, *choshen mishpat*, "breastplate of justice"

אֵפוֹד, *ephod*, "ephod"

כְּתֹנֶת תַּשְׁבֵּץ, *k'tonet tashbeitz*, "knitted tunic"

bells and pomegranates on hem

linen pants (מִכְנְסֵי בָד, *michn'sei vad*) from the waist to the knee were worn as an under garment

no shoes or sandals described

אַבְנֵטִים, *'avneitim*, "sashes"

Note the difference in English Translations:

NASB	NIV	KJV
ruby	ruby	sardius
topaz	topaz	topaz
emerald	beryl	carbuncle
turquoise	turquoise	emerald
sapphire	sapphire	sapphire
diamond	emerald	diamond
jacinth	jacinth	ligure
agate	agate	agate
amethyst	amethyst	amethyst
beryl	chrysolite	beryl
onyx	onyx	onyx
jasper	jasper	jasper

Urim & Tummim (הָאוּרִים וְהַתֻּמִּים) literally means "lights" and "perfections." Most think they were stones used in some manner to descern God's specific will in a given situation.

The text does not specify which stone was for which tribe. If we presume the tribes were engraved in birth order, and that the order went across from top to bottom, then the following arrangement would ensue. The Sages give at least four different arrangements, including this one:

ruby	Reuben
topaz	Simeon
emerald	Levi
turquoise	Judah
sapphire	Dan
diamond	Naphtali
jacinth	Gad
agate	Asher
amethyst	Issachar
beryl	Zebulun
onyx	Joseph
jasper	Benjamin

Parashah 66
Triennial Cycle

Exodus 29:1–46

Haftarah: Isaiah 61:7-62:5 | Apostolic: Hebrews 2:10-18

Filling the Hands of Aaron & His Sons

Our *parashah* this Shabbat outlines the "ordination" of Aaron and sons as the priests to HaShem. It is instructive for us to remember that the Hebrew term usually translated "ordain" is לְמַלֵּא יָדִים, "to fill the hands." In fact, the sacrifice described as the ordination offering is also called the מִלֻּאִים, *milu'im*, "filling" offering. What does it mean to "fill the hands" when describing the ordination of Aaron and his sons to the priestly office of service? It no doubt emphasizes that the service to which they were ordained was not for themselves, but for others. They were to have their hands full of the offerings the Israelites would bring. Their energies and work would be for the benefit of others, not themselves.

The same lesson is emphasized by the use of unleavened breads in the offerings of ordination. In this case, as in the Pesach offerings, unleavened cakes describe the situation of servanthood, while leavened bread (prescribed in the Shavuot offering) symbolizes the life of freemen whose time is their own, and who can therefore wait for bread to rise before baking. The priestly life is one of service to others, not to self. The priests would not have an inheritance in the Land, nor would they have their own means of support—they would have to depend upon the obedience and faithfulness of the people they served for their food and support.

We should be careful in making applications from this passage not to fall into the trap into which the emerging Christian Church fell prey, i.e., thinking that this describes the leaders of the believing congregation, whom they called "priests" as well as "fathers." For the typological application of Aaron and his sons is not to the leaders of the believing congregation, nor to the congregation itself, but to Yeshua specifically who alone is our High Priest. If we look carefully at the specific ceremony detailed for the inauguration of the High Priest we are confronted once again with Mashiach and His unique work.

Note that the first action taken upon Aaron and his sons is that they are washing in a *mikveh* (29:4). This is a symbol of purity, of ritual acceptance to do the work to which they are being ordained. When Yeshua first emerges to do His public work he requests that John the Baptizer officiate at His public *mikveh*. He is visibly being inaugurated as a priest Who would engage in the business of atonement for His people.

After clothing the priests in their vestments, oil was to be put upon them as an anointing (וּמָשַׁחְתָּ אֹתוֹ, *umashachta 'oto*, "and you shall anoint him"). They were to be *meshuchim* (cf. Num 3:3), anointed ones foreshadowing Mashiach, the Anointed One. When Yeshua came up out of the water of the *mikveh*, the Ruach descended upon Him in the form of a dove (the sacrifice described for the very poor, cf. Lev 14:30). His anointing by the Ruach once again marks Him as being ordained for His priestly function. Psalm 133 describes the oil of anointing upon Aaron's head, running down upon his beard and upon his robes. When the Head is anointed, the body is likewise anointed.

The next activity in the ordination process of Aaron and his sons was a sacrifice for their own iniquity (29:10-14). The writer of Hebrews makes it clear that Yeshua needed no sin-offering for His own sins, for He was without sin (7:27ff).

Two rams were set apart for the inauguration of the priests: one as a whole-burnt offering (עֹלָה, *'olah*) and one as a wave-offering (תְּנוּפָה, *tenuphah*). The whole burnt offering is an offering of complete and full dedication to HaShem. This in every way characterized the life of Yeshua. From His earliest years when He recognized that the Father's purpose in Him was His divine priority (Luke 2:49), to His final submission to death, His life was in every way characterized as an *'olah*.

The *tenuphah* (wave-offering) is specifically described as a "sweet smelling aroma" to HaShem. The *tenuphah* signals the acceptance of the offering before God, an offering which He willingly accepts and is therefore satisfied with its outcome. Do we not hear the *bat kol* (heavenly voice) of HaShem directed to Yeshua: "This is the Son I love, listen to Him" (Matthew 17:5)? Yeshua as the High Priest to HaShem is a "sweet smelling aroma," His life of holiness and purity was, in every way, befitting the Father He served.

From this second ram, the *tenuphah* offering, the blood was to be put upon the lobe of the right ear, upon the right thumb and the right big toe. In this case, the application of the blood signals dedication, or sanctification unto HaShem. The ear attaches to the Hebrew concept of "hearing" which signifies "to obey." The priest would thus listen to the words of God and perform them. Blood on the ear bespeaks obedience to God and Yeshua is the only perfect example of that. All that He "heard" He did. His "ear" was in every way perfectly sanctified.

The blood of the *tenuphah* offering was also put on the right thumb and the right big toe. In ancient times, conquering enemies would sever thumb and toe to debilitate their captives. The thumb and toe were recognized as necessary for one's full ability to carry out life's tasks. The thumb governs the work of the hands, and the big toe makes the feet strong for work. Putting blood on each signified that the work of hands and feet were to be sanctified to HaShem. The Priest's life energies were to be expended in service to the Lord.

How well we see this exemplified in our High Priest, Yeshua. He clearly stated that He did all that the Father directed Him to do (John 8:28, 38; 14:10, 31). All that was symbolized in the inauguration of Aaron is realized in the life of Yeshua.

But it is not only realized in His life, but also in His death. Consider the agony of the Incarnate One, mystery beyond our comprehension: Son of God, son of man. "And He went a little beyond them, and fell on His face and prayed, saying, "My Father, if it is possible, let this cup pass from Me; yet not as I will, but as You will." (Matt. 26:39) Here the sanctified One obeys even to the point of death, and death on an execution stake. His obedience is perfect. "Having loved His own, He loved them fully" (John 13:1).

The fat of the *tenuphah* ram is put upon the altar and burned up in a quick flash of flame to HaShem (29:22ff). In this sacrificial display the full inner angst of dedication is symbolized. See in this the words of Yeshua's cry from the execution stake, "it is finished."

But the *tenuphah* is not entirely consumed. The priest would receive his due: the breast and the right-thigh, the choice portions of the sacrifice would belong to the priest for his food, for his enjoyment, for his sustenance.

Consider the remarkable words in the Epistle of Hebrews 12:2, "fixing our eyes on Yeshua, the author and perfecter of faith, Who for the joy set before Him endured the cross, despising the shame, and has sat down at the right hand of the throne of God." Here the phrase "who for the joy set before Him" should be translated "who in exchange for the joy set before Him," the Greek word ἀντὶ, *anti*, having its primary meaning "instead of," "in the place of," and is used in this way in v. 16 where Esau gives his birthright *for* ("in exchange for") a bowl of soup. Thus, Yeshua exchanges the sufferings of the cross for the joy set before Him—His portion, what He receives from the sacrifice. And His portion is nothing less than the people for whom He died, who would forever be His. It may be difficult to comprehend, but we are the "joy" for which He was willing to suffer. It is in this that we find our true "self-worth," for we are the joy of His heart, redeemed by His blood, purified by His intercession, and made ready for eternity with Him in the world to come.

Note carefully that not only does the Priest enjoy his portion of the *tenuphah* offering, but all who obtain atonement by the sacrifice also eat of it. The only one who is excluded is the foreigner (זָר, *zar*, a term often describing something illicit, or having connection to idolatry), the one outside of the covenant. The place of forgiveness, the place of atonement—the place of fellowship and shalom is only within the covenant, not outside of it. Only covenant members can partake of the life the High Priest offers in the sacrifice. "I am the way, the truth, and the life–no one comes to the Father but through Me" (John 14:6).

The *parashah* ends with a description of the תָּמִיד, *tamid* (daily) offerings. Why? Why are these put next to the ordination of Aaron and his sons? Because the lessons learned from that event are to be rehearsed every day—the coming of the High Priest was to be the central event in all of the daily activities in the Temple. The whole story is about Yeshua—the entire priestly service was given as a foreshadow of the Messiah. If we miss this, we miss the primary and most important lessons God intends us to see in the Tabernacle and Priesthood.

Ordination of Leaders

As noted above, the primary lesson we are to learn from the ordination of the Aaronic priest is that of Yeshua's own unique position as our *cohen gadol* (high priest). But we should not overlook the fact that in God's historic unfolding of His plan of redemption, revealed through the Tabernacle and Temple, and the priestly service that took place there, He selected men (priests) to serve the people, and He did so by setting them apart through the ceremony of ordination ("filling the hands"). Similar rituals of setting apart leaders and kings are noted as well. Kings were anointed (1Sam. 15:1; 2Sam. 2:4; 5:3; 1Kings 1:34; 19:15-16; 2Kings 23:30; Psa. 18:50) as were prophets (1Kings 19:16; 1Chr. 16:22; Psa. 105:15) in public ceremonies.

In an interesting ceremony, Moses, just before he dies, passes his authority to Joshua:

> Now Joshua the son of Nun was filled with the spirit (Spirit?) of wisdom, for Moses had laid his hands on him; and the sons of Israel listened to him and did as the LORD had commanded Moses. (Deut 34:9)

Here, the laying of Moses' hands upon Joshua, symbolically endowed him with the authority to lead the people of Israel in the place of Moses. The text makes it clear that the endowment of the "Spirit of wisdom" to Joshua came as a result of Moses laying his hands upon him (כִּי־סָמַךְ מֹשֶׁה אֶת־יָדָיו עָלָיו). [All of the English translations use a lower-case "s" on "spirit," but it seems warranted, in the context, and with other biblical parallels, that we should understand the word here to be speaking of the רוּחַ אֱלֹהִים, *ruach Elohim,* the Spirit of God.] The verb סָמַךְ, *samach,* means "to lean upon," an act that symbolically transferred the "weight" of one's authority to another person. Numbers 27 also describes the ceremony of commissioning Joshua:

> 18 So Adonai said to Moses, "Take Joshua the son of Nun, a man in whom is the Spirit, and lay your hand on him; 19 and have him stand before Eleazar the priest and before all the congregation, and commission [צָוָה] him in their sight. 20 You shall put some of your authority on him, in order that all the congregation of the sons of Israel may obey him. 21 Moreover, he shall stand before Eleazar the priest, who shall inquire for him by the judgment of the Urim before Adonai. At his command they shall go out and at his command they shall come in, both he and the sons of Israel with him, even all the congregation." 22 Moses did just as Adonai commanded him; and he took Joshua and set him before Eleazar the priest and before all the congregation. 23 Then he laid his hands on him and commissioned [צָוָה] him, just as Adonai had spoken through Moses.

Here, then, Moses commissions Joshua to stand "in his place." The people were to accept the leadership of Joshua as equal to that of Moses. It would seem evident that the ceremony of "laying on of hands" was taken from the same action done when one brought a sacrifice (e.g., Lev 1:4). When the offerer "laid hands" upon the head of the sacrificial animal, he was symbolically transferring himself upon the animal, so that the animal now represented the one bringing the offering. In the same way, when Moses laid hands upon Joshua, he was stating that Joshua would now rule in his stead.

This ceremony of Moses' laying hands upon Joshua became the template for later rabbinic ordination. Using this same ritual as their guide, the Sages also ordained or commissioned their students through the "laying on of hands," called סְמִיכָה, *s^emichah,* from the same verb סָמַךְ, *samach,* "to lean upon." Though there is no clear evidence that such an ordination ceremony was extant among the Sages of the 1st Century, it is clear that so-called "rabbinic ordination" was common by the Talmudic era. The point of Rabbinic ordination is that when the Sage ordained his disciple, he gave to that disciple the right to speak *in his name.* Thus, even if the disciple were to teach something that his mentor had never taught, it was to be received *as though* his mentor had, in fact, taught it. Of course, a disciple would never think of absolutely contradicting the mentor who had ordained him. If it appeared that he had contradicted his mentor, later interpreters went to great lengths to show that the two were, in reality, non-contradictory.

It is interesting to parallel the times in the Apostolic Scriptures where the idea of "laying on of hands" is found, taken no doubt from the pattern of ordination given described in our *parashah*. Throughout the book of Acts, for instance, the laying on of hands conferred gifts of the Spirit. Note the following examples:

> Then they began laying their hands on them, and they were receiving the Holy Spirit. (Acts 8:17)

> So Ananias departed and entered the house, and after laying his hands on him said, "Brother Saul, the Master Yeshua, who appeared to you on the road by which you were coming, has sent me so that you may regain your sight and be filled with the Holy Spirit." (Acts 9:17)

> When they heard this, they were baptized in the name of the Master Yeshua. And when Paul had laid his hands upon them, the Holy Spirit came on them, and they began speaking with tongues and prophesying. (Acts 19:5–6)

The obvious background to these texts are the examples of "laying on of hands" found in the Tanach, and in our Torah *parashah* specifically. Even as Moses' commissioning of Joshua resulted in Joshua being "filled with the Spirit of wisdom" in order to fulfill the office to which he was being appointed, so the similar events noted in Acts resulted in the enabling power of the Holy Spirit.

In the Pauline epistles, we find notice that Timothy was commissioned by the "laying on of the hands of the council of elders" (1Tim 4:14; 2Tim 1:6). Interestingly, by this ceremony, Timothy received a "spiritual gift," apparently given to him for the task to which he had been appointed, namely, carrying on the apostolic duty of teaching and training teachers in the Apostolic message (1Tim 1:3ff; 2Tim 2:1ff). Likewise, Paul and Barnabas are commissioned for their mission through the laying on of hands by the leaders at Antioch:

> While they were ministering to the Lord and fasting, the Holy Spirit said, "Set apart for Me Barnabas and Saul for the work to which I have called them." Then, when they had fasted and prayed and laid their hands on them, they sent them away. (Acts 13:2–3)

Thus, in the Apostolic Scriptures, we see that the pattern first begun by Moses commissioning Joshua is followed in the commissioning of men for leadership positions and ministry within the messianic communities. The post-destruction rabbinic Judaism incorporated a similar ceremony of ordination for those men granted teaching authority, but there is no indication that the rabbinic ceremony was seen as endowing the one being commissioned with a specific endowment of the Ruach.

The biblical "laying on of hands" apparently accomplished two things: 1) it endowed the man with the spiritual gifting necessary for his appointed tasks, and 2) it publicly commissioned or ordained him with the authority to accomplish his duties.

We should note several important aspects in the commissioning or ordaining of men for leadership and mission. First, there were no "lone rangers." Joshua did not rise to leadership by his own prowess or campaign. He received his commission from Moses at the direct command of God. Likewise, the men chosen to care for the widows in Acts 6 were commissioned by the Apostles. They did not personally take the responsibility upon themselves. And even Paul and Barnabas were duly commissioned by the leaders of the congregation that sent them forth. In the same manner, Timothy was commissioned by the council of elders (perhaps from Lystra, Acts 16:1ff) for the work he was to do at Ephesus. Thus, the authority of leadership within the believing community is conferred by the existing leaders and community itself—it is not something anyone can rightfully obtain on his own.

Second, those ordained to positions of leadership or ministry are chosen because they have demonstrated the necessary character and giftings to accomplish the task. The men chosen in Acts 6 were those who were "full of the Spirit and of wisdom, whom we may put in charge of this task" (Acts 6:3). In like manner, Timothy was admonished to find "faithful men" (2Tim 2:2) to whom he could entrust the Apostolic message and *halachah*.

Third, the commissioning of men to leadership and ministry was a recognition that God had appointed them for this task. When Moses laid his hands upon Joshua, it was because God had chosen Joshua to take Moses' place. And when Paul and Barnabas were commissioned for their mission, it was because the Holy Spirit had indicated that He had separated them (sanctified them) for this task. Thus, ordination to leadership and ministry is first and foremost a public recognition of the evident will of God for the one ordained. His commission is first and foremost from God as it is recognized and thus verified by the community.

Finally, the ordination of a man to a position of leadership or ministry is part of the necessary equipping of that man for the duties to which he is commissioned. Timothy received a "spiritual gift" as a result of the laying on of hands by the council of elders, and Joshua received the "Spirit of wisdom" through his ordination by Moses. I take this to mean, not that Joshua lacked the presence of the Spirit before his ordination, but that by the laying on of hands, he received the confirmation of God Himself, and was therefore assured that the Spirit would aid Him in completing his duties. I would think that the same was true for Timothy. Thus Paul reminds Timothy of his having been commissioned by the laying on of hands (2Tim 1:6), a commissioning that confirmed God's pleasure in the matter, and he could therefore be confident that God would provide divine help and assistance for his work. As such, a man who is commissioned to the task of leading God's people must see his duties as first and foremost the fulfillment of a divine appointment. This being the case, in the same way that a man is commissioned to an office of leadership by authority outside of himself, so he is not free to leave that position of responsibility apart from being released by those same authorities. The phenomenon common in our day in which leaders, from their own desires and initiative, move from one congregation to another, finds no basis in the Scriptures.

In summary, then, God is pleased to use common people, equipped through the gifting of His Spirit, to accomplish His work and purposes. In the case of those who take on leadership positions, the authority they acquire as leaders is bestowed through the public recognition of God's will in appointing them as leaders, being ordained to their tasks by the existing leadership and confirmed by the voice of those they lead.

PARASHAH 67
TRIENNIAL CYCLE

EXODUS 30:1–10

HAFTARAH: MALACHI 1:11-2:7 | APOSTOLIC: REVELATION 8:1-5

The Altar of Incense

Our *parashah* this Shabbat deals exclusively with the altar of incense: "Moreover, you shall make an altar as a place for burning incense…" The altar of incense is one cubit square (1 cubit = approx 18-21 inches), standing two cubits high. It was made of acacia wood (שִׁטִּים) overlaid with gold. Like the Altar of Sacrifice, the table for the Bread of the Presence, and the Ark, the Altar of Incense was fitted with rings and poles for carrying.

The placement of the Altar of Incense is stated to be "in front of the veil that is near the ark of the testimony, in front of the mercy seat that is over the ark of the testimony, where I will meet with you." The veil is said to be "near the ark of testimony" but the Hebrew has לִפְנֵי הַפָּרֹכֶת אֲשֶׁר עַל־אֲרֹן הָעֵדֻת, (literally) "before the *parochet* which is upon the ark of the testimony." Rashi notes that the description of its placement was so that it would not be moved away from the veil. The Talmud notes (b.*Yoma* 33b) that this description marks its placement between the menorah and the table. The point is surely that its placement was to connect it with the Ark of Testimony, the idea being that the incense burned daily was to be vitally connected to the once-a-year activity (on Yom Kippur) when the *cohen hagadol* would apply the blood to the *kaporet* or mercy seat. In this the lesson is learned that the atonement made at Yom Kippur was continually accepted by HaShem throughout the year, the incense a constant reminder that the Almighty was willing to dwell among the children of Israel on the basis of this atonement that He had accepted.

It is not difficult to see how this foreshadowed the saving work of our Messiah Yeshua. For though His atoning death was a one-time event, its atonement is constantly applied to His people through His constant intercession. In this picture the intercessory work of Messiah is linked to His sacrificial death. "He always lives to make intercession for us" (Hebrews 7:25).

We should also note that the Altar of Incense was to have horns on its four corners, like the Altar of Sacrifice. The "horn" (קֶרֶן, *keren*) in the Hebrew culture was a symbol of "strength." For instance, Hannah, in her prayer of thanksgiving to HaShem (1Samuel 2) says: "My horn is exalted in HaShem" (v.1, cf. v. 10), meaning that her strength had been realized in His promise to her that she would, indeed, have a son. "Horn" is regularly used in the Psalms as a symbol of strength (Psalms 18:2; 75:4-5; 89:17,24; 92:10; 98:6; 112:9; 132:17; 148:14).

The message, then, that we should learn is that the Altar of Incense, with its continual fragrance before the Almighty, had strength or power. Indeed, HaShem willingly acted toward Israel on the basis of the very atonement symbolically present in the burning incense. And this speaks directly to its ultimate fulfillment in the intercessory work of Yeshua as our Great High Priest. For it is by His constant intercession that we have ready access (through Him) to the Father. HaShem's favor toward us is the proof that Messiah's work is powerful, for it satisfies the infinite holiness of the Father. In His gracious acts toward us who are sinners, His justice never is diminished, for the work of Yeshua in His intercession is powerful to save.

The *haftarah* also emphasizes this aspect of the incense, for it is in the burning of the incense (along with the other sacrifices) that HaShem's Name is seen to be great. Surely the greatness of our God is manifest in the world around us, for He is the Maker of the heavens and the earth. This is a regular point made in the Psalms (Psa. 115:15; 121:2; 124:8; 134:3; 135:6; 136:5; 146:6). But His greatness is seen in even more significant ways when one recognizes the power of His grace in making atonement for sinners. For though the creation required His speech, and the Torah required the writing with His finger, redemption was accomplished "with an outstretched arm" (Ex 6:6; Deut 4:34; 5:15; 7:19; 9:29; 11:2; 26:8; 1Kings 8:42; 2Kings 17:36; 2Chr 6:32; Ps 136:12; Jer 27:5; 32:17,21; Ezek 20:33-34), symbolic of a great exercise of power and energy.

Our Apostolic section makes an interesting application of the Altar of Incense. Here, in Revelation 8:1-5, the incense put upon the golden altar is specifically said to be the prayer of the pious ones: "Another angel came and stood at the altar, holding a golden censer; and much incense was given to him, so that he might add it to the prayers of all the saints on the golden altar which was before the throne. And the smoke of the incense, with the prayers of the saints, went up before God out of the angel's hand."

Here we see that the intercessory work of the high priest, symbolized in the Altar of Incense, is combined with the prayers of the pious ones as they petition HaShem. This is a very important insight: our prayers reach the Almighty because they are "intermingled" with the prayers of our *cohen hagadol*, Yeshua. Paul hints at this when he writes in Romans 8:26ff, "In the same way the Spirit also helps our weakness; for we do not know how to pray as we should, but the Spirit Himself intercedes for us with groanings too deep for words; and He who searches the hearts knows what the mind of the Spirit is, because He intercedes for the saints according to the will of God." Through the Ruach HaKodesh, our petitions and heart-needs are brought into the very presence of the Almighty by the intercessory work of our High Priest.

Here, then, is a beautiful picture of the intersection of our need for diligence in prayer and the faithfulness of our Savior in His intercession for us. It is not an "either-or" but a "both-and." We are not blessed only because Yeshua works on our behalf, nor are our blessings solely dependent upon our faithfulness. It is in the intersection of our obedience and His faithfulness that blessing comes to us. And since He is faithful to intercede for us, we will persevere and we will grow in our obedience to Him. The one guarantees the other. "For He who has begun a good work in you will perfect it (i.e., bring it to completion) with a view to the very day of Messiah Yeshua's appearance" (Philippians 1:6).

Note the strict prohibition against burning "strange incense" upon the Altar of Incense or offering any kind of sacrifice on it (v.9), "You shall not offer any strange incense on this altar, or burnt offering or meal offering; and you shall not pour out a drink offering on it."

What exactly is "strange incense?" We know that the sons of Aaron were struck dead by the Almighty because they offered "strange fire" to the Lord (Lev. 10). The Hebrew is קְטֹרֶת זָרָה, *k'toret zarah*. The Sages understand this to mean incense provided by an individual and not made specifically for the purpose (Rashi) or incense made with unauthorized ingredients (Ibn Ezra; Ramban). But *zarah* is the common word for "stranger (usually of idolators)," and thus "strange incense" most likely means "incense used for pagan worship." This might fit the description of "strange fire" offered by Nadav and Avihu, in that it appears they were mixing pagan worship into the service of the Tabernacle.

But notice also that the offering of any sacrifice upon the Altar of Incense is prohibited. What should we understand by this? Simply that the Altar of Incense was to foreshadow the intercession of Yeshua *after* His sacrifice, not an ongoing sacrifice. That is to say, Yeshua died once for all time, never to die again. The Roman Catholic teaching that the Messiah is constantly dying is not only unbiblical, it totally misses the point of His death in the first place. Yeshua died once for all time and in that death obtained eternal redemption for all of His people. Note Heb 9:12 – "and not through the blood of goats and calves, but through His own blood, He entered the holy place once for all, having obtained eternal redemption." If there were sacrifices offered on the Altar of Incense, this would ruin the picture and the foreshadowing of Yeshua's death for us as acted out in the once-a-year Yom Kippur sacrifice.

Furthermore, the prohibition of "strange incense" teaches that the intercession symbolized by the incense is of a unique quality and cannot be duplicated or copied. All other forms, regardless of how "beautiful" they may be, are not accepted. This speaks to the uniqueness of Yeshua's person and work. There is one way and only one way to find full acceptance before HaShem, and this is only through His Son, our Messiah Yeshua. Throughout the symbolic teaching of the Tabernacle, this fact is emphasized over and over again. God desires to dwell among His people, but He can do so only as His people can approach Him in holiness. Represented by the *cohen hagadol*, the people of Israel come into the presence of God through the sacrificial cleansing and atonement. But all of the regulations and prescriptions teach us that there is only one way for this to happen, and it is God's way. All other attempts or designs will be rejected. Yeshua said: "I am the way, the truth, and the life. No one comes to the Father but through Me" (John 14:6).

Consider, then, the mystery of this picture: Yeshua, the eternal Messiah, acts as our *cohen hagadol*, takes our prayers and our concerns before the Almighty in the majesty of His person, on the merits of His own sacrifice, and with full confidence that His every request will be granted. It is in this that we have bold confidence to approach the "throne of grace" (Heb 4:16), for we know that we have received grace "in the beloved one" (Eph 1:6).

In John's Gospel, he gives us an inspired preview of our Master's heavenly intercession for us. It is as though we are allowed to peek through a crack in the opened door of heaven, and witness the activity of our High Priest in His intercessory prayer on our behalf. In John 17, we hear the words of Yeshua just hours before He would be tried, condemned by man, and crucified. Yet in v. 11, Yeshua states: "I am no longer in the world," while in v. 13 He says, "these things I speak in the world." Apparently Yeshua had, in His prayer, transported Himself beyond the cross, beyond the tomb, beyond His ascension, to His abode with the Father in glory. He begins His prayer (v. 1) by saying, "I glorified You on the earth, having accomplished the work which You have given Me to do" (v. 4). As such, His prayer in this text stands as a model of His intercession, and affords us the opportunity to understand what it is that He requests of the Father on our behalf.

We may note a number of preliminary aspects of His prayer. First, He says that He is not praying for the world, but for those given to Him (v. 9): "I ask on their behalf; I do not ask on behalf of the world, but of those whom You have given Me; for they are Yours." Like the *cohen gadol* in Ancient Israel, who carried the names of the tribes upon His chest and shoulders as he burnt the daily incense, so our High Priest prays for those who are His—His chosen ones.

Secondly, we see that Yeshua's intercession is based upon His having accomplished the work of redemption for which He was sent (v. 4). That His requests will be granted is based upon the fact that His sacrifice was already accepted by God. In His intercession, He applies the merits of His sacrifice to those for whom He died.

We may summarize the requests of His prayer as follows:

1. Glorify Your Son, that the Son may glorify You (v. 1).

The glory of the Father is the ultimate goal and result of Yeshua's prayer. It is when the Son is glorified in accomplishing the work of redemption for His people, that the Father will be glorified. One cannot honor the Father, if one does not honor the Son. "He who hates Me hates My Father also" (John 15:23, cp. 5:23).

2. Keep them in Your name, which You have given Me, that they may be one, even as We are (v. 11).

Yeshua's prayer secures that all who were given to Yeshua will be kept or guarded so as not to be lost or taken from Him. Our redemptive relationship with God is the work of God. We are not kept by our own power or even by our own faithfulness. It is God's omnipotence that maintains our relationship with Him. Our salvation is as secure as is the relationship of the Son to the Father. "… He who began a good work in you will perfect it with a view to the day of Messiah Yeshua (Phil 1:6).

3. Keep them from the evil one (v. 15)

Our warfare is not against flesh and blood, but against wicked spirits and demonic forces (Eph 6:12). Apart from Yeshua's intercession on our behalf, we would be powerless to fight and win in the battle against the enemy of our souls. But because Yeshua always lives to make intercession for us, we may be confident that we will win this battle. We need never fear that somehow we will be defeated by our enemy. The victory is ours because Yeshua is praying for us. "Simon, Simon, behold, Satan has demanded permission to sift you like wheat; but I have prayed for you, that your faith may not fail…" (Luke 22:31–32).

4. Sanctify them in the truth; Your word is truth (v. 17)

Yeshua prays that we will be set apart by knowing and applying the eternal truth of God's word. In other words, He is praying that we will understand and apply the Scriptures to our lives. Our hunger for the word of God, and for knowing what it means and how it applies, is the direct result of Yeshua's intercession on our behalf. We hold in our hands the eternal words of the Almighty—the Creator of this universe, and our own King! And we may have every confidence that as we study and search the Scriptures, they will be unfolded to us by the Spirit as He implements the requests of our High Priest. We may therefore come to the Scriptures with the full anticipation that in them, we will find the answers to the deepest questions of life, and discover in them the shalom that God intends us to enjoy. "…you will know the truth, and the truth will make you free" (John 8:32).

5. I ask…that they may all be one, even as You, Father, are in Me and I in You…that the world may believe (vv. 20-21).

Being "one" means striving for unity. Unity is not "sameness," as though we all have to be clones of a single mold. Unity means the ability to remain one by affirming the essential truths, while allowing differences in the non-essentials. It does not mean that we find a oneness in reductionism, but that we all strive together to know the truth, and to live it out. Realizing that we are all seekers of truth, not manufacturers of it, enables us to strive together for the single goal of becoming like Yeshua. It is this ability to remain together in the midst of our differences, that forms a strong witness to the world. "By this all men will know that you are My disciples, if you have love for one another" (John 13:35).

6. Father, I desire that they also whom You have given Me be with Me where I am (v. 24).

In ancient times, a ship that was making its way to the harbor during a storm, may have been unable to navigate the narrow opening of the harbor in the tempest. For that reason, they would send a smaller boat, with the anchor, into the harbor, to keep the ship from being blown back out to sea. Yeshua has taken the anchor of our souls with Him as He ascended to the Father, and thus our safe haven in the harbor of the world-to-come is secure. "This hope we have as an anchor of the soul, a hope both sure and steadfast and one which enters within the veil…" (Heb. 6:19). The fact that there is a "man in heaven" today (cf. 1Tim 2:5) means that, as the first-fruits from the grave, He is the guarantee that a great harvest will follow. Nothing could ever overthrow this request of our High Priest: we will one day come into the presence of His glory, to abide forever in the world-to-come, because He is praying that this will be a reality. "For I am convinced that neither death, nor life, nor angels, nor principalities, nor things present, nor things to come, nor powers, nor height, nor depth, nor any other created thing, will be able to separate us from the love of God, which is in Messiah Yeshua our Lord" (Rom 8:38–39).

7. ...that the love wherewith You did love Me may be in them and I in them (v. 26).

While we remain in this life, we are assured of God's love, not in some theoretical or philosophical sense, but in a deep reality that cannot be fully explained in words. Our corporate worship of song and prayer is one way of expressing the reality of this love. In the "ups and downs" of life, we nonetheless experience the abiding presence of God's love for us, because Yeshua continues to intercede on our behalf, that this might be so. "...that you, being rooted and grounded in love, may be able to comprehend with all the saints what is the breadth and length and height and depth, and to know the love of Messiah which surpasses knowledge, that you may be filled up to all the fullness of God" (Eph 3:17–19).

Parashah Twenty-One
כִּי תִשָּׂא – Ki Tissa'

"WHEN YOU LIFT UP"

Exodus 30:11-34:35

In the Triennial Cycle
there are three Parashot

30:11-38 | 31:1-32:14 | 32:15-34:26

Note: the final *parashah* in the Triennial Cycle does not complete the Annual Cycle for this *parashah*. 34:27–35 are included in the next Triennial *parashah*.

Parashah 68
Triennial Cycle

Exodus 30:11–38

Haftarah: 2Kings 12:1–16 | Apostolic: 2Corinthians 9:6-11

The Half-Shekel, the Laver, the Anointing Oil, and the Incense

Our *parashah* combines instructions regarding taking a census of the people by counting a designated contribution given by the men who were 20 years old and up, with the commandments pertaining to the Laver, anointing oil, and incense. Why would God have given Moses the instructions regarding the census in the midst of the instructions regarding the construction of sacred articles of the Tabernacle? At first, the commands regarding the census seem out of place. But they are put here to remind us that while the people are represented by the priests in the whole matter of the divine service, they are not passive. They too are required to participate. Thus, the census was not done by merely counting the people, but by counting a contribution (תְּרוּמָה, *termumah*) given by the adult males as representatives of their respective families. (According to later rabbinic Judaism, 20 was the normal age for a man to be married, cf. *Avot* 5:21).

Moreover, the command regarding the contribution for counting states: "The rich shall not pay more and the poor shall not pay less than the half shekel, when you give the contribution to Adonai to make atonement for yourselves" (v. 15). In offering the contribution of counting, all Israelites were considered equal—all were of equal value and importance in terms of the makeup of the entire nation. Regardless of their lineage, economic status, or assigned duties, all were equally important for the success of the whole. The Sages note that it is important to understand how vital this principle is. The strength of Israel does not reside in the talents or acumen of a few individuals, but in the corporate solidarity of the nation as a whole. Each individual must see himself or herself as an essential part of the whole. This is likewise emphasized in the writings of the Apostles when they liken the people of God to the human body. Paul speaks of the "body of Messiah" as made up of many parts, but each is a necessary, essential part of the whole. Note Eph 4:14–16,

As a result, we are no longer to be children, tossed here and there by waves and carried about by every wind of doctrine, by the trickery of men, by craftiness in deceitful scheming; but speaking the truth in love, we are to grow up in all aspects into Him who is the head, even Messiah, from whom the whole body, being fitted and held together by what every joint supplies, according to the proper working of each individual part, causes the growth of the body for the building up of itself in love.

Thus, the blessing for Rosh Chodesh includes the phrase "all Israel are companions" (חֲבֵרִים כָּל יִשְׂרָאֵל). At the renewal of every month, we are reminded that each of us has an important part to play in the *chavurah* (fellowship; community) of God's chosen people.

The command to number the people found in our *parashah* seems to be contrary to what the Tanach teaches elsewhere, namely, that God was angry when David took it upon himself to number the people. In 2Sam 24, when David numbers the people, he realizes that he has sinned and seeks God's forgiveness. Yet even though God does spare David's life, He sends a severe punishment upon the nation for the King's actions in which 70,000 were killed. How are we to reckon this apparent contradiction? The answer comes in the *way* the people were counted. While the nations around Israel numbered the people by simply counting them, no doubt in order to ascertain the strength of the adult men who would form the standing armies, God had decreed that a census in Israel should be conducted by counting their *contributions.* In other words, the *purpose* for the census in Israel was to demonstrate their corporate solidarity, not to offer a reliance upon their military strength. Israel's strength was to be seen in her willingness to contribute to the on-going maintenance of the Tabernacle or Temple, and the sacred service that was conducted there. This, the worship of God and service to Him, was the real source of their might. Thus, Israel's strength was in God's willingness to be her protection, symbolized in the abiding *Shekinah* and in the priestly service of sacrifice and intercession, something that the contribution for counting (census) emphasized.

The exact value of a half-shekel is disputed. Modern scholars usually consider a shekel to be 8.26 grams. Our text indicates that a shekel is equal to 20 *gerahs,* but the exact weight of a *gerah* is also disputed. The rabbinic literature puts the weight of 1 *gerah* at 1.14 grams. This would make the shekel 22.8 grams. A troy ounce (used to calculate the value of silver in our day) is equal to 31.1 grams, making the shekel .73 troy ounces. Given these calculation, and the average value of silver as $21.24 per troy ounce (as of Feb., 2014), the value of a shekel of silver would be approximately $15.50, and a half-shekel $7.75.

Rashi and Rambam calculate the shekel at 13.33 grams, however, making it equivalent to .43 troy ounces. Using the same average value of silver, this would make the half-shekel equal to $4.57.

In the Second Temple period, the shekel was increased to 24 *gerahs*. If we accept that the *gerah* was 1.14 grams, this would put the shekel at .77 troy ounces, with a value of $16.35, and a half-shekel equal to $8.18. Thus, even though we cannot be sure of the precise weight of a shekel of silver, it is clear that the half-shekel would have been well within the means of everyone.

But this emphasizes another principle: even though the required payment for each family representative was relatively small, when combined together with the contribution from every family, it was a sizeable amount! The Sages emphasize this by noting that a *half*-shekel was the requirement, meaning that each person's contribution depended upon another's contribution to form the whole shekel. In seeking to accomplish the work God has given us, each of us needs one another to make up what we lack.

Another issue confronts us in this *parashah*. The giving of the half-shekel is said to effect atonement: "each one of them shall give a ransom for himself to Adonai" (v. 12); "when you give the contribution to Adonai to make atonement for yourselves" (v. 15); "You shall take the atonement money from the sons of Israel and shall give it for the service of the tent of meeting, that it may be a memorial for the sons of Israel before ADONAI, to make atonement for yourselves" (v. 16). Does it not appear that the giving of a half-shekel effected atonement? But how is this possible? Was atonement effected by paying the yearly contribution?

The answer lies in understanding v. 16. There it becomes clear that the giving of the half-shekel was for the maintenance and support of the Tabernacle and the service that was carried on there by the priests on behalf of the people. Furthermore, the silver that was given by the people is said to function as a "memorial" (זִכָּרוֹן, *zikaron*) before Adonai. The Sages suggest that much of the silver was used to form the silver sockets in which the columns and boards of the Tabernacle and the surrounding fence of the courtyard were placed. So in giving the half-shekel, the people enabled the construction and maintenance of the Tabernacle where the service of atonement was carried on. In this way, they enabled the atoning work of sacrifice and intercession by the priests.

Furthermore, we should understand that atonement, as it is portrayed in the Tabernacle and Temple, had both a temporal as well as an eternal dimension. In terms of temporal atonement, the obedience of the people, and the service of the priests, was an on-going demonstration of their trust in God's promise to protect and keep them. Or to put it another way, as they obeyed God and walked in His statutes, they were "cleansed" (the basic meaning of "atonement") and thus received divine protection from their enemies. God promised His blessing for their obedience, and their willingness to build and maintain the Tabernacle as the central place of worship was an act of obedience to God. It was rewarded with God's giving them the temporal blessings He had promised. Through the sacrificial requirements, the people were able to be cleansed of ritual impurities, giving them access to the Tabernacle as the designated place of worship, which in turn strengthened their faith in God and their relationship with Him, both individual and corporate. In being obedient to His commands, they received the blessings He had promised in the covenant, one of which is His promise to save them from their enemies.

We often forget that even the word "saved" or "salvation" likewise carries a temporal sense at times. For instance, in James 5:15 we read that the prayer offered in faith will "restore" the one who is sick, but actually the word is "save" (σώζω, sōzō) the sick. This does not mean salvation in an eternal sense, but in a temporal way. When God brings healing, it is part of what He does in terms of "saving" the one who is sick. In the same way, when Israel experiences "atonement," we should not automatically think that it involves eternal salvation, that is, the forgiveness of sins in a final and eternal dimension.

Yet the method by which God does effect eternal and lasting atonement, through the forgiveness of sins and the imputation of everlasting righteousness, was first demonstrated fully in the service of the Tabernacle and the Temple. Thus, when the Israelites brought the half-shekel as a contribution for counting, they were contributing to the Tabernacle as the very revelation by which eternal atonement would be made, that is, through the complete and final sacrifice of Yeshua to which the sacrificial service pointed.

Our *parashah* goes on to detail the construction and purpose of the Laver (כִּיּוֹר, *kiyyor*). It was to be made of bronze, with a base of bronze upon which it would sit. It is specifically stated to be for washing the hands and feet of the priests before they entered into their daily duties. It was not to make them ritually clean, since they could not enter into the courtyard until they were clean. Rather, it was to be a constant reminder that in their duties, they were to be set apart or sanctified from their common, daily work. The Targum translates "to wash" (לְרָחְצָה, *lirachtzah*) as "to sanctify" (לְקִדּוּשׁ, *l'qidush*) for this very reason. That the priests were to wash hands and feet emphasizes this aspect of being set apart, for the hands and feet are symbolic of one's common activities—one's daily walk and actions. Thus, in their washing, the priests were reminded that they were entering into a service that was set apart from their other, common activities. Moreover, since the laver was situated between the altar of sacrifice and the Mishkan proper, it was to symbolize that their priestly duties, both outside of the Tabernacle proper as well as within, were to be sanctified as holy to Adonai.

It is clear that the sanctification of the priests to do their duties was of utmost significance to Adonai. He prescribes the death penalty for those who would neglect this important ritual. Here, once again, we see the emphasis put upon the unique aspects of worship and service that God had prescribed for Israel. There was not to be any admixture of pagan practices within the sacrificial ceremonies of the Tabernacle. As the priests washed their hands and feet, they were to be reminded that God had given specific details regarding their service and the manner in which they were to offer the sacrifices and represent the people of Israel before the Holy One. They were not free to be creative, nor to incorporate other rituals and ceremonies from the pagan nations. In their being set apart to HaShem, they were likewise set apart to His way of worship.

Continuing with the emphasise upon the sanctification of the Mishkan and Aaron and his sons, our *parashah* details the manner in which the anointing oil was to be made. The Sages teach that this same oil was used to anoint the Kings during the days of the 1st Temple. The text opens with "And now you take for yourself" (וְאַתָּה קַח-לְךָ) which seems to indicate that this was to be done by Moses himself, or at least personally supervised by Moses. The anointing of the priests was therefore connected directly to Moses who alone entered the cloud on Mt. Sinai. In this way, the anointing was to be understood as coming directly from God Himself. In other words, it was to be understood that the sanctification of the Tabernacle and the priests came directly from God through Moses. God was the One who had set apart the Tabernacle and its ministry from that which was common—it gained its holiness by the very anointing of God. As the priests were anointed, it was to remind them of at least two aspects: 1) their service was primarily directed to God, Who is Himself holy, and 2) they were to serve with supreme devotion to Him. They were not to accomplish their duties for their own benefit.

All of the items of the Tabernacle that were anointed, as well as Aaron and his sons, were considered "most holy" (קֹדֶשׁ קָדָשִׁים) because of the anointing. They attained the same level of sanctity that the inner sanctuary had. Verse 29 seems to indicate that anything that touched the anointed vessels would likewise become holy: "You shall also consecrate them, that they may be most holy; whatever touches them shall be holy." However, the last phrase, כָּל-הַנֹּגֵעַ בָּהֶם יִקְדָּשׁ, "whatever touches them will be holy" could just as well be understood as "whatever touches them *must* be holy." In other words, the command is that only substances that were ceremonially clean could be put into the vessels or come in contact with the items that had been anointed. Like the *cohen gadol*, who alone could enter the Most Holy Place, only after he himself was fully consecrated, so only those things that were deemed ritually clean could come in contact with the anointed vessels. In this way, the sanctity of the vessels insured the sanctity of all other substances used in connection with them. What is emphasized by this is that one cannot approach God in service or worship in an unholy state. God is not Himself unclean, nor does He commune with that which is unclean. Without holiness (sanctification), "no one will see the Lord" (Heb 12:14). This likewise emphasizes that only as we are clothed with the righteousness of the Messiah, are we able to draw near to God.

The fact that the anointing oil signified those who were set apart by God Himself to engage in priestly intercession also made it necessary that the anointing oil not be made into a common commodity. Therefore, it is strictly prohibited for anyone to duplicate this oil or to apply it to an "alien" (זָר, *zar*). The word *zar* most often denotes a foreigner who was an idolater. Once again, God reveals Himself as the One who divides between the holy and the profane. The holiness of God cannot be mixed together with the profane.

Our *parashah* ends with the details regarding the manufacture of the pure and holy incense, burnt upon the golden altar of incense which stood before the veil, just in front of the ark that contained the stone tablets of the Testimony or the covenant. Once again, the precise ingredients, and the amounts for each, is detailed, and it is strictly prohibited for anyone to duplicate this incense and use it in a common way. Thus, as sanctified for the specific use in the Tabernacle, it too is designated "most holy" (קֹדֶשׁ קָדָשִׁים, *kodesh kodeshim*). As we noted in the last *parashah*, the incense was symbolic of the priestly intercession on behalf of the people, and particularly of the ultimate work of intercession accomplished for His people by Messiah, Yeshua Himself. Like the anointing oil that sanctified the Tabernacle and Aaronic priesthood to their unique ministry on behalf of Israel, so the incense symbolized the unique ability of their intercession to effect acceptance before the Holy One of Israel. This comes from the idea of a "soothing aroma" (רֵיחַ נִיחֹחַ) used often of the sacrifices. The incense, in a similar metaphor, filled the sacred space of the Tabernacle or Temple with an aroma bespeaking the very presence of the Almighty. Its fragrance reminded all who came in as well as all who came near, that God was pleased to dwell among His people.

Once again we see that the goal of these carefully defined regulations is the revelation of the Messiah. For He is Immanuel, "God with us," and "He is the radiance of His glory and the exact representation of His nature, and upholds all things by the word of His power" (Heb 1:3).

The *haftarah* that accompanies our Torah *parashah* has clear parallels. First, the fact that under the reign of Jehoash (יְהוֹאָשׁ), though he did right in the sight of Adonai, he failed to remove the high places (הַבָּמוֹת). As a result, the people were still sacrificing and burning incense at these pagan shrines. The subtlety of syncretism had remained, and the clear teaching of our Torah *parashah* against such syncretism is therefore highlighted.

Second, however, Jehoash was zealous for the repair of the Temple. As a result, he made a wooden chest in which the contributions for the Temple were to be placed. Apparently, the priests were taking the contribution money and keeping it for themselves. Jehoash put a stop to that, and the gathered funds were used to hire workers in wood and stone to make repairs to the Temple. Only the funds gathered in respect to the trespass offerings and the sin-offerings were given to the priests. But what were these? In the trespass offering, a fifth of the value (determined by the priests) was to be added to the offering (Lev 5:16, cf. Num 5:9), and apparently this was kept by the priest for his maintenance. No such law pertains to the sin offering, however. Most likely, it became a common thing for someone who was bringing a sin offering to make a voluntary contribution to the priest who offered the sacrifice, and it was this money that is spoken of in our *haftarah* passage.

Our Apostolic portion emphasizes the correct attitude or heart condition for anyone who gives to the work of the kingdom of God. Gratefulness to God was to be the over arching perspective whenever an offering was given, even those that were mandatory (as the half-shekel contribution in our Torah *parashah*). Obedience to HaShem is done out of a heart of thanksgiving for all that He has done for us. But Paul also applies another Torah principle: that of reaping and sowing. The one who sows sparingly, reaps sparingly, but the one who sows generously, also reaps generously. The point he is making is quite simple: since all we have comes from God ("He supplies seed to the sower and bread for food"), we need not fear when we are urged to contribute to the work He intends to accomplish. When we willingly give of our own substance, the One Who has supplied what we have in the first place will also make the seed we sow abound. This does not mean, as so many teach in our day, that giving to the work of the Lord is a kind of monetary investment: the more you give, the more you'll get back. Our motivation in giving is one of gratefulness to HaShem and a desire to see His work flourish resulting in the expansion of His kingdom.

Thus, as we give contributions to the work of the Lord, we may trust HaShem to continue to meet our needs, and we may also take much joy in knowing that as the seed is sown, it will bring forth a lasting harvest.

Parashah 69
Triennial Cycle

Exodus 31:1-32:14

Haftarah: Ezekiel 20:1–7 | Apostolic: Colosians 3:1-5

This week's section contains three lines of thought. It begins with the notice that Bezalel, Oholiab, and other craftsmen would be filled with the Ruach HaKodesh in order to perform their tasks of constructing the various articles of furniture and ornamentation for the *Mishkan*, the Tabernacle.

The second section centers on the Shabbat as an eternal sign between God and Israel (31:12-18), followed thirdly by the narrative of how Israel sinned with the golden calf. Are these sections related, or were they simply pasted together without much attention to literary transition by the final editor?

My own belief is that if there were a "final editor" of the Torah, he or they were as much guarded by the Ruach as was Moses in the original compilation. Thus, I would take it as a given that not only the words, sentences, and paragraphs were inspired, but also the order in which they were recorded. Thus, my initial query is to find the relationship between these three sections in our *parashah* for this week.

And, it is not difficult to see the connection. The opening strain focuses attention upon the fact that God would supernaturally empower the craftsmen to make the necessary articles of the *Mishkan* so that His commands to Moses would be carried out perfectly, and so the people would be able to worship as He intended. Thus, the first line of thought in our section focuses upon the means of worship.

The second paragraph reiterates (with some interesting additions) the former commandments regarding the Shabbat. Yet in this context the Shabbat is said to be given to Israel for a specific purpose (v. 13), "…that you may know that I am Adonai who sanctifies you." In other words, the Shabbat is also given as a means—a sign, a reminder—to set Israel apart to the Lord. After all, this is the essence of worship, to serve Him wholly. (Remember that the Hebrew term most often translated "worship" is the word עֲבוֹדָה, *'avodah*, the basic meaning of which is "to serve.") The

Shabbat keeps this thought in focus. Our redemption from Egypt had one primary purpose, that we should be forever worshipers of God. So the empowering of the craftsmen to create a place for worship, and the giving of the Shabbat as a constant reminder that our purpose in life is to be worshipers, are linked together.

The final section is striking in comparison, and in connection with the first two. In the golden calf event we see a vivid picture of an ugly reality. Israel, indeed, mankind, even given the best of all possible advantages to appreciate and worship God, inevitably chooses to worship the creation rather than the Creator, Who is blessed forever (cf. Rom 1:25). The three themes of our *parashah* remind us that even when God has prepared a place and day for worship, until He changes the heart of a person, no true worship will take place.

This, in itself, has profound implications for us today. First, we should not despise careful preparation of time and space for worship. These are God ordain and honored. God does not change, nor do His precepts change. His Torah stands as an eternal revelation of His character, thoughts, and will. Thus, the God of Abraham, Isaac, and Jacob is the same God Who endowed the craftsmen with ability and gave very specific instructions regarding the place of corporate worship, the *Mishkan*. But secondly, we must remember that neither a place set apart for worship, nor the recognition of the ordained day for worshipful rest, guarantee true worship. Unless the Lord quickens our hearts—enlivens our souls—rebirths us by the water and the Spirit (John 3:5), our worship will be false, self-centered, and even idolatrous. The prophet Isaiah teaches us this in the first chapter of his prophecy, by commanding the Israelites of old to stop bringing their sacrifices (their acts of worship) since in truth these were nothing more than false worship—the kind of thing that stinks in God's nostrils.

How is it that our hearts can be changed? How may we prepare to worship in spirit and truth? The inward work is done by the Ruach on the basis of the sacrifice of Yeshua, linked to the heart by faith. Without faith in the crowning sacrifice of Mashiach, without the cleansing (atoning) of His blood, without His priestly intercession—there is no true worship. For no one may approach the Father but through Him, and worship is nothing more nor less than communion with the Father and the Son of His love, by the sanctifying work of the Ruach.

Let us look briefly, now, at each of the sections. 31:1-11 describes the supernatural ability given to the craftsmen by the *Ruach HaElohim* (Spirit of God). This ability was not merely in the hands, but first (and perhaps foremost) in the heart and soul. V. 3—"I have filled him with the Spirit of God in wisdom, understanding, and knowledge." These three terms (which form the basis for the acronym CaBaD, חָכְמָה, בִּין, דַעַת) speak of spiritual vigor, of a life filled with Torah study and application to life. These craftsmen therefore constructed their items in accordance with what they knew about God. This in itself is a tremendous lesson for each of us. Let the work of our hands, empowered by the Ruach, show forth the truth about God in wisdom, understanding, and knowledge.

How might these terms be simply defined? Wisdom is being able to know what God has said—being able to approach life with His viewpoint as revealed in the Torah. Understanding is the ability to apply this viewpoint to the specific situations of life (to say it another way, to be able to derive *halachah*). Knowledge is the ability to derive new applications from the wisdom and understanding gained from the Torah—to be able to make application of a given precept to a situation that is new. Spiritual knowledge makes the eternal and ancient wisdom always relevant.

The second paragraph of our section reiterates the centrality of the Shabbat. There are several things I will point out by way of overview. First, note that here the Sabbath is declared as a sign (אוֹת, *'ot*) between Adonai and Israel forever (v. 13). A sign must point to some reality. In this case, it is the unique relationship that God has with Israel on account of His having chosen them to be His covenant nation, and thus having redeemed them from Egypt to be His own people. Therefore, the Shabbat is to be a sign that God has set Israel apart, sanctifying the nation to Himself. The Shabbat is a sign that Israel is special to the Lord, that they have been marked out (sanctified) for Him. This does not, of course, exhaust the meaning of the Shabbat as a sign, but in this context it is the primary emphasis. This is all the more significant in light of the up coming golden calf event. God has claimed Israel for Himself, they belong to Him. The Shabbat is proof of this, and the Shabbat is a creation reality—it cannot change as long as the heavens and earth remain. In like manner, even though Israel will sin and turn their back upon God, the unique status of their being His chosen people cannot change any more than the course of the earth around the sun can change. It is fixed (cf. Ps 89:37).

A second thing I might point out from this passage is that "being cut off from your people" is equivalent with capital punishment, v. 14. The Hebrew is emphatic: "surely be put to death" (מוֹת יוּמַת, *môt yûmat*). But this phrase is parallel to the next one, i.e., "shall be cut off from his people" (וְנִכְרְתָה הַנֶּפֶשׁ הַהִוא מִקֶּרֶב עַמֶּיהָ). In this case, being cut off from one's people is done through the death penalty, whether administered by appointed judges or by God Himself.

A third matter: the term for "work" is not the common word עֲבוֹדָה, *'avodah*. It is rather the term מְלָאכָה (*m^elā'chāh*), the same word used in the Gen 2 account which gives us the first notice of Shabbat. While עֲבוֹדָה may include any kind of activity that is labor, מְלָאכָה has as its primary meaning "business, occupation, employment." The two are clearly different. In the broadest of strokes, what is prohibited on the Shabbat is the continuation of business, of employment, of seeking to make wages, or to gain economically. It is not *activity* that is prohibited. Rather, the activity which is enjoined upon us for the Shabbat is precisely those kinds of things which direct our attention as fully as possible to the fact which we always affirm, i.e., that God is the One who supplies all of our needs, and that even that which we gain through our weekly business is, in fact, from Him.

This fact is emphasized again in v. 16. Here the language is that the sons of Israel are to "do" (לַעֲשׂוֹת, *la'asôt*) the Shabbat (translated "celebrate" in some English bibles). So Shabbat is not a lack of doing—it is doing those things that set the day of Shabbat apart from the other days of work, and which draw us together as a community to the worship of God and an appreciation of who we are in Messiah as His chosen people.

Our *parashah* ends with the well-known story of the golden calf. But from the time of the earliest commentaries on this text, the story has raised a number of obvious questions. First, it seems beyond belief that Aaron, who had such partnership with Moses as the spokesman for God, could have been so easily persuaded to make an idol for the people. What is more, had he been guilty of leading the people in idolatry, it would seem that he would be the most culpable, yet when the punishment comes upon the people for their sin, Aaron is entirely spared, and then goes on in the subsequent story to be the primary figure in the service of the Tabernacle before HaShem as the *cohen gadol* (High Priest). Later, God charged Aaron with the sin of joining Moses in striking the stone (Num 20:12). Yet here, it appears as though Aaron entirely escapes any punishment for the sin of idolatry!

The Sages felt this difficulty, and attempted to give various explanations why Aaron, in fact, was not guilty of idolatry. They suggest that he simply tried to stall to give time for Moses to reappear. They note that before Moses ascended the mountain, he had appointed Hur as a co-leader with Aaron in his absence (Ex 24:14). Since there is no mention of Hur in the current pericope, the Sages conclude that the people had already killed him because he had refused their request to fashion an idol. Thus, they suggest, Aaron's actions should be seen in light of the fact that he feared they would kill him as well. His actions in reference to the golden calf, therefore, are interpreted as attempts to delay the people's request in order to give time for Moses to come back from the mountain.

The Sages also posit that there was a contingency of Egyptians who had joined Israel in her exodus, but had done so not out of a fear of God, or a willingness to turn from their idolatry to trust the God of Israel, but because they considered the events of the Passover as magic (putting the blood on the door, leaving in haste, considering Moses to be a sorcerer, etc.). According to the Sages, this group of Egyptians, who had never truly confessed HaShem to be the One, true God, constituted the "mixed multitude" (עֵרֶב רַב, *'eirev rav*, cf. Ex 12:38) who came out of Egypt. They were the ones who incited the people to idolatry, and they were the 3000 who were eventually put to death.

While it is clear that there are some interesting points in our text which are usually overlooked by many commentators, and which may seem at first to give some credence to the interpretation of the Sages on this passage, in the final analysis, the Sages simply could not bring themselves to admit that the Israelites could be guilty of such blatant idolatry, especially since they had so recently witnessed the wonderful power of God on their behalf in bringing them from Egypt, and in giving them the very words of God in the Torah. It is typical, then, for the rabbis to blame non-Israelites for the transgression. Yet it the obvious is inescapable, if we allow the text its plain meaning, that the people were, in fact, moved to idolatry in the moment of their despair. To try to come up with alternate explanations actually obscures the hard but important lessons we are to learn from this text.

The opening verse of this story (32:1) relates that the motivation of the people was to replace Moses, since they feared he may have died, having lingered on the mountain longer than they thought he should have. Their words are insightful: "Come, make us a god who will go before us; as for this Moses, the man who brought us up from the land of Egypt, we do not know what has become of him." Obviously, Moses was not the one who brought them up from the land of Egypt! God was their Deliverer! Here we see an all important perspective: whenever we assign to a leader, regardless of how important or powerful that leader may be, those things that are the work of God, we open the door to idolatry. Surely God had appointed Moses, and surely he was a prophet unlike any other. Yet he was God's servant. It was not his leadership, or even the strength of his character, that had effected Israel's deliverance from Egypt. Somehow, the people had put their trust and allegiance in man rather than in God.

Next, it appears that Aaron acted out of fear. The Hebrew of 32:1 has וַיִּקָּהֵל הָעָם עַל־אַהֲרֹן, which the English versions translate, "the people assembled about Aaron," but the preposition עַל used with קָהַל, "to gather," always carries hostile connotations. We should understand this to mean that the people gathered "against" Aaron. In other words, the people had formed into a mob who were hostile to Aaron. If, as the Sages suggest, Hur was already somehow taken out of the picture, one could well understand Aaron's fear. How could he single-handedly expect to withstand the force of a mob? In his fear, he gave into a plan that he hoped would buy him some time until Moses reappeared.

At first, given this scenario, we might empathize with Aaron. What else could he have done? Yet it is at the point of crisis that a leader must stand upon the clear principles of truth, and leave the outcome to God. Aaron's actions, while understandable from a human point of view, were not worthy of his position and responsibility as God's appointed leader. It is precisely at the point of crisis where mature faith in God's way of doing things is manifest. Standing on true principles and leaving the outcome to God should have characterized Aaron's actions. Instead, he came up with his own plan, which apparently he thought would work. In the end, however, it caused great harm to the people he was commissioned to lead. Moses' assessment of Aaron's leadership is given in 32:25, "Now when Moses saw that the people were out of control—for Aaron had let them get out of control to be a derision among their enemies...."

Aaron, giving into the pressure of the people, instructed them to gather the gold they possessed in ear rings. Perhaps he thought this would have taken them a few days. But instead, they return almost immediately with gold in hand. The use of the verb פָּרַק, *paraq*, "to tear," in 32:2 may highlight the fact that Aaron hoped the process would be difficult for the people, yet the next verse uses the same verb, indicating that the people were willing to do anything necessary to fashion the idol.

When the people brought the gold, 32:4 relates that Aaron took a engraving tool (חֶרֶט, *cheret*), and fashioned the gold into a golden calf (עֵגֶל מַסֵּכָה, *'ēgel masēchah*), literally, a "calf of a molten image." The way that this text relates the event is much different than what Aaron tells Moses later on (34:24), "I said to them, 'Whoever has any gold, let them tear it off.' So they gave it to me, and I threw it into the fire, and out came this calf." The Sages suggest that the demonic power of the Egyptians was actually responsible for making the idol—that Aaron threw the gold into the fire in hopes that a malformed glob of gold would be left, and the people would be discouraged about ever having an idol made of it. Yet the previous text tells us that Aaron took an engraving tool and fashioned (צוּר, *tzur*) the idol. Moreover, in the initially telling (v. 4) the text says that Aaron "took" the gold from the hands of the people (וַיִּקַּח מִיָּדָם, *vayiqqach miyadam*) while in Aaron's retelling he says "they gave it to me" (וַיִּתְּנוּ־לִי, *vayit^enu li*). From a strictly *halachic* perspective, Aaron took legal possession of the gold when he "took it" or drew it to himself. When he later relates the events to Moses, he tries to distance himself from having owned the gold that eventually became the idol. Such disparity between the two accounts gives every indication that Aaron was attempting to rationalize what he knew had been an egregious sin on his part.

After fashioning the molten image, we read in v. 4, וַיֹּאמְרוּ אֵלֶּה אֱלֹהֶיךָ יִשְׂרָאֵל אֲשֶׁר הֶעֱלוּךָ מֵאֶרֶץ מִצְרָיִם, "and they said, 'These are your gods, O Israel, who brought you up from the land of Egypt.'" There a couple of important things to note in this phrase: 1) the demonstrative pronoun (אֵלֶּה, 'ēle) is plural, thus "these are"; 2) אֱלֹהִים, elohim, may be translated as a plural, "gods" (though cf. Neh 9:18); 3) the people, not Aaron, are the ones making this pronouncement, "they said." (Note variants in the Lxx, which has the singular except in a few Mss.). It appears, therefore, that there was a group of people who had put themselves forward as leaders in some fashion. They were the ones who made an "official" proclamation regarding the molten image. And it appears that the rest of the people were willing to follow their lead, since no one comes forward to challenge them. It may be that the construction of the calf or bull was considered as a way to bring God close to them—a way to "get God's attention" by constructing a throne for His feet or a kind of pedestal for His enthronement. That the image of bulls in pagan religions of the Ancient Near East were apparently used in this manner may give credence to this interpretation. Regardless of exactly how the molten image was viewed, it was considered a means of controlling God—to bring Him near when it appeared that He remained aloof and distant, or to assembly Him along with the local gods believed to be in control of that region. Here we see the heart of all idolatry: an attempt to control God because He is viewed as less than good. The spirit of idolatry goes back to Satan's lie: "has God said?" Once the people came to believe that God was selfish (like the pagan gods), they resorted to means they thought could manipulate Him to do their bidding.

Aaron's next action is interesting. It appears that in order to persuade the people away from their idolatry, he constructed an altar in front of the idol (לְפָנָיו, l'phanav), and declared that "Tomorrow shall be a feast (חַג, chag) to יהוה." If in fact Aaron's intentions were to draw the people back to the worship of HaShem, we can only say that his motivations were honorable. But here again, we learn an important lesson: using the wrong methods in an attempt to achieve an honorable goal never works. God is the One Who decreed the mo'edim, the appointed times of the festivals. In Aaron's desperation to bring the people back to their senses, he quickly adds a festival. From a human point-of-view, this seems logical. After all, if the festivals are a means of focusing attention upon what God has done, and especially His role as our Deliverer and King, then engaging in a festival would seem the right thing to do. But the error of Aaron's rationale was in trusting that the *emotional* aspects of a festival would turn the people back to a *right way of thinking*, when in fact just the opposite is true. Truth is the fountainhead of Godly emotions, not visa versa. Instead of proclaiming a festival, Aaron should have called the people to repentance and to a return to the truth.

The fruit of this backwards rationale is highlighted in 32:6. The people did, indeed, show up for the festival. They engaged in the emotional festivities, but it did not turn them to confess the error of their ways. Instead, the text states: "So the next day they rose early and offered burnt offerings, and brought peace offerings; and the people sat down to eat and to drink, and rose up to play." They "rose early"—they were eager to engage in the festivities. They offered false offerings, and then sat down to eat, drink, and engaged in "play." The Hebrew word translated "play" is צחק, "to laugh," which can sometimes denote "dancing" (Ex 32:19; Judg 16:25) but also at times carries the idea of sexual activity (Gen 26:8; 39:14, 17). Instead of the festival returning the people to a true recognition of God, it carried them away into further sin, perhaps even engaging in Canaanite fertility rites.

God is the first to alert Moses to the situation (32:7ff). His assessment is clear: 1) they have corrupted themselves, 2) they have turned aside from the commandments of God, 3) they have committed idolatry, 4) they are an obstinate people. When God's anger burned against the people, He suggests that He would destroy them, and begin a fresh with Moses, from whom He would make a "great nation." This is neither a test for Moses, nor an indication that God could actually lie in regard to His covenant promises. Rather, this section is given to us so that we might understand the manner of an intercessor. Moses, in the face of God's anger, stands firm on what God has said, and reminds Him of His promises. As Moses is a foreshadow of Messiah as our Intercessor, we are given insight into His intercession for us. He constantly pleads the merits of His own sacrifice, and the eternal promises that rest upon it. Like Moses, the intercession of our Messiah is based upon the eternal faithfulness of God.

When Moses returns to the mountain to intercede a second time for the people, he says: "But now, if You will, forgive their sin—and if not, please blot me out from Your book which You have written!" Once again, we are taught the method of an intercessor. Yeshua pleads in the same way: the merits of His own righteousness form the basis of His requests on our behalf. When we are said to be clothed in His righteousness (Is 61:10; 1Cor 1:30; Phil 3:9; 2Pet 1:1), it means that before we could ever be declared unrighteous, the Father would need to find some flaw in our Intercessor, for His righteousness has been reckoned to us. To the extent

Ki Tissa' • כי תשא 31:1-32:14 • 213

that Yeshua is righteous, to that extent all who are "in Him" are likewise righteous.

The final paragraph (the golden calf story) is at once a heart wrenching account of sin, as well as having many lessons for us. Here are a few.

1. In times of disappointment, people often attempt to "control God"

   - It appears that the people were first of all asking for a substitute for Moses.
   - Apparently they thought that if they did not have Moses, they could not rely upon God.
   - The making of the golden calf should be seen in the context of idol worship in the Ancient Near East. Idols were considered the thrones of the gods, and used as a way to bring the gods into proximity with the people. (note verse 4, "these are your gods...)
   - How do we "build golden calves" in times of disappointment?

2. Aaron's sin was that of syncretism. He thought he could appease the people with a little sin, in order to keep them from the greater one.

   - Is it possible Aaron was trying to "buy time" in hopes Moses would come and bring the people under control? (v. 2)
   - Note the text specifically says "<u>they</u> said, 'These are your gods, O Israel....'" (v. 4). It was not Aaron who made this statement. [Some Sages suggest it was Nadab and Abihu, which is why they are later destroyed by God, because the entered the Most Holy Place without confessing their sin and offering sacrifices for their guild.]
   - The text of v. 4 should probably read "These are your gods, O Israel ..." not "This is your God, O Israel ..." since the verb "brought you up" is plural, and it is hardly possible that Israel could have thought the golden calf just fashioned was the God of the exodus. Rather, they were putting Baal (often represented by a calf) and Adonai together in the exodus work. The altar Aaron built was for Adonai, the calf was the symbol of Baal. (Note v. 6, "The people sat down to eat and to drink, and rose up to play." This may well be euphemistic language for the sexual unchastity associated with the fertility cults.)
   - Perhaps Aaron thought the altar he built to Adonai would dissuade the people from worshiping the golden calf, but instead they worshiped both. Aaron's compromise "back-fires." Compromising worship to HaShem always "back-fires."

3. God refuses to be any part of syncretism.

    - Note well the emphasis in v. 7: "Go down at once for <u>your</u> people, whom <u>you</u> brought up from the land of Egypt, have corrupted themselves."
    - God refers to Israel as the people of Moses, for they are not worthy to be called His people, and He refuses to honor them with the blessing of His work in the exodus while they worship a pagan god.

4. God requires complete allegiance, like that of Moses.

    - Beginning in verse 9, God tests the allegiance of Moses. He suggests destroying Israel and making a people from Moses instead. Moses shows unbending allegiance to the word of God:
    –He brings before God the mighty work of redemption in the exodus.
    –He brings before God the great witness the exodus was to the nations and the honor of His name.
    –He brings before God the covenant promises established with the fathers.
    - In this passage we have Moses as an excellent type [foreshadowing] of Messiah, Who also intercedes for His people on the exact same bases:
    –He brings before God the mighty work of redemption He accomplished on the cross.
    –He brings before God the manner in which His name will be honored through those He has redeemed.
    –He brings before God the covenant promises established to Him through His completed work of redemption.
    –Our standing before the Father is as sure as the position of Yeshua before Him! (cp. vv. 30ff)

5. Often God uses extreme measures to bring His people back to Him.

    - Note that only the priests (tribe of Levi) sided with Moses when he called for repentance. Lesson: idolatry begins as a means to an end, and ends up as the end itself. The people turned to idolatry because Moses was gone. Now Moses is back, yet only the Levites are willing to follow him!
    - 3000 were slain before the people were ready to listen to the words of Moses (v. 28)
    - This does not mean that the punishment was over. Apparently v. 34 indicates that God would reserve judgment for Israel until a future

Ki Tissa' • כי תשא   31:1-32:14 • 215

time. He guarantees that they will possess the land, but he forestalls the punishment into the future. Lesson: present peace does not necessarily put the stamp of God's approval on present actions.

6. What might have been the future punishment to which God refers in v. 34? ("Now, go and lead the people to where I have told you. Behold! My angel shall go before you, and on the day that I make My account, I shall bring their sin to account against them.")

- If the plural "they" refers to Nadab and Abihu, then the accounting comes when they attempt to enter the Most Holy Place (apparently on Yom HaKippurim) and are executed by God Himself.
- If the punishment is for the nation as a whole (as appears more likely), is it possible that the veiling of Moses' face (34:29ff) was a Divine hiding of the revelation of Messiah, the initial method use by God to keep Israel from seeing and believing (as the prophet Isaiah would later describe, Is 6:9f)?
- It appears in 2 Cor 3 that this is Paul's understanding of the veil. In Ex. 34 there is no clear reason given for Moses' wearing the veil, though it appears on a surface reading that it was to assuage the fear of the people. Yet the fear of the people seems to be overcome by Moses simply talking to them (Ex 34:31). In 2 Co 3:13, the reason which Paul suggests for the veil over Moses' face is so that the people would not see the significance of the glory. [Note: the Greek term usually translated "fade," "fading," which is καταργέω, *katargeō*, never means "to fade," but "to abolish," "destroy," "render inoperative," "render insignificant."] The word "end" in 2 Co 3:13 should probably be understood to mean "goal" or "significance" (as in Rom 10:4, "Messiah is the goal of the Law").
- If this understanding of 2 Co 3:13 is correct, then the glory which was shining on the face of Moses was nothing less than the glory of Messiah Himself. This is implied by Paul in 2 Co 4:3-6, where the veiling of Moses' face is analogous to the veiling of the gospel to Israel, while those who believe have the "light of the glory of God in the face of Messiah." The glory which shone on the face of Moses was the direct revelation of the Messiah, but because of the rebellion and repeated rebellion of the people, Messiah's glory on the face of Moses was hidden from them. This was punishment indeed! Note 2 Co 3:14, "But their minds (Israel's) were hardened; for until this very day at the reading of the old covenant the same veil remains unlifted, because it is removed in Messiah."

- The blindness prophesied by Isaiah has its beginnings in the veiling of the face of Moses, God withholding the very revelation of the Messiah from the nation as a whole, though He would reveal Him to individuals who would make up the "remnant" in every generation. Cp. Lk 10:21ff; Rom 11:1-15
- We may therefore emphasize the converse, namely, that the revelation of the Messiah is God's supreme act of blessing. Nothing compares to the privilege of knowing the Messiah Who has been sent by the Father to accomplish eternal redemption for all of His elect.

PARASHAH 70
TRIENNIAL CYCLE

EXODUS 32:15-34:26

HAFTARAH: 2SAMUEL 22:10-51 | APOSTOLIC: ROMANS 9:14-16

The Trap of Idolatry

Sometimes we shake our heads as we read the history of Israel in the Tanach! How could they have been so ignorant, so hard hearted to have somehow missed all of the mighty acts of God in Egypt, to have forgotten the death of Egypt's first-born, the crossing of the Sea, the drowning of Egypt's finest—how is it possible that only a relatively short time after Moses and the rest ascend the mountain, the people are ready to revert to idolatry as a means of trying to find personal security?

What is more, our text is very explicit that Moses was coming down from the mountain with the tablets which contained the very writing of God, words recognizable because they were in God's own script (וְהַלֻּחֹת מַעֲשֵׂה אֱלֹהִים הֵמָּה וְהַמִּכְתָּב מִכְתַּב אֱלֹהִים הוּא חָרוּת עַל־הַלֻּחֹת, "and the tablets were the handiwork of God, and the writing was the writing of God, inscribed upon the tablets.") God has sent His revelation via the hand of Moses, His servant, and the people are engaged in seeking the help of gods who do not exist, who neither speak nor write! In seeking to find their own security, they have failed to prepare to receive the revelation from God, a revelation which would give to them the very path of life.

How had they come to this place? What was it that brought the people of Israel to seek the aid of a stupid idol rather than relying upon the God they knew was there?

Several factors might be sited, but I'll mention only a few. First, they had, over the course of their long stay in Egypt, *absorbed the culture and religion of that place.* We suspect, for example, that they had adopted the Egyptian circumcision which did not remove the foreskin, but only made an incision. After leaving Egypt, they "rolled away" the reproach of Egypt (a euphemistic play on "Gilgal" meaning "wheel" and the circular cutting of circumcision) at Gilgal by being circumcised as God had instructed. To what extent the people had become accustomed to various aspects of the Egyptian religions we are not sure, but it seems very possible that they had retained some "fear" of the gods of Egypt, for the golden calf may well be connected to the Apis Bull. The Satanic culture of Egypt had become an accepted "background" for religious thought in general. Certain aspects may have become "normal" for the Israelites.

Secondly, *they had considered their security to be more in the hands of Moses than in the hands of God.* Notice carefully that they were concerned with the fact that Moses has tarried upon the mountain, not that God had forsaken them. Perhaps they thought that if God had destroyed Moses, then He was angry at them, and so they sought other gods for their protection. But rather than seeking God, they resorted to seeking a false god. They had been led astray by the same sin with which Satan tempted Chavah (Eve)—"has God said?" which is understood to mean, "aren't you suspicious that God is not really looking out for your best interests and that maybe He's just using you?" Instead of seeing themselves as the servants of God, they viewed themselves more as the people of Moses. This is a kind of idolatry, perhaps not as blatant as constructing an idol and bowing to it, but idolatry nonetheless. Because idolatry is putting someone else in God's place.

Just previous to this event God had tested Moses with this very thing: would he be willing to exchange the God of Israel for a self-serving God—a god who is unjust but gives me what I want? "I shall make your descendants countless as the stars...." Moses would have nothing of it. Either the God of Israel is the true God, or there is nothing left. Genuine faith in God is singular faith—a faith that relies upon the God of Israel and upon Him alone.

In the initial punishment meted out by Moses upon the people, he burns the idol (since it was most likely made of wood overlaid with gold, it burnt easily), grinds it to powder, sprinkles it over water (cp. Deut 9:21, "the brook that came down from the mountain"), and makes the people drink it. Drinking the ashen water reminds one of the test for the unfaithful wife (Num 5), in which the dust from the floor of the Tabernacle and ink from a scroll is mixed with water and then the woman is made to drink the mixture. At Sinai, Israel, as the unfaithful wife of Adonai, is similarly made to drink water mixed with the ashes. Such an ordeal was no doubt humiliating, and Moses clearly humiliates the Israelites by making them "drink their god." Rather than delivering them from their dilemma, their idol god would end up in the latrine.

But even more severe measures are taken: Moses makes an offer to the people to prove their repentance. He asks them to commit to the Lord, but only the Levites make such an open confession. As a result, the Levites are sent, not by Moses, but by God, to go through the camp and slay the idolaters. About 3000 are killed before the massacre stops. This emphasizes a third factor that led the people to idolatry: *they had not understood how much God hates idolatry.* Even Moses, returning to the mountain and offering himself as a substitute for the people (32:32), pleads for God's forgiveness. But while God forestalls His punishment, He nonetheless promises retribution upon those who had rebelled against Him.

This same theme is continued in chapter 33, though it may not be apparent. Idolatry is not only bowing to a false god, or putting a man in the place of God, *it is also thinking or living as though there is really no need for God.* Israel was to be the primary example of how God relates to His people, so she was the nation redeemed from Egypt and she was the nation among whom the Lord would dwell. Her ability to be a "light to the nations" (Is 42:6) consisted in her willingness to be obedient to God as an open demonstration of who God is (cf. Deut 4:6–8). When the suggestion is made to Moses that an angel would go ahead of them to route out the enemies of Israel, but that God Himself would not dwell with the people—this was not acceptable to Moses. He was a man who had come to know God, and was known of Him ("I know you by name," 33:17). Moses had established an intimate understanding of who God is and had entered into personal covenant with Him. On this basis Moses makes the incredible statement: "…if You do not go Yourself, do not send us up from here" (33:15). Moses could not even think of proceeding with the journey unless he was assured that God would be making Himself known in the midst of the people, abiding with them and thus protecting them along the way. This suggests a fourth factor which led the people into idolatry: *they had been satisfied with a corporate relationship with God.* Moses, on the other hand, had come to understand that God is not only the God of the nation, but also of the individual. This is boldly displayed when Moses makes the straightforward request (33:18): "Show me Your glory." The interesting thing is that Moses' definition of God's glory and God's own definition may not have been the same. It seems at least possible that Moses was looking for a visible phenomenon ("show me…") while God clearly teaches that His glory is summed up in the whole of His attributes—His own revelation of Himself known through His written word (Torah) and His works.

The Name of God is the single summation of all that He is—of the sum of His attributes. Thus, when God puts Moses into the cleft of the rock, He first pronounces His ineffable Name, and then proceeds to reveal His glory by describing His attributes. God's glory is contained in His goodness (33:19), which is another way of saying His character or attributes (34:6f). It is superfluous to say that one loves God but has no desire to know Him as He has revealed Himself. To be satisfied with the pop-culture definition of God is likewise to engage in idolatry, for the worship of the god which the culture has defined is the worship of "another god." The same may be said of Yeshua and the definitions which our modern day has attempted to attach to the historical Messiah. Yeshua is the One with whom Moses communicated (Ex 24) for He had visible form (including feet) and ate with him and the others. This One described in our *parashah* is one with Yeshua. We therefore must strive to know Yeshua as He is revealed in Scripture, not as modern society has redressed Him to fit the needs of the time. Our golden calves may be less obvious, but they are there nonetheless.

How, then, can we guard against idolatry? How can we prepare ourselves now for the unknown events of the future, regarding which we may feel the panic to make our own security and create our own substitute for God? 1) refuse to accept the idolatry of our culture, regardless of how subtle or pervasive it may be; 2) recognize that God's appointed leaders are given to lead the people to God, not to replace Him; 3) recognize how much God hates idolatry; 4) don't be satisfied with a corporate relationship with God—seek a personal one; 5) accept only the self-revelation of God, not the man-made model. This revelation of God is to be found in the Scriptures, in the creation (cf. Ps 19:1ff; Rom 1:19f), and in the person of the Messiah (cf. Heb 1:1–4).

The Presence of God

Moses sought the Presence (literally "face") of God to be among the people. He realized that apart from God's presence among the people, there was no reason to go any further. "If Your Presence does not go along (with us), do not bring us forward from here" (33:15). Mere religion is content to travel the journey without God; true worship, based as it is in a covenant relationship with God, recognizes that without His Presence, the outward signs of piety are nothing but an empty shell.

Our *parashah* teaches us that Moses erected a "tent of meeting" (אֹהֶל מוֹעֵד) far outside of the camp. Here he would go to meet with God in order to receive from Him direct instructions for the people. Apparently Joshua would also go with him, for the text indicates that when Moses would come out of the tent, Joshua would remain within it (33:11). Interestingly, the Hebrew calls Joshua יְהוֹשֻׁעַ בִּן־נוּן, *Yehoshua bin Nun*. While this spelling for "son" (which is usually בֵּן, *bein* or בֶּן *ben* in construct form) is not uncommon (found 17x in the Tanach), the Sages remark that it is most often found in those places where "understanding" is emphasized (analogous to Hebrew בִּין, *bîn*, "to understand"). They make a midrash on Joshua's name: בִּינוּן means "a person of understanding," and suggest that Joshua, as the chosen disciple of Moses, had been granted the particular gift of understanding as he was preparing eventually to assume leadership after the death of Moses.

If we might be allowed our own midrash, it seems interesting to me that the scenario presented in our *parashah* models the mysterious inner workings of God Himself. The tent of meeting, set up outside of the camp, clearly portrays an incarnational model. That is, the sanctity of Mt. Sinai is transported to the earth through the tent of meeting, where the Presence of God is revealed in the "face to face" meetings with Moses. The text is clear that Moses' relationship with God was different than other prophets. While they received God's revelation in dreams or vision, when they were not in the full use of their faculties, Moses converses with God while fully conscious, as a man speaks with his friend (cf. 33:11). In this capacity, Moses foreshadowed the Messiah Himself, Who could claim that "All things have been handed over to Me by My Father, and no one knows who the Son is except the Father, and who the Father is except the Son, and anyone to whom the Son wills to reveal Him" (Matt 11:17; Lk 10:22). The relationship of the Messiah to the Father was unique, foreshadowed by the unique relationship that Moses had with God. But in a typical or midrashic sense, what is foreshadowed by Joshua? Perhaps it is not too far-fetched to see in Joshua the work of the Spirit, Who aided the Messiah in His work, and Who gives *understanding* to the words of Messiah (cf. Jn 14:26). When Moses leaves the tent of meeting, Joshua remains. This is illustrative of the teaching of Yeshua, that though He would depart and return to the Father, He would send the Spirit Who would remain with His followers and lead them in the truth.

As Moses petitions the Almighty on behalf of Israel, He seeks God's assurance that He will, indeed, go with them—that He would graciously abide (reveal His Presence) in their midst. God grants the request of Moses based upon the unique relationship he has with the Almighty: "I will also do this thing of which you have spoken; for you have found favor in My sight and I have known you by name" (33:17). As a portend of the Messiah's own intercession, we are reminded that God's grace to us comes, not because of what we have done, but because of who Messiah is. God grants the requests of our Intercessor, and as a result, we are blessed.

God instructs Moses to ascend the Mountain again, and to bring with him two new tablets upon which He would re-write the Ten Words, since the first set of tablets was destroyed because of the people's disobedience (34:1). This time, Moses goes up alone, leaving Joshua in the camp. When he arrives at the top of the mountain, God descends in the cloud, and fulfills His promise to reveal His glory to Moses. This He does not only in a visual way, but in declaring His Name to Moses, that is, describing

Himself in attributes of mercy. The Sages enumerated Thirteen Attributes from this text (34:5–7), though they differed slightly on how the various terms should be grouped, and exactly what was meant by each of the terms. The most common enumeration is found in b.*Rosh Hashanah* 17b.

We note first of all that the Tetragrammaton is given twice. The Masoretic accentuation indicates that the first occurrence stands alone, while the second is combined with אֵל, thus, יהוה, יהוה אֵל, "ADONAI, ADONAI (Who is) God."

1. יהוה - the Eternal, Ineffable Name of God reveals His eternal, unchangeable character, and therefore His utter faithfulness to His word. His promises are secure, because He never changes (Mal 3:6). As the God of Abraham, Isaac, and Jacob, He has promised to abide with His people, and to fulfill in them all of His sovereign designs.

2. יהוה אֵל - The combination of יהוה with אֵל emphasizes the power of God. Not only is He the eternal, unchangeable One (infinite in time and space), He is also all-powerful (infinite in power). He will perform all of His holy will because He is able to do so. He orders the events of the universe, and is able to bring all things to their appointed end. "For from Him and through Him and to Him are all things. To Him be the glory forever. Amen!" (Rom 11:36).

3. רַחוּם - Compassionate. God's mercies are demonstrated continually, for they are new every morning (Lam 3:23). In His compassion, He forestalls His condemnation of sinners, and provides payment for their sin through the substitute sacrifice of His own Son. God's compassion is fully seen in Messiah's work on our behalf.

4. וְחַנּוּן - and Gracious. God is gracious to the undeserving. He understands the distresses that come upon His people, and He comes to them with grace, with aid for their troubles.

5. אֶרֶךְ אַפַּיִם - Slow to anger. Both with the righteous and the unrighteous, God is patient. Instead of immediately enacting the punishment that sin deserves, He gives them time to consider their actions and to seek repentance. Through His word, He makes known what is right and wrong, and calls sinners to repent.

6. וְרַב-חֶסֶד - and Abundant in Lovingkindness. The word חֶסֶד, *chesed* may have a connection to "covenant faithfulness." Even when His people are faithless, He remains faithful to His covenant, because He cannot

deny Himself (2Tim 2:13).

7. וֶאֱמֶת - and Truth. God is abundant in lovingkindness and truth. The two terms (חֶסֶד and אֱמֶת) may function as a hendiadys (two terms combined to give one thought), emphasizing that God is faithful to His covenant promises because He is always true. He never speaks falsehood. All of His words are eternally true.

8. נֹצֵר חֶסֶד לָאֲלָפִים - Preserver of lovingkindness to thousands. God's grace is infinite. He intends to bring to Himself a host of people that no one can number, of every tribe, kindred, and tongue (Rev 5:9). God's grace is not limited by man's rebellion. He is able to change the heart of man, and bring all of His chosen ones to Himself (Jn 6:37).

9. נֹשֵׂא עָוֺן - Forgiver of Iniquity. God is said to forgive in three categories, and each of these have been traditionally taken as a separate attribute of God. In this case, iniquity is usually understood to be intentional sins, and specifically sins against one's fellow man. God forgives even intentional sins for those who seek His forgiveness and who repent of their sin.

10. וָפֶשַׁע - and Transgression. This word is taken to emphasize sins of rebellion against God in particular. God is willing to forgive those who sin directly against Him if they seek His forgiveness and turn from their rebellion.

11. וְחַטָּאָה - and Sin. The Sages suggest that the emphasis of this word is that of "sin done out of carelessness or apathy." These may be sins committed out of ignorance or weakness. Yet even these are sins, for if a person were diligent to know the gravity of defying God's will, they would not sin through carelessness. Still, God is willing to forgive such sins if one seeks His forgiveness and is committed to a life of righteousness.

12. וְנַקֵּה - and Cleanses. When one seeks forgiveness from God through the work of His Son, Yeshua, and turns from his sin, God cleanses him of that sin, meaning He wipes the record of that sin away. "If we confess our sins, He is faithful and righteous to forgive us our sins and to cleanse us from all unrighteousness" (1Jn 1:9). "As far as the east is from the west, so far have I removed your transgressions from you" (Ps 103:12).

13. לֹא יְנַקֶּה פֹּקֵד עָוֺן - He will not cleanse *but* visits iniquity. God's mercy and grace do not overturn His justice. He deals justly with iniquity. Yet He

"visits" the iniquity of the fathers upon the children and grandchildren to the third and fourth generation. While the word פָּקַד. *paqad*, can have the sense of "punish" or "bring judgment," it can also have the sense of "make careful inspection," as well as to "instruct, command, urge." The sins of the fathers affect their children. Yet God, in His justice does not punish the children for the sins of their fathers (Deut 24:16). He recognizes that the sins of the fathers have a negative affect on their children, and so He comes "visiting" them with instruction, giving them His Torah of truth by which they will know His will and be able to discern what is right and wrong. Still, if the children refuse to turn from the sins of their fathers, and if they walk in the ways of their fathers, God's justice will prevail. Each generation will reap what they sow.

Parashah Twenty-Two
וַיַּקְהֵל – Vayaqheil

"and he assembled"
Exodus 35:1-38:20

In the Triennial Cycle there are two Parashot

34:27-36:38 | 37:1-38:20

Note: the first *parashah* in the Triennial Cycle begins a few verses before Annual portion of

Parashah 71
Triennial Cycle

Exodus 34:27-36:38

Haftarah: Jeremiah 31:31-40 | Apostolic: 1Corinthians 12:1-13

The Glory of God Shining in the Face of Yeshua

In this *parashah* we learn of the final meeting of Moses with the Almighty upon Sinai, the re-issuing of the Ten Words (עֲשֶׂרֶת הַדְּבָרִים, *'aseret hadevarim*) written upon two stone tablets, the descent of Moses from the mountain to the people, and the subsequent construction of the Tabernacle and its furnishings in accordance with God's instructions. It is noteworthy that the Sages of old collated the reading from Jeremiah 31 as the *haftarah* for this Torah portion in the triennial cycle. In so doing, they recognized that the New Covenant prophesied by Jeremiah fit the re-writing of the Torah (as summarized in the Ten Words) after Moses destroyed the first set of tablets in the face of Israel's disobedience at the Golden Calf incident. In their minds, the re-writing of the Torah upon the heart of Israel was pictured in Moses returning to the people with the re-written words upon the new tablets. Moreover, the response of the nation, in bringing their abundant contributions for the construction of the Tabernacle, evidenced their willingness to receive the Torah. Furthermore, our Torah portion reiterates seven times that the people contributed as their hearts were "stirred" or as their hearts "moved them" (Ex. 35:5, 21-22, 26, 29, 34; 36:2), corresponding to Jeremiah's promise that the Torah would be written upon the heart in the establishment of the New Covenant. Even as the Ten Words were written by the finger of God (we should understand the phrase in 34:28, "And He wrote on the tablets the words of the covenant, the Ten Commandments," to refer to God), so the writing of the Torah upon the heart is likewise the work of the Almighty.

In 34:28 the notice is given that Moses remained upon the mountain for 40 days and 40 nights, a number that is usually symbolic of a period of testing (the deluge of the flood; the wilderness wandering of Israel; periods of rest during the days of the Judges; the taunting of the Philistines with Goliath as their champion; the temptation of Yeshua in the wilderness). Later on (Deut. 9:25; 10:10) Moses explains to the people of Israel that he was two times upon the mountain for 40 days and 40 nights as he interceded for the people, imploring God that He would not destroy them for their sin. Once again, Moses stands as a foreshadow of the Messiah Who would likewise undergo testing, and would emerge victorious as the intercessor for His people.

When Moses descended from the mountain, he was not aware that his face was shining, the result of talking "face to face" (cf. Ex. 33:11; Deut. 5:4; 34:10) with God. The glory of God was shining in the face of Moses. The Hebrew uses the verb קָרַן (found only here in the *qal*, cf. Ps 69:32 for its use in the *hitpael*) to describe this phenomenon. The context, as well as the parallel with Hab 3:4 ("He has rays flashing from His hand") suggests that the meaning of this verb is "rays of light" that went out from the face of Moses, as likewise interpreted by the Lxx, Peshitta, and Targums. The verb, however, is related to the noun קֶרֶן (*keren*) meaning "horn" or "strength," which was most likely used here as a direct negation of the golden calf. The *power* of God is revealed in His Torah, not in a molten image. Recognizing the connection to the word for "horn," the Vulgate translated the verb with *cornutus,* "having horns," which in turn gave rise to Michelangelo's famous statue of Moses with horns.

It is instructive to note carefully what happened as a result of the shining of Moses' face. At first, Aaron and the rulers were afraid to come near to him. But after Moses calls to them, they return and he relates to them the commandments he had received while on the mountain. Then, after he had finished speaking with the people, Moses put a veil over his face, but the text does not explain why. Many commentators have suggested that he did so in order to assuage the fear of the people, but this hardly seems reasonable. Apparently they were not afraid of the brilliance of his face, for after Moses calls to them, they return and listen to his words. Furthermore, the text goes on to explain that whenever Moses would go into the tent of meeting to inquire of God, he would remove the veil, and when he emerged from the tent, the people would see that his face was shining. He would thus replace the veil over his face until he entered the tent again to speak with God. Thus, the text before us gives no clear indication regarding the purpose of the veil.

It is this ambiguity that gives rise to Paul's midrash on our portion in 2Cor 3. We know, from Exodus 24, that the One with whom Moses spoke was none other than the Messiah, Who is the physical representation of God, and in Whom is the "radiance of His glory" (Heb 1:3). As such, the glory that shone in the face of Moses was, in fact, the glory of Messiah. With that in mind, Paul understands the veil over Moses' face midrashically. Since Moses can stand as a metonym for the Torah itself (cf. 2Cor 3:15, "…Moses is read"), for Paul, the glory of Messiah shines forth from the Torah (cf. Rom 10:4, "For Messiah is the goal of the Torah..."). But in order to see the glory of Messiah in the Torah, one must have one's eyes opened by the work of the Spirit. When the Spirit "unveils" the glory of Messiah in the Torah, those who read and hear it see and put their trust in the Messiah. But apart from this work of the Spirit, the glory of Messiah in the Torah is veiled. This corresponds to the words of Isaiah 6:9–10, "He said, 'Go, and tell this people: keep on listening, but do not perceive; keep on looking, but do not understand. Render the hearts of this people insensitive, their ears dull, and their eyes dim, otherwise they might see with their eyes, hear with their ears, understand with their hearts, and return and be healed.'" Yeshua refers to this text to explain why He taught in parables (Matt 13:14; Mk 4:12; Lk 8:10; Jn 12:40, cf. Acts 28:26–27).

Unfortunately, the English translators of 2Cor 3 have been influenced by yet another interpretation of why Moses wore a veil. From ancient times, Christian commentators have suggested that the reason Moses put on the veil was because he did not want the people to see that the glory or shining of his face was fading or diminishing with time. Thus, many newer translations speak of the glory in Moses' face as "fading away" (cf. 2Cor 3:7, 13). But the word translated "fading" (καταργέω, *katargeo*) means "to render ineffective," "to annul," "to do away with," but it never means "to fade." In reality, what Paul is saying in his midrash is that the veil upon Moses face was for the purpose of rendering the glory "ineffective." Instead of seeing the glory of God, which would bring a person to believe, the veiled glory had no effect. Thus, the NET Bible has it correctly translated: "and not like Moses who used to put a veil over his face to keep the Israelites from staring at the result of the glory that was made ineffective" (2Cor. 3:13). The veil was put over the face of Moses (and by analogy, over the Torah) so that the glory of Messiah could not be seen. But whenever the Spirit of God takes away the veil, the glory of Messiah is seen (=known), and thus received. While God allowed the veil to remain so that the nation of Israel would not see the glory of Messiah in the words of Moses, in the Apostle's proclamation of the Gospel, God was removing the veil and many were seeing and receiving the Messiah Yeshua.

Chapter 35 of our Torah *parashah* gives a brief summary of the words spoken by Moses to the people after he descended from the mountain. It consists of primarily two sections: the first is a reiteration of the Sabbath commandment, and the second is the instructions for the people to bring contributions for the construction of the *Mishkan* (Tabernacle). Why would Moses first reiterate the Sabbath commandment, and then admonish the people to bring their offerings? The purpose seems clear:

the bringing of the materials for constructing the *Mishkan* was to be done from a heart of gratitude for the covenant God had made with Israel. The Sabbath was the sign of the covenant (Ex 31:12ff), and the Tabernacle was the central revelation of God's way of salvation within the covenant (through the work of a mediator [priest] offering sacrifices). The arrangement of our text, in which the Sabbath commandment precedes the request for contributions, teaches us that access to the Tabernacle was available only to those who were covenant members. One could not be an outsider to the covenant and expect to have communion with God via the Tabernacle. Or to put it another way, one could not expect to enjoy the fellowship offered in the Tabernacle if one was not willing to accept the covenant as God had revealed it. Here, as is the case throughout the Scriptures, obedience and faith are wed together as inseparable partners of a single reality.

In this reiteration of the Sabbath commandment, Moses adds "You shall not kindle a fire in any of your dwellings on the Sabbath day" (35:3). The Sages understood the verb בָּעַר (*ba'ar*, used here in the *piel*) to mean "begin a fire anew," and ruled that it was permissible to use a fire that was kindled before the Sabbath. This gave rise to the rabbinic rule that one was obligated to kindle a fire prior to the Sabbath, which most likely was the basis for instituting a blessing over the kindling of fire (as seen in the blessing for lighting candles on the eve of Sabbath). The Karaites, however, reacting to the rabbinic interpretations, spent the Sabbath day in darkness (see the comments of Sarna, *JPS Torah Commentary: Exodus*, p. 222 and n. 2). Some later Karaites, however, broke with their traditions, and accepted the rulings of the Sages regarding fire on the Sabbath.

In attempting to understand the meaning of this prohibition, one might cross-reference Jer 7:18, "The children gather wood, and the fathers kindle (מְבַעֲרִים, *m^eva'arim*) the fire, and the women knead dough to make cakes for the queen of heaven; and they pour out drink offerings to other gods in order to spite Me." Here, the kindling of a fire is linked to the process of gathering wood. If we collate that with the incident in which a man is caught gathering wood on the Sabbath (Num 15:32ff), a transgression that received the death penalty, we may understand that the prohibition for kindling a fire was given as an example of the kind of work that was to be suspended on the Sabbath. In this way, kindling a fire would be seen as the "common work" of the six days, which was to be set aside on the Sabbath.

The admonition to the people, that they bring offerings of goods and materials needful for the building of the Tabernacle and its furnishings, was met with happy compliance. The people were so moved in their hearts that they gave abundantly. So great was the outpouring of the free will offerings, that Moses was forced to constrain the people: "So Moses issued a command, and a proclamation was circulated throughout the camp, saying, 'Let no man or woman any longer perform work for the contributions of the sanctuary.' Thus the people were restrained from bringing any more" (36:6). This notice is in stark contrast to the heart of the people as they engaged in the idolatry of the golden calf. There, they were entirely consumed with their own needs. Here, they willingly give of their wealth in order to construct the Tabernacle according to God's instructions.

This illustrates an important principle made clear by the teaching of our Savior: "… for where your treasure is, there your heart will be also" (Matt 6:21, cp. Lk 12:34). The treasures we have are not only our material wealth and money but also our time and our life energy. Our *parashah* is a sober reminder that as our hearts are more and more given over to loving God, we will willingly use our treasures to accomplish the advancement of His kingdom and the sanctification of His Name upon the earth.

The remainder of our *parashah* is essentially a reiteration of the instructions for constructing the Tabernacle and its furnishings, now changed to narrate the actual construction. The point of such a repetition is that the Tabernacle was constructed precisely according to the instructions of God. This is the connection with our Apostolic portion. In 1Cor 12, Paul speaks of each member of the community being endowed with particular ability given by the Spirit. Even as the people of Israel each contributed to the building of the Tabernacle, so each member of the body of Messiah contributes to the building up of the community in Yeshua. Not everyone has the same task, but everyone's task is important. Even as Bezalel and Oholiab were singled out as leading craftsmen in the production of the Tabernacle, so there are those in the body of Messiah who may have a more conspicuous duty within the community. But this in no way diminishes the high importance of the work done by those whose contribution may not be so public. Paul uses the metaphor of the human body itself: not everyone is an eye, or a hand, but every part is necessary for the proper functioning of the whole. "But now God has placed the members, each one of them, in the body, just as He desired" (v. 18). By way of illustration, then, we may ask ourselves how we are contributing to the growth and building up of the community of Yeshua. Do we have the same heart demonstrated by Israel of old, to bring our "willing contributions" (i.e., to function in the manner in which God has gifted us by His Spirit) in abundance?

As I noted above, the Sages saw a clear connection between the rewriting of the Torah upon the new tablets that Moses brought with him the second time, and the writing of the Torah upon the heart of Israel as prophesied by Jeremiah. Our *haftarah* contains the only occurrence of the term "New Covenant" (בְּרִית חֲדָשָׁה, *bᵉrit chadāshāh*) in the Tanach. It is to this text that Yeshua refers when He identifies the cup of redemption in the Pesach seder as representing the "new covenant in My blood" (Lk 22:20, cf. 1Cor 11:25), meaning that His subsequent sacrifice upon the execution stake would procure everything necessary to bring about the New Covenant as prophesied by Jeremiah. Likewise, Paul identifies himself as a servant of the "new covenant" (2Cor 3:6), because in His proclamation of Yeshua as the Messiah, the New Covenant would be realized through the salvation of God's chosen people. In this same way, the writer to the Hebrews identifies Yeshua as the "mediator of the New Covenant," (9:15; 12:24).

But what exactly is the "New Covenant?" Unfortunately, this terminology has become so common place in Christian theology that people regularly talk about the "New Covenant" without really considering what it actually is. Usually, the New Covenant is viewed as opposite of the "Old Covenant," which many people identify with the "Old Testament." In fact, the designations "Old Testament" and "New Testament" are nothing more than another way of saying "Old Covenant" and "New Covenant" (since our English word "testament" is derived from the Latin *testamentum* meaning "covenant"). Thus, the Christian Church has regularly taught that the "Old Covenant" or "Old Testament" was the precursor of the "New Covenant" or "New Testament," and that since Yeshua has established the "New Covenant," the "Old Covenant" has been abolished or relegated to an inferior position. Given such a theology, it is no wonder that the "Old Testament" always takes a "back seat" to the "New Testament." In fact, in many churches, the "Old Testament" is essentially neglected, with the exception of the Psalms and few of the prophetic passages.

In reality, the designations "Old Testament" and "New Testament" are the fruit of Replacement Theology formulated by the early emerging Church. Believing that God had abandoned Israel, and that He had replaced her with the new, "spiritual" Israel, the Scriptures of Israel were considered antique (old) while the Scriptures of the Church (those of the Apostles) were received as relevant (new). The Hebrew Scriptures constituted the Bible for "old Israel," while the Apostolic Scriptures were received as the Bible for the "new Israel." It is not uncommon to hear the teaching that "as Christians, the New Testament alone is what we obey." Thus, if something is found in the "New Testament," it is received as normative (or at least it is supposed to be received as normative), while the instructions and commandments of the "Old Testament" are relegated to bygone eras. The oft heard slogan is: "the New is in the Old contained; the Old is by the New explained." But if we were to accept this as true, we would have to say that before the canonization of the "New Testament," no one was able to explain the "Old Testament," and we know that is not the case. The so-called "Old Testament" was the very Bible used by the Apostles in their proclamation of the Gospel, and the Hebrew Scriptures were the means by which all true believers came to faith in the centuries before the Apostles. In fact, the teachings of the Apostles cannot be understood apart from the Hebrew Scriptures. Rather than the "New Testament" shining light back upon the "Old," the Tanach is a light shining forward to illuminate the teachings of the Apostles.

In view of this, we do well to reconsider the words of Jeremiah and seek to understand how he defines the New Covenant. First, we see specifically that the New Covenant is made "with the house of Israel and with the house of Judah" (31:31). Yet in v. 33, the New Covenant is made "with the house of Israel," without mention of "the house of Judah." What the prophet is indicating is that the New Covenant is made at a time subsequent to his own, when the dispersed tribes of Israel will be regathered and reunited as the single people of Israel. Even to this day, that has not yet happened.

Second, Jeremiah contrasts the New Covenant with the "covenant which I made with their fathers in the day I took them by the hand to bring them out of the land of Egypt, My covenant which they broke..." (v. 32). As he demonstrates in the following verses, the contrast is not in the substance of the covenant itself, but in the response of the house of Israel to the covenant. The covenant of Sinai was broken, not by God (for He gave it as an eternal covenant), but by the generation of Israel that came out of Egypt. In contrast, Israel will be faithful to the New Covenant.

Third, the reason Israel will be faithful to the New Covenant is because God will sovereignly write it upon their heart: "I will put My Torah within them and on their heart I will write it" (v. 33). God does not have two different Torahs! The Torah that He will write upon the heart of Israel in the day of their salvation is the same Torah that He wrote on tablets of stone, and put into the hands of Moses. It is this same Torah that is written on the heart of everyone He brings to salvation. Thus, Paul could confess: "I joyfully concur with the Torah of God in the inner man" (Rom 7:22) and David could say: "Your word I have treasured in my heart, that I may not sin against You" (Ps 119:11).

Fourth, this sovereign work of writing the Torah upon the heart of the nation of Israel is the fruit of Yeshua's work in procuring salvation for the elect. Jeremiah indicates that the essence of the New Covenant is to be found in the forgiveness of sins: "for I will forgive their iniquity, and their sin I will remember no more" (v. 34). We know that there is no forgiveness of sins apart from the payment of sin offered by the death of the sinless One on the cross. The New Covenant, then, as Jeremiah foresees it, occurs at a time when the House of Israel has come to receive God's forgiveness for their sins. This means that on a national scale, Israel will receive Yeshua as their true Messiah—as the only means for them to stand righteous before God. Once again, it is clear that even up to our own times, this has not occurred.

Finally, the result of the establishment of the New Covenant is that the nation of Israel will be faithful to God: "They will not teach again, each man his neighbor and each man his brother, saying, 'Know ADONAI,' for they will all know Me, from the least of them to the greatest of them," declares ADONAI" (v. 34). Here, the idea of "knowing ADONAI" should be understood in a covenant sense: to "know ADONAI" means to have intimate, faithful relationship with Him in the context of a covenant of marriage (note v. 32, "even though I was a husband to them"). Once again, such a covenant faithfulness *on a national scale* has never been seen in Israel.

But all of these characteristics have been the norm for the believing remnant in every generation. Every true believer, then, has participated in the New Covenant as the first fruits of the final harvest. But the fulfillment of the New Covenant is yet future, for it awaits the national revival and salvation of the physical offspring of Jacob. It is to this that Paul points when he writes: "For I do not want you, brethren, to be uninformed of this mystery…that a partial hardening has happened to Israel until the fullness of the Gentiles has come in; and so all Israel will be saved" (Rom 11:25–26). When this comes to pass, something new indeed will have taken place, for the remnant of Israel, enlarged by the ingathering of the elect Gentiles from the nations, will at last include not a part but the whole of the Jewish nation.

Parashah 72
Triennial Cycle

Exodus 37:1-38:20

Haftarah: 1Kings 8:8-22 | Apostolic: 1Peter 2:4-10

Furnishing the Mishkan

In our *parashah* this Shabbat we see the actual completion of the articles commanded by God to be in the *Mishkan* (מִשְׁכָּן, "tabernacle") itself: the ark (הָאָרֹן, *ha'aron*), table (הַשֻּׁלְחָן, *hashulchan*), menorah, (הַמְּנוֹרָה, *ham{e}nôrāh*) and altar of incense (מִזְבֵּחַ הַקְּטֹרֶת, *mizbeiach haq{e}toret*), along with the articles to be placed in the courtyard (מִזְבַּח הָעֹלָה, *mizbeiach hā'olāh*, altar of whole burnt sacrifice, הַכִּיּוֹר, *hakiyôr*, the laver, הֶחָצֵר, *hechatzeir*, the courtyard with all of its screens, posts and sockets.)

The articles in the *Mishkan* itself were, first of all, the Ark which is considered the throne of Adonai, for the Scriptures speak of Adonai as "dwelling" (יָשַׁב, *yashav*) or enthroned between the cherubim (1Sam 4:4; 2Sam 6:2; Ps 80:1; 99:1; Is 37:16). The שְׁכִינָה *shekinah* shone forth above the Ark, being a visible representation of the presence of the Almighty. The Ark was the focal point of atonement, that place at which sinful Israel and Adonai Most Holy met and were reconciled through the placement of the blood (כִּפֶּר, *kipeir*) upon the cover or top of the Ark. It is, at the same time, the very focal point of the covenant, for the Ten Words of the Torah made between Israel and HaShem are guarded safe within the Ark. So redemption and covenant are forever wed in the symbolism of the Ark and the atonement made there. The presence of God at the point of atonement shows that His desire to dwell among His people is the ultimate and final purpose of the covenant itself.

It is highly significant that the Apostles chose the same Greek term used by the Lxx to translate כַּפֹּרֶת (*kapporet*), the "mercy seat" or "cover" of the Ark (37:6) to describe the concept of "propitiation," ἱλαστήριον (*hilstērion*), applying it to Yeshua Himself Who is "our propitiation" (Rom 3:25). Likewise, the writer to the Messianic Jews (Hebrews) uses this word to describe the "mercy seat" of the Ark (Heb 9:5). The point is obvious: Yeshua is the covering of the Ark, the place where the blood is put in the ritual atonement on Yom Kippur—a covenant dramatization of the eternal reality that would be secured in the death of Yeshua as the

Lamb of God. Even as ADONAI walked with Adam and Chavah in *Gan Eden* before they rebelled against Him, so He purposes to restore mankind to Himself in order that He might dwell with us. The three-times holy God has purposed to be Immanuel, "God with us."

But it is not enough for just the generation of Israel who came forth from Egypt to experience this *reproachment* with the Almighty in the renewal of friendship that the *Mishkan* afforded. Had the Tabernacle only contained the Ark, one might surmise that the whole concept of atonement was limited to the physical seed of Jacob—that they alone would be the recipient of God's forgiving grace. But the articles of furniture that fill the Holy place paint a different picture. Here the cycle of life is seen, bespeaking a generational reality. Here there is need for constant maintenance and refurbishing, day-by-day, week by week, season to season and generation to generation. The bread of the Presence (לֶחֶם פָּנִים, *lechem panim*) has to be changed weekly; the wicks on the *menorah* must constantly be trimmed and the oil replenished; the fire of the altar of incense must constantly be renewed and new incense spread upon its coals. And year after year the *Cohen Gadol* enters on Yom Kippur to enact the sacred rituals. In other words, the eternality of the Ark with the eternal *Shekinah*, illumines the temporal, and defines the mission once again. The glory of ADONAI is to be taken by Israel into her daily living and must shine forth upon a world that is in darkness and therefore does not enjoy the very purpose for which God created all peoples. We are to be, as it were, the bread of life to a dying and hungry world; we are to be the light shining forth to those who live in darkness; and we are to be that sweet-smelling savor of life to a world trapped in the stench of hatred and rebellion (cf. 2Cor 2;15). We, in the cycle of our temporal lives, are to show forth the reality of the eternal One, and shed the light of an eternal friendship with our Creator, a friendship made possible through the blood of the innocent victim—through the awful ordeal of sacrifice.

Here, then, is yet another major theme of our Pesach celebration which is soon upon us. If we have been freed from slavery, then we have a message for the whole world about the true God, namely, that He is not for slavery, and that He intends men to live free. Paul takes this metaphor and fills it out beautifully in Rom 6 in which he reminds us that we were slaves to sin, but now we have become slaves to righteousness. He has the Pesach theme in mind, for our redemption from Egypt was not to render us autonomous to do whatever we wished, but to render us free so that we might serve Him. Freedom is not the unrestrained ability of self-determination, but the divinely given ability to serve HaShem in ways we never could have while enslaved. We are redeemed to go and serve our Redeemer.

But while the inward, heart freedom is surely foundational and all-important, we miss something vital if we fail to realize that in the redemptive plan of God, so beautifully displayed in the Pesach story, there is a call to freedom in our physical as well as spiritual world. It is surely true that apart from renewed hearts of faith no freedom is possible, but it is equally true that where salvation reigns in the hearts of people there will be a natural concern that freedom as God defines it reigns upon this earth. It seems that often this very issue is where the Christian and the Jewish communities are at odds. Rabbi Greenberg writes:

> "…in as much as the Exodus occurred in history, so will the messianic age also remain in history. This idea is in contrast to the development of Christian messianism. The early Christians experienced Jesus as the redeemer in their midst. Having experienced the Messiah's 'actual presence,' the Christians were tormented by the contradictions between his coming, which should have brought the Exodus for all, and the reality of a world that was still unredeemed. One way to resolve this conflict was by denying that the Messiah had come. But for some, the experience of his coming was too strong to deny. Another interpretation was then explored. Somehow the nature of messianic redemption had been misunderstood; the true messiah was not in the external physical world but in the internal spiritual world. Driven by the dissonance of the continued existence of a suffering world in which abuse of power remained unchecked, Christians ended up changing the very notion of messianism. They translated the concept of messianic redemption into a state of personal salvation, thus removing it from the realm of history. In coming up with this solution, they were acting on the Jewish Exodus model but resolving its tensions in a manner that eventually turned them away from Judaism. (*The Jewish Way: Living the Holidays*, p. 37).

What should we make of this claim? Is Greenberg right? Did Yeshua and His disciples teach that redemption and freedom are entirely an internal reality within the scope of individual salvation? Is Pesach fulfilled in the redemption of the soul without consideration for the body?

When we listen to Greenberg's assessment of Christianity, and then compare them with the words of Yeshua, we are struck by the obvious fact that how Christians live and talk often does not harmonize with the very admonitions of the One she confesses as her Messiah. We hear Yeshua (Matt 25:31ff) describe the categories upon which He will judge the sheep and goats in the last day, and we are amazed at the utter lack of systematic dogma or church creeds! "For I was hungry, and you gave Me to eat; I was thirsty, and you gave Me drink; I was a stranger, and you invited Me in."

It is clear that we have understood forgiveness of sins and right standing with God to be only through the shed blood of Yeshua, our Messiah. But if we forsake our ties with history—forgetting that we have been grafted into the olive tree and that Abraham is the father of us all—this will result in neglecting to realize that each of us, as it were, came out of Egypt. And, if we neglect to apply this personally, we may also forget that God's intentions are to remake this world and society into a world were wickedness is banished and righteousness reigns—a world where the fatherless and widow are cared for as they ought to be, and where injustice is punished and righteousness exalted; a world where the truth of God and His actions in history are seen and experienced in the everyday events of eating (the Table), smelling (altar of Incense), and seeing (Menorah), so that freedom and shalom are a reality for both body and soul. Shabbat and the Festivals always speak to this duality: the soul rest through having sins forgiven, but they also require a rest of body—a cessation from work. God is vitally interested in both soul and body.

Our *Haftarah* portion today speaks to the same issue. Here, in the dedication prayer of Solomon for the Temple, he emphasizes the presence of God in connection with the Ark as it is placed into the Most Holy place. The Temple will be the focal point of prayer for the nation of Israel, as well as for the individual within Israel. But if the full context is read, (vv. 41ff), the Temple is also the focal point for the prayers and worship of the foreigner who is "not of your people." From the very beginning Israel is redeemed from her slavery in order that God's great Name should be proclaimed among the nations, and so that the nations themselves would experience true freedom, that is, freedom to join themselves to God's chosen nation and to obey God, becoming therefore an appropriate place for His dwelling.

The same is true of our Apostolic section in which Peter, using the analogy of the Temple, teaches that each believer is like a stone used to construct the dwelling place of HaShem. We might be tempted to read Peter as R. Greenberg suggests we have, i.e., discounting any physicality and concentrating entirely upon the non-physical, "spiritual" side of being "living stones" and built into a "spiritual house," offering up "spiritual sacrifices." But Peter does not have such a bifurcation of physical and non-physical in mind, for just a few verses later (2:12), he is urging his readers to live in such a way as to bring the Gentiles (here clearly unbelievers) to the point where they will glorify God in the final day of judgment. What is more, he admonishes us to follow in the footsteps of Yeshua, who suffered for righteousness sake yet committed Himself to HaShem who judges righteously (2:21ff). Yeshua constantly demonstrated in His earthly walk a concern for the outcast, a care for the needy, and one who sought justice for the oppressed.

All too often we have been unsuccessful as believers in Yeshua in keeping these two realms in balance—the salvation of the soul and the salvation of the body. We have often slipped into an emphasis upon one to the exclusion of the other. Evangelicals tend to do well at telling the good news of sins forgiven in Yeshua, but are not always known for promoting social justice and peace. Liberals, on the other hand, having forsaken the Scriptures as antique and therefore irrelevant for us in our modern world, fashioned the "social gospel" and have tried to feed the hungry, aid the oppressed, etc., without recognizing that one's soul constantly affects one's body. Changing the social status of an individual without changing the heart never works. In fact, social injustice and oppression can inevitably be traced back to the influences of sin—a soul issue. How do we find the balance in all of this?

I would suggest that here the Messianic believers have a great contribution to give to the Church at large, if only we can give it with the right heart and spirit. Namely, that our faith is tied to history. This we demonstrate through the continual celebration of the festivals, all rooted in history, but all therefore anticipating the coming of Yeshua to restore in history what has been broken. Pesach, which is now upon us, is the beginning of our cycle of God's appointed times. Pesach calls us back to earth, to the realities of history, and to the obvious longings of God's heart regarding such things as oppression, slavery, freedom, justice, etc. In the wonderful rehearsal of our eternal salvation, we are brought back down to earth where we now live, and the responsibilities of showing God's love and righteousness in a world enslaved by sin, and the poverty, injustice, and pain which that sin brings.

We must therefore resolve to live out the truth of who we are: covenant members with ADONAI, displaying His righteousness in our words, deeds, and motives. But we must know that we will be able to do this only as we rely upon the leading of the Spirit as He conforms us more and more to be like Yeshua.

The Ark of the Covenant

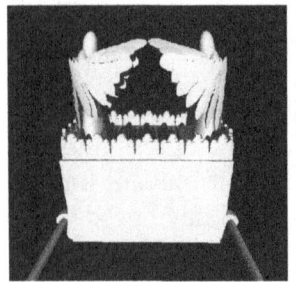

2.5 cubits long
(3ft. 9 in.)

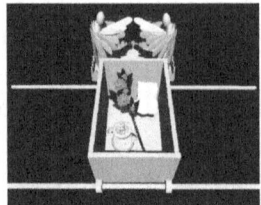

1.5 cubits wide
(2 ft. 3 in.)

Made of acacia wood overlaid with pure gold. Acacia (*Acacia raddiana*) is native to the Mediterranean, with four basic varieties being attested. It is a particularly dense wood and very strong. It has been found in use for clamps on mummy coffins, and used for fuel, hand tools, and structural posts. Cf. Ex 26:15; Num 25:1; Josh 2:1; Is 41:19; Mic 6:5.

The Menorah

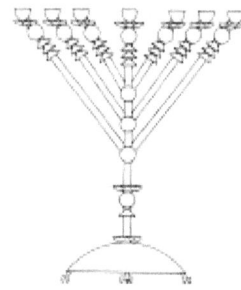

Majority opinion of how the menorah looked

Maimonides' understanding of the menorah

Ex 37:24 indicates that the menorah was made from a talent of gold. Talent measures of the Ancient Near East were consistently between 28.38 and 30.27 kg. (a kg. = 2.2 lbs., thus a talent would be between 62 1/2 lbs. and 66 1/2 lbs.) At $1304.00 a troy ounce of gold (as of 8/2014), in today's standards the menorah would be worth approximately $1.2 million.

Table for the Bread of the Presence

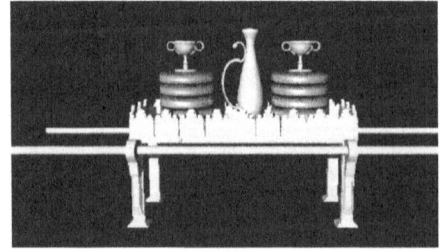

2 cu long x 1 cu wide x 1.5 cu high
(3 ft long x 2ft, 3 in wide x 18 in high)

The Table for the Bread of the Presence was made of acacia wood overlaid with gold. Two poles, also of acacia wood overlaid with gold, were held by rings attached close to the rim of the table's top. The Bread of the Presence was constantly to be placed on the table, located in the Holy Place before the veil.

The Golden Altar of Incense

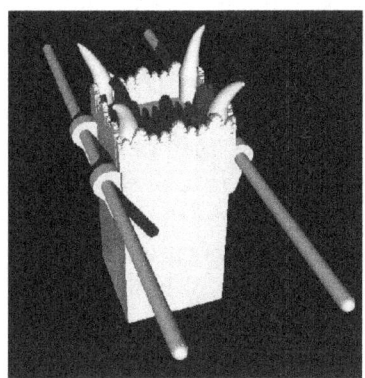

2 cu high; 1 cu square
(3ft high x 18 in square)

The actual placement of the Altar of Incense has been disputed by scholars. The text could be read to mean that, in the Tabernacle and Solomon's Temple, it was placed in the Most Holy place, before the Ark of the Covenant (Ex 40:5; Lev 16:11-14). The writer to the Messianic Jews (Hebrews) seems to use similar language (Heb 9:3,4). In the 2nd Temple (built by Zerubbabel and enlarged by Herod), the Altar of Incense was apparently placed in the Holy place (Luke 1:9, 10). Josephus likewise describes the Altar of Incense as situated in the Holy place along with the Menorah and Table of Bread (*Antiq.* 3.6.8). Rabbinic sources also consider the Altar of Incense to be situated in the Holy place, opposite the Ark but separated by the veil (Rashi on Ex 30:6; many places in the Mishnah, e.g., m.*Yoma* 2.3, Mid. Rab. *Num* 4.16, etc.). Since the Scriptures teach that no one was allowed into the Holy of Holies except the High Priest, a problem exists if the Altar of Incense is in the Holy of Holies—how can the common priests burn incense on it morning and evening? The resolution to this apparent difficulty is to understand that on Yom Kippur, for all practical purposes, the Altar of Incense was taken into the Most Holy Place by the High Priest, in the form of a golden censor containing coals from the Altar of Incense itself. It could therefore be spoken of as in the Holy of Holies when the Day of Atonement was in mind. Furthermore, since it was near the veil, it stood closest to the Ark of the Covenant, and no doubt filled the Holy of Holies with its fragrant aroma. In fact, when we look more closely at the language employed in the Tanach regarding the placement of the Altar of Incense, we discover that the author of Hebrews is very precise in his language.

> Behind the second veil there was a tabernacle which is called the Holy of Holies, having a golden altar of incense and the ark of the covenant covered on all sides with gold, in which was a golden jar holding the manna, and Aaron's rod which budded, and the tables of the covenant; (Heb 9:3–4)

The key to understanding these words is to recognize that the golden altar of incense is always connected with the ark of the covenant, for it is said to be placed "in front of the mercy seat that is over the ark of the testimony" (Exodus 30:6, cf. 40:5). This vital connection between the golden altar of incense and the ark of the covenant is clearly stated in 1Ki 6:22—"... He (Solomon) also overlaid with gold the altar that belonged to the inner sanctuary." The golden altar "belonged" to the Most Holy Place, because its placement in the Holy Place was directly in front of the ark, with the veil separating the two. The idea that the golden altar belonged to the Most Holy Place emphasizes that its primary function was in relation to the ark of the covenant, which is particularly seen on Yom Kippur when its coals and incense were taken into the inner sanctuary by the High Priest. In fact, the author of Hebrews carefully reproduces the language of 1Ki 6:22 by writing: "...the Holy of Holies, *having* a golden altar of incense." Earlier, in v. 2, he utilized the preposition "in" (ἐν, *en*) to note the location of the menorah and the table of the bread of the Presence in the outer sanctuary. But in regard to the altar of incense, he utilizes the verb "to have," (rather than the preposition "in") when connecting the golden altar and ark of the covenant to the Most Holy Place. By doing so, he conveyed the language of the Tanach which consistently connects the altar of incense with the ark of the covenant: the altar of incense *belonged* to the Most Holy Place.

Furthermore, the Greek word our author used, which nearly all the English versions translate as "altar," is θυμιατήριον (*thumiaterion*), the same word used in the Lxx to denote a censer or pan used for burning incense (2Chronicles 26:19; Ezekiel 8:11; 4Maccabees 7:11). Some have argued that the censers were made of bronze, not gold, and that therefore a "golden censer" could not be what our author has in mind. However, though the Torah does indeed mention censers made of bronze (Ex 38:3; Num 16:39), these are specifically said to be the utensils of the altar of sacrifice (the brazen altar), not the altar of incense which was overlaid with gold. In fact, we do find that golden utensils connected with incense existed in the Tabernacle, for in the dedication of the altar, each tribe presents incense in golden dishes (Num 7:14ff). Moreover, in the historian's account of the destruction of the Temple by Nebuchadnezzar and his commander Nebuzaradan, we read: "The commander of the imperial guard took away the censers (הַמַּחְתּוֹת, *hamachtot*) and sprinkling bowls—all that were made of pure gold or silver." So in Solomon's Temple there were censers made of gold.

What is more, our author's perspective, that a golden censer was used for taking the coals into the Most Holy Place on Yom Kippur accords with the rabbinic tradition:

> Every day he [the High Priest] would scoop out the cinders with a silver fire pan and empty them into a golden one. But today [Yom Kippur] he would clear out the coals in a gold one, and in that same one he would bring the cinders into the inner sanctuary. (m.*Yoma* 4.4)

The author of Hebrews, rather than being "mixed up" about the Tabernacle and Temple service, is extremely accurate, utilizing language that directly corresponds to the wording of the Tanach when describing the golden altar of incense as belonging to the Most Holy Place. This vital connection between the altar of incense and the Most Holy is seen by the fact that a golden censer is taken into the Most Holy on Yom Kippur, something corroborated by the Sages as well.

The Altar of Sacrifice

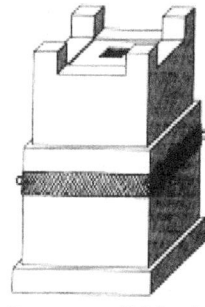

5 cu square (7.5 ft sq)
3 cu high (4.5 ft high)

Copper, Bronze, or Brass? Various translations of the text which speak of the the Altar of Sacrifice utilize different words for the metal used in the altar. Which is correct? The Hebrew word is נְחֹשֶׁת, *nechoshet*, which can mean either copper or bronze. Bronze is an alloy of tin and copper, and is more suited for casting due to its greater fusibility. The use of bronze has been found from dwellings dated as early as 3700 BCE. Indeed, the vast use of bronze between 3200 and 1200 BCE has resulted in this era being labelled the "Bronze Age". Brass, an alloy of tin, zinc, and copper, was not used by the ancients until 1500 BCE and after.

The Altar of Sacrifice was no doubt made of bronze, since bronze's fusibility and higher melting point would make it suitable for a firebox, able to withstand the temperatures of an open fire.

The Laver

The physical description of the laver: made of bronze, with a bronze base; No dimensions are given; the Hebrew word כִּיּוֹר, *kiyor*, suggests a "round" shape; there is no mention of poles and rings for carrying. It was made from the bronze mirrors of the women who ministered at the entrance of the tent of meeting.

The description of the Laver in the Tabernacle is not detailed at all. Such is not the case with the Laver which Solomon built in the First Temple. Like everything else in Solomon's Temple, the dimensions are increased! The Laver was 5 cubits high, 10 cubits in diameter, and 30 cubits in circumference (cf. 1 Ki 7:23-24). It rested upon four groups of three bronze oxen, each group facing one of the four compass points. Some have estimated that the weight of the entire Laver and stand was over 30 tons! Obviously, in a situation where the Tabernacle was portable, the Laver was a great deal smaller!

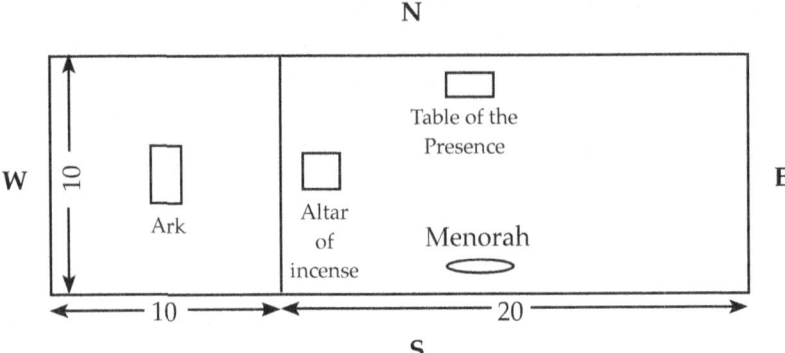

The Mishkan (Tabernacle)

Parashah Twenty-Three
פְּקוּדֵי – Pequdei

"THE NUMBERS"
Exodus 38:21–40:38

In the Triennial Cycle
there are two Parashot

38:21-31 | 39:1-40:38

Parashah 73
Triennial Cycle

Exodus 38:21-31

Haftarah: Jeremiah 30:18-22 | Apostolic: Romans 12:1-13

"…that I might dwell among them"

The texts chosen for this Shabbat's readings all focus on the matter of building a place fit for the dwelling of God. This, in itself, is an amazing concept: that the Almighty should dwell among His people. But perhaps even more amazing is that He puts into the hands of His people the responsibility of building the place where He will reside. This is in striking contrast to the norm of the Ancient Near East where Kings displayed their power and wealth by building for themselves mansions of splendor. Each monarch sought to outdo his predecessor, making his palace more ornate and costly.

Now surely the King of all the Universe could have miraculously built a palace for Himself that would have caused all others to pale in its glory. But instead, He solicits the work of craftsmen, and utilizes the building materials that the people would bring. Granted, He endows the craftsmen with the power of His own wisdom and ability by sending His Spirit to aid them. Yet the Tabernacle, in all of its finery, was still a moveable tent (*mishkan*). Its beauty was to be seen in an entirely different fashion, in the way that His presence enabled the people of Israel to walk in righteousness. He used the "common stuff," brought by the people themselves, to fashion a place for His dwelling. Yet in their bringing the materials for the construction of the Tabernacle, they did so with hearts of gratefulness and worship. In doing so, the common materials were transformed into the palace of the King. God takes the work of our hands, and recreates it into something of eternal value. One cannot help but be mindful of the words of our Master when He taught:

> Do not store up for yourselves treasures on earth, where moth and rust destroy, and where thieves break in and steal. But store up for yourselves treasures in heaven, where neither moth nor rust destroys, and where thieves do not break in or steal; (Matt. 6:19-20)

In our *parashah*, it is interesting to note that the gold and silver brought by the people is labelled a *tenuphah* (הַתְּנוּפָה), that is, a "wave offering." What exactly is the significance of a "wave offering?" Generally, the wave offering was that part of the peace offering (those offerings in which all were allowed to participate) that belonged to the priest. It was waved as unto the Lord, since the priest functioned as His servant to perform the sacred duties in the Tabernacle. The *tenuphah* is found in connection with the guilt offering of the cleansed leper (Lev 14:12, 21, 24), the sheaf of First Fruits (Lev 23:15), the two loaves at Shavuot (Lev 23:17, 20), and even the Levites themselves are designated as *tenuphah* in as much as their entire lives were given over to the service of HaShem.

What should we learn from the fact that the silver and gold donated by the people for the building of the Tabernacle is designated as a "wave offering?" The obvious significance is that the Tabernacle was not first and foremost for the people, but for God. Their gift of silver and gold was not so that they could have a wonderful "cathedral" to set themselves apart from other peoples. The Tabernacle was a dwelling place for the presence of the Almighty—a place in which He could dwell among His people. It was first and foremost for Him and for His glory.

This speaks to the motivation for giving the gold and silver in the first place—it was given as a *tenuphah*, a wave-offering, which by its very description is an offering given to God for His purposes. All too often we fall into the trap of man-made religion in which our "cathedrals" are the outcomes of our efforts rather than the glory of God. People are more impressed with their religion than they are with their Maker. But if we are living out Torah as God intends, this will cause those who see us to marvel, not at our "religious corporation" or our magnificent buildings, but at the One Who gave us such wonderful wisdom for life and community:

> See, I have taught you statutes and judgments just as Adonai my God commanded me, that you should do thus in the land where you are entering to possess it. So keep and do them, for that is your wisdom and your understanding in the sight of the peoples who will hear all these statutes and say, 'Surely this great nation is a wise and understanding people.' For what great nation is there that has a god so near to it as is Adonai our God whenever we call on Him? Or what great nation is there that has statutes and judgments as righteous as this whole Torah which I am setting before you today? (Deut. 4:5–8)

Our *parashah* is called *Pekudei* (פְּקוּדֵי) in the annual cycle of readings, after the first distinct word in the portion. *Pekudei* means "reckonings." In other words, Moses made a careful accounting of all the silver, gold, and bronze that people were bringing. This tells us something about leadership, for the people into whose hands the precious metals were entrusted were leading, trustworthy men. Ithamar, the son of Aaron, along with Bezalel and Oholiab are noted as those with authority in keeping the donated materials. We noted in the previous *parashot* that Bezalel and Oholiab were, in particular, endowed with the Spirit of God for their work. So if these leaders were men of integrity and character, why did Moses feel the need to keep an accurate accounting of the precious metals?

Two answers may be given. First, the integrity of the leaders, including Moses himself, is known by fact, not by assumption. Leaders must be above reproach, and the manner in which they handle the funds that come into their possession must be accounted for. A great many leaders in our day have suspicion hanging over them because of the way they have gathered wealth from the people of God.

Second, an accurate reckoning of the costly materials that the people brought gave witness of God's miraculous work among them. The Sages note something interesting in our text. All of the silver and gold that was gathered is entirely used in the various implements of the Tabernacle. Usually, during the process of casting and shaping, some metal is wasted. But the text indicates that the amount collected equalled the weight of the objects made—none was lost. The only explanation the Sages can give is that the ability to make the parts of the Tabernacle was given supernaturally to Bezalel and Oholiab by the Ruach HaKodesh. This reminds of the necessary "ingredient" in preparing any dwelling for the Almighty—the Ruach HaKodesh must be active in the work. In our modern world the work of the Ruach is constantly counterfeited or manufactured with smoke and mirrors. How do you know when the work you are doing—the "tabernacle" you are building—is energized by the Ruach? The sure mark of His work is that He accomplishes what no mere mortal can.

Let us consider our own community—the "building" we hope is fit for the presence of the Almighty. Is the Ruach's work evident among us? The fruit of His work is: love, joy, peace, patience, kindness, goodness, faithfulness, gentleness, self-control. Are these the supernatural qualities we find more often than not in our shul? Have we learned true love for Him and for each other? Are we patient, kind, faithful? These are not the characteristics of man-made "tabernacles," but they are the inevitable reality in the "tabernacle" built by those endowed with the Ruach's skill.

Let us consider, for a moment, the "fruit of the Spirit" as the silver and gold we bring for such a "tabernacle." Paul, in Gal 5:22–23, heads the list with "love." This begins with love for God, and extends to love for our neighbor. Love for God means love for His truth, for one cannot rightly love God while living in error. How tenacious are we for God's truth? Are we willing to stand firm for the truth, not being swayed to the left or right to accommodate the fleeting trends of our day? Do we stand firm on convictions, regardless of what it may cost us? If we do, then we will also express a genuine love for our neighbor—a love displayed in care and support, but a love that also is willing to be "tough" and enduring.

Next in the list is "joy." Our tenacious holding onto the truth does not make us into somber kill-joys who walk about under a cloud of despair. We know the true meaning of joy that surpasses common understanding. We are able to rejoice even in the storm, because we have tasted of God's goodness. By the grand gift of faith, God has endowed us with a spiritual ability to relax and rest in the greatness of His sovereign love. We know how to trust Him for the future, because we have experienced His faithfulness in the past. And so, even in the midst of trouble, we find deep-seated joy in His greatness, and in the bounty of life He has granted us.

Paul continues the list with "peace." Shalom is a gift of God, and nothing equals the contentment of faith. Our lives are not characterized by the morose darkness of this fallen world. We have died with Messiah, and are hidden with Him in the heavenlies (Col 3:3). As such, we take from the future and live it out in the present. The glory of our reigning King encompasses our lives with shalom. We know how the story ends, and we live in the reality of that now.

Next is "patience." Patience is the spiritual ability to leave the outcome to God. When life and relationships seem like a tangled mess of fishing line in the bottom of the boat, we resist the temptation to proceed with scissors. We know that cutting and tying will not yield a suitable outcome, so with patience we seek to untangle the mess and return it to its rightful state. We demonstrate patience when we allow God to work according to His schedule, not ours.

Paul continues with "kindness." The word itself is built upon the root meaning "grace." Having recognized the grace that God has shown to us, we willingly extend grace to others. We learn the spiritual exercise of forgiveness, because we know what it means to be forgiven.

Then comes "goodness." The word itself may emphasize a quality that is seen or known, rather than a mere innate quality. Thus, there is an outward "beauty" to our lives. A good person is one who is characterized by doing good things. He is not a chameleon who changes colors in accordance with his environment. He is single hearted, striving toward the goal of that final day, when he will hear the words "well done, good and faithful servant" (Matt 25:21–23).

Paul continues with "faithfulness." Faithfulness is the ability to remain at one's post. God has given each of us a task to perform for His glory. "It is required of stewards that one be found faithful" (1Cor 4:1). The stewardship we have received is a sacred trust, with which we must be faithful. As husbands, wives, fathers, mothers, sons, and daughters, will we perform the God-given duties we have received and remain faithful? These are the materials we bring to build a place for His dwelling.

Next in the list is "gentleness." The word itself means "the quality of not being overly impressed by a sense of one's self-importance." Gentleness and humility are partners, because an honest assessment of oneself yields the conclusion that one is fraught with deficiencies. Recognizing our own foibles makes us gentle when we see lacks in others. We know how to help someone who has fallen, because we have also fallen and have been given a helping hand.

Paul concludes with "self-control." Maturing faith is not impulsive. Faith relies upon wisdom, because faith is bound to the truth. Wisdom seeks God's solutions to the troubles life presents. It does not react from emotions, but seeks to reign in the first impulses, and patiently puts into practice the wisdom that comes from above (James 3:17).

These spiritual characteristics, then, are the silver and gold we bring to build God's dwelling among us. By His grace, and through the work of His Spirit, we are partners with Him to build the tabernacle of His dwelling.

I might go further in the midrash and suggest that the "tabernacle" built by the Ruach is also beautiful. Try to imagine what the *Mishkan* must have looked like: silver and gold, bronze and tapestries, *techeilet* and scarlet—when it was finally erected it must have been stunning to say the least. It was therefore attractive—the kind of thing that arrested one's attention.

Is that true of us? We are a building of living stones which should evoke the "ooh's" and "aah's" of passers-by? Granted, we are weak—He chose to grace the weak and despised of this world with His presence. Yet in spite of our weaknesses, the glory of His work shines forth, and bespeaks a deeper reality which the world longs to have. Do they see it in us? In our families, in our gatherings, in our community? Do they see it in the way we treat each other, talk about each other, care for each other? "By this all men will know that you are My disciples, if you have love for one another" (John 13:35).

And our children—they are being molded after the patterns they see in us. How are they being shaped? It is an interesting fact to contemplate that, unlike the two Temples that were subsequently built, and eventually destroyed, the Tabernacle never is captured or ransacked by Israel's enemies. Granted, we have no clear notice in the biblical text what became of the Tabernacle, but we likewise never see its demise in the biblical history. Will our children enhance the "building of God's presence" as they grow into adulthood and carry the truth into the next generation? May God grant us that we will, like the Spirit-endowed craftsmen of old, build a beautiful place where God's presence is pleased to dwell לְדוֹר וָדוֹר, from generation to generation.

Yet another lesson is learned from our *parashah*: a good deal of the silver came from the half-shekel tax paid by every male over 20. The lesson in this is clear: everyone has the same to contribute, and when these contributions are combined, the net effect is a significant outcome for HaShem. "But," you might respond, "surely some have much more to contribute than others!" In reality, this is only how it appears. Like the half-shekel tax, each one is able to "build" only as God enables via His Spirit, and each one who is truly born from above is gifted by the Spirit for this work. Thus, as each one, in accordance with the Spirit, adds his or her craftsmanship to the dwelling place of God's presence, it takes on the beauty He intends. In this way, He receives the "applause" and not the workers themselves.

It is not as though the workers are unimportant. In our *parashah* Bezalel and Oholiab are both listed along with the tribe from which they came. In other words, the workers gain recognition as the servants of God. He does not intend to accomplish His work apart from us—though He certainly could if that's what He wanted. Rather, HaShem has designed (for His own divine reasons) to complete His purposes through the efforts of His chosen ones. He calls them, endows them with spiritual abilities, and instructs them how to "build." Then, in obedience to Him, each servant partners with Him to do His work, and to do it His way. The end result? A tabernacle fit for His presence—the very dwelling of God in the midst of His people.

All of this comes to us with a question: how am I building? We should begin this questioning within our own families, for this is the foundation of the whole building. If someone were to evaluate how I spend my most valuable resources (time, energy, finances), would they see that I have put my family as the top priority? Am I consistently working hard to utilize the gifting with which God has endowed me, first in the lives of my spouse and children? in the lives of my parents and extended family? From here we can move to the larger community. How am I contributing to the overall "building" of the community with which I identify? By this I do not mean a physical building (though the facility we use is important and a necessary element of our growth as a community) nor the size of our community (as though a growing number who attend indicates some special success). What I mean by "building the community" is that we more and more understand ourselves as a "place," a community where God's presence is known—where His covenant righteousness is manifest in the way we treat each other, care for each other, bear each other's burdens, and especially in the way that the truth of God in Messiah Yeshua is lived out day by day, year by year, generation to generation.

It is clear why the Sages chose the *haftarah* for our Torah portion. Jeremiah prophesies of the future when the dwelling place of God will be re-established within the midst of Israel, and we will worship in peace and thanksgiving. Moreover, like the silver and gold that was "reckoned" and none went missing, so the children of Israel will be multiplied and "not diminished." Thus the faithfulness of God brings about the very goal of the covenant itself: "You shall be My people, and I will be your God."

The Apostolic section was chosen for this *parashah* because it likewise describes the building of the community of faith in which God's presence is known. Paul begins this passage by noting that the manner in which we live out God's commandments and serve one another constitute "living and holy sacrifices." He clearly has the Tabernacle or Temple in mind as a metaphor of the assembly of Yeshua. He further emphasizes the need for each member to contribute to the functioning of the whole, through the gifts that God has bestowed. Interestingly, in the listing of the gifts, only one is included in the list he provides in 1Cor 12, that is, "prophecy." The remainder of the gifts find no direct parallel elsewhere as spiritual gifts. What is more, it appears that the majority of the gifts listed in our Apostolic *parashah* are the common functions of those within the body of Messiah who are intent upon serving each other: "service," "teaching," "exhorting," "giving," "leading," and "showing mercy." One wonders if the gift of "serving" (διακονίαν, *diakonian*) is not a general heading for all that follow, for those who teach, exhort, give, lead and show mercy are, in each of these, serving others.

What is remarkable is that each of these, while clearly the work of the Spirit as an outflow of God's grace (12:6), is not viewed as miraculous. In other words, the way each one utilizes his or her gifts for the profit of the whole is the "common" activity that goes on in the body of Messiah. Moreover, these are not clear, distinct categories, for the one who prophesies must surely be involved in some aspect of teaching, as is the one who exhorts. Leaders "teach" by example, as do those who give and those who show mercy. Likewise, one who teaches often exhorts, and engages in the prophetic spirit of declaring the mind of God. It may be, then, that Paul is giving us a picture of how those who are led by the Spirit utilize their God-given abilities for the common good. Just as Bezalel and Oholiab were surely craftsmen before they were endowed by the special gift of the Holy Spirit, so we take our individual talents and use them for the success of God's work in our midst.

In this regard, note Ex 31:6, "...and in the hearts of all who are skillful I have put skill, that they may make all that I have commanded you." The craftsmen who built the Tabernacle were already skilled, yet God gave them additional skills for the specific work to which they were summoned. In the same way, when we came to faith in Yeshua, the Spirit, who was instrumental in creating us in the first place, added to our individual talents His ability to utilize these talents for the glory of Messiah, and the building up of the *kehilah* for the sanctification of God's name upon this earth.

We are therefore left with this important question: how are we doing in the building of a place for God's dwelling?

> According to the grace of God which was given to me, like a wise master builder I laid a foundation, and another is building on it. But each man must be careful how he builds on it. (1Cor 3:10)

Parashah 74
Triennial Cycle

Exodus 39:1-40:38

Haftarah: Isaiah 33:20-34:8 | Apostolic: Ephesians 2:17-22

A Place for the Dwelling of God

In this final parashah of Shemot (Exodus) we are struck by the repeated refrain "according to all that God had commanded, so they did" (or something similar). No less than 18 times in our text for this Shabbat is it noted that the people and Moses did just as the Lord commanded. Perhaps never before, and never again (until the return of Messiah), would the nation as a whole operate in such an obedient way. What is to be derived from this remarkable emphasis? What should we learn from it?

First, the conclusion of *Shemot* is clearly focused to teach us that the primary purpose of the exodus and of the Tabernacle with its services and priesthood, was that God should dwell among His people. Here, in our section, we have the crowning event, the descending of the *Shekinah* (שְׁכִינָה, God's dwelling presence) to fill the Tabernacle with the glory of HaShem. The glory which had been displayed upon the mountain in the sight of Moses, Aaron and the others would now come to dwell in and over the Tabernacle so that all could see His presence. Now we understand why the oft repeated phrase of Israel's obedience to God's commandments in constructing the Tabernacle is found here: preparing a place for God's presence begins with the obedience of His people.

In our pluralistic society we have unwittingly fallen prey to the *Zeitgeist*, the "spirit of the times"—we have begun to think that there is a little bit of good in all things, in all modes of thinking. We're hesitant to teach and more hesitant to believe that God is the God of separation, that He refuses to dwell among the rebellious and wayward, among the spiritual harlotry of man-made religion. Consider Is. 57:15, " For thus says the high and exalted One Who lives forever, whose name is Holy, 'I dwell on a high and holy place, and also with the contrite and lowly of spirit in order to revive the spirit of the lowly and to revive the heart of the contrite.'" Or Is. 66:2 – "For My hand made all these things, thus all these things came into being," declares the Lord. "But to this one I will look, to him who is humble and contrite of spirit, and who trembles at My word." God does not wait for people to be perfect to take up His abode with them (else He would only dwell with His people in eternity). He rather provides redemption for them, and then asks for humble and contrite hearts—hearts that tremble at His word, meaning that there is a ready spirit of obedience toward the Lord. "just as He commanded, so they did"—this is an essential element of preparing a place for God's presence.

A second element is evident as we read of Moses erecting the *Mishkan* (Tabernacle): the people had contributed abundantly to make the final product a reality. We are stunned by the amount of gold, precious stones, fine materials of woven cloth, etc. which went into the making of the *Mishkan*. (Conservative calculations would put the value of the materials for the Tabernacle at 20+ million dollars if valued by today's standards.) In 35:5, 20, 21 the text indicates that the people gave out of "willing hearts." The Hebrew is נָדִיב (*nᵉdiv*), which could mean "noble." In 35:21 a second expression is found, translated "whose heart stirred him," literally "whose heart lifted him" (נְשָׂאוֹ לִבּוֹ, *nisā'ô libbô*).

These expressions would indicate that the people had a genuine desire for companionship with God. They were willing to give sacrificially in order to prepare a place for God's presence to be manifested. It is worthwhile for us to inquire of our own hearts how much we desire friendship with God. What a remarkable statement of James (2:23) that Abraham was "a friend of God!" Do we desire to have this kind of relationship with the Almighty? If so, our willingness to sacrificially prepare a place for His presence will characterize our lives.

How might we assess our heart's desire for God's presence? Might I suggest two simple questions: 1) How high a value do I put on things? and 2) What takes priority in my schedule? Wealth and Time—the two most valuable commodities in our lives—God asks us to put His friendship above both. It doesn't mean that these things are unimportant, or somehow "evil." On the contrary! Our *parashah* put a high value upon the materials that were used for the construction of the Tabernacle, as well as the skill and time of those who did the actual building. The issue is a matter of priority.

The principle of the tithe attaches to the issue of "things," while the appointed times (Sabbath and festivals) attach to the matter of our "time." Would we have been willing to give up our savings account in order to prepare the *Mishkan*, a place for God's *Shekinah*? Would we have conformed our schedules to match God's requirements? It is very interesting that God prescribes exactly when the *Mishkan* was to be erected: "On the day of the first new moon, on the first of the month...." God asks us to demonstrate the level of our desire for His presence by submitting to Him the two things we value the most: our material possessions and our time. Even in the building of the articles for the *Mishkan*, God's appointed times (Sabbath) were to be kept (35:1-9), and the people were expected to give from their own possessions in order to make the *Mishkan* a reality. All this teaches an important principle: God dwells among those who put Him first—who desire His presence above all else.

A third element in preparing a place for God's presence is evident in our text: God desires the abode of His presence to be one of beauty. One can only imagine what the High Priest must have looked like as he ventured out of the *Mishkan* into the courtyard. Had the sun been shining, the golden clasps, rings, chains, engravings, etc. would have illuminated the deep, rich colors of his vestments. He would have struck an imposing image. Likewise, the *Mishkan* itself, with its fine linens and weavings, the gold and silver, and the embroidery—all of it would have made the place a mini-mansion.

It is no secret why such elaborate measures were ordained for the priestly vestments and the Tabernacle itself—all of these foreshadowed the person and work of Yeshua, our Great High Priest. And here we find a simple yet profound truth: for the Father nothing is more beautiful than His Son, Yeshua. If you want to be near the *Shekinah*, find the Son, for the Father and the Son dwell together as one. Would our hearts be fashioned as place for the *Shekinah*? Would we invite the very presence of HaShem to dwell in the contrite halls of our hearts? Then we must be conformed to the image of His Son if we would erect a place of beauty for His dwelling. When I am "in Messiah" and He is in me, then surely the *Shekinah* will take up His dwelling where such beauty resides. This is the metaphor used by the Apostles. We are being built into the very abode of His dwelling as we are more and more conformed into the image of the Son.

How are we conformed to the image of Yeshua? Some might point to the life of obedience which Yeshua manifested—that as we obey the Torah we become more and more conformed to the image of Yeshua, and this, of course, is correct. But it is too easy to list those things of the Torah to which we are willing to be conformed, and to neglect that heart of the Torah that Yeshua Himself emphasized, namely, loving God by loving our neighbors; showing submission to God by submitting to our authorities; showing our reliance upon God by loving our enemies, and doing good to those who hate us. Our desire to become like our Lord Yeshua must mean a desire to live out the Torah not by the letter (i.e., devoid of the Spirit) but by the Spirit through whom the letter will be followed in a spirit of humility and love, being patient with those who are learning, and caring about those who need to learn. Nothing, it seems to me, is more anti-Torah than to fail to be conformed to the pattern of Yeshua in His Torah observance (cf. 1Cor 9:21 where Paul speaks of "the Torah of Messiah"). Rather than writing the masses off, He grieved over them, longing that they should know the truth. And when He disagreed with the teachers of His day, He confronted them directly while still evidencing a willingness to submit to God's ordained authority.

A fourth element I wish to emphasize as we see the manner in which the people prepared for the *Shekinah* is that they were ready to be lead by the *Shekinah*. It is one thing to sacrifice and prepare for the presence of the Lord, and another thing to commit oneself to following wherever the presence of God leads. I could imagine some who were eager for the "event," the descent of the Cloud upon the *Mishkan*, but who had not thought beyond the grandeur of the event itself. Yet our *parashah* goes on to describe how the people travelled when the Cloud lifted, and they remained encamped when the Cloud remained stationary. They submitted to the will of God as He dwelt in their midst.

How wonderful it would be if we had such a tangible guide—to know precisely whether to turn to the left or right in the decisions of our lives by simply waiting to follow a visible cloud. Yet through the eyes of faith we are led by the Spirit. To the extent that the presence of God dwells with us, to that extent we can be assured of His guidance in life and in life's decisions. Consider once again Prov 3:5, 6:

> Trust in Adonai with all your heart
> And do not lean on your own understanding.
> In all your ways (*halachah*) acknowledge Him,
> And He will make your paths straight.
> (Proverbs 3:5–6)

חֲזַק! חֲזַק! וְנִתְחַזֵּק!

Index of Haftarah Readings – Triennial Cycle

Haftarah	Torah	Parashah No.	Page
2Samuel 22:10–51	Exodus 32:15–34	70	217
1Kings 8:8–22	Exodus 37:1–38:20	72	235
2Kings 12:1–16	Exodus 30:11–38	68	197
Isaiah 19:1–17	Exodus 10:1–12:12	52	57
Isaiah 21:11–22:4	Exodus 12:29–51	54	71
Isaiah 27:6–13	Exodus 1:1–2:25	46	15
Isaiah 33:20–34:8	Exodus 39:1–40:38	74	255
Isaiah 40:11–19	Exodus 3:1–4:13	47	21
Isaiah 45:20–25	Exodus 15:19–16:24	57	89
Isaiah 46:3–13	Exodus 13:1–20	55	75
Isaiah 49:1–6	Exodus 22:5–23:33	61	137
Isaiah 55:12–56:7	Exodus 4:14–6:1	48	29
Isaiah 58:13–14	Exodus 16:25–17:16	58	97
Isaiah 60:16–61:19	Exodus 24:1–18	62	145
Isaiah 61:1–6	Exodus 18:1–20:26	59	103
Isaiah 61:7–62:5	Exodus 29:1–46	66	179
Isaiah 66:1–13	Exodus 25:1–26:30	63	155
Isaiah 34:11–35:4	Exodus 8:20[16]–9:35	51	51
Jeremiah 30:18–22	Exodus 38:21–31	73	247
Jeremiah 31:31–40	Exodus 34:27–36:38	71	227
Jeremiah 34:1–14	Exodus 21:1–22:24	60	129
Jeremiah 46:13–28	Exodus 12:13–28	53	65
Jeremiah 49:1–22	Exodus 13:21–15:18	56	81
Ezekiel 16:10–19	Exodus 26:31–27:19	64	163
Ezekiel 20:1–7	Exodus 31:1–32:14	69	205
Ezekiel 28:25–29:21	Exodus 6:2–7:18	49	39
Hosea 14:4–9	Exodus 27:20–28:43	65	173
Joel 3:9–21 [Hebrew 4:9–21]	Exodus 7:19–8:19[15]	50	47
Malachi 1:11–2:7	Exodus 30:1–10	67	187

Index of Apostolic Readings – Triennial Cycle

Apostolic	Torah	Parashah No.	Page
Matthew 26:27-28	Exodus 24:1–18	62	145
Mark 2:27–28	Exodus 16:25–17:16	58	97
Luke 4:16–30	Exodus 18:1–20:26	59	103
John 1:29–34	Exodus 10:1–12:12	52	57
John 6:31–51	Exodus 15:19–16:24	57	89
Acts 7:35–37	Exodus 4:14–6:1	48	29
Acts 10:9–28	Exodus 3:1–4:13	47	21
Acts 17:17–22	Exodus 6:2–7:17	49	39
Romans 9:14–16	Exodus 32:15–34:26	70	217
Romans 9:17–18	Exodus 7:19–8:19[15]	50	47
Romans 12:1–13	Exodus 38:21–31	73	247
Romans 6:1–2	Exodus 1:1–2:25	46	15
1Corinthians 6:9–11	Exodus 21:1–22:24	60	129
1Corinthians 6:12–20	Exodus 25:1–26:30	63	155
1Corinthians 12:1–13	Exodus 34:27–36:38	71	227
2Corinthians 9:6–11	Exodus 30:11–38	68	197
Ephesians 2:17–22	Exodus 39:1–40:38	74	255
Colossians 1:13–14	Exodus 12:13–28	53	65
Colossians 1:15–23	Exodus 13:1–20	55	75
Colossians 3:1–5	Exodus 31:1–32:14	69	205
1Thessalonians 4:13–18	Exodus 12:29–51	54	71
Hebrews 2:10–18	Exodus 29:1–46	66	179
Hebrews 4:14–16	Exodus 27:20–28:43	65	173
Hebrews 8:1–6	Exodus 26:31–27:19	64	163
Hebrews 11:23	Exodus 1:1–2:25	46	15
Hebrews 12:14–17	Exodus 8:20[16]–9:35	51	51
James 1:26–2:4	Exodus 22:5–23:33	61	137
1Peter 2:4–10	Exodus 37:1–38:20	72	235
Revelation 8:1–5	Exodus 30:1–10	67	187

Made in the USA
Coppell, TX
22 January 2026

69106443R00144